Exploring Communication Ethics

PETER LANG
New York • Washington, D.C./Baltimore • Bern
Frankfurt am Main • Berlin • Brussels • Vienna • Oxford

Exploring Communication Ethics

Interviews with Influential Scholars in the Field

**Edited by
Pat Arneson**

PETER LANG
New York • Washington, D.C./Baltimore • Bern
Frankfurt am Main • Berlin • Brussels • Vienna • Oxford

Library of Congress Cataloging-in-Publication Data

Exploring communication ethics: interviews with influential
scholars in the field / edited by Pat Arneson.
p. cm.
Includes bibliographical references and index.
1. Communication—Moral and ethical aspects.
2. Communication—Philosophy. I. Arneson, Pat.
P94.E97   175—dc22   2006022390
ISBN 978-0-8204-8824-0

Bibliographic information published by **Die Deutsche Bibliothek**.
Die Deutsche Bibliothek lists this publication in the "Deutsche
Nationalbibliografie"; detailed bibliographic data is available
on the Internet at http://dnb.ddb.de/.

Cover design by Lisa Barfield

© 2007 Peter Lang Publishing, Inc., New York
29 Broadway, 18th floor, New York, NY 10006
www.peterlang.com

All rights reserved.
Reprint or reproduction, even partially, in all forms such as microfilm,
xerography, microfiche, microcard, and offset strictly prohibited.

J. G. M.

Contents

Acknowledgments ix

Introduction xi

A Conversation about Communication Ethics with ...

    Christopher Lyle Johnstone 1

    Sharon L. Bracci 21

    Richard L. Johannesen 37

    Ronald C. Arnett 53

    Josina M. Makau 69

    Clifford G. Christians 89

    Michael J. Hyde 105

    Julia T. Wood 117

    Kenneth E. Andersen 131

Communication Ethics: The Dialogic Turn
    Ronald C. Arnett, Pat Arneson, and Leeanne M. Bell 143

Contributors 185

Index 191

Acknowledgments

I would like to thank Duquesne University for granting a sabbatic leave that enabled me to pursue work on this project. I am grateful to faculty members in the Department of Communication & Rhetorical Studies for enriching conversation and professional opportunities that have profoundly influenced my scholarship.

This project emerged from the 8th National Communication Ethics Conference, co-sponsored by the National Communication Association Communication Ethics Division, McAnulty College & Graduate School of Liberal Arts NEH Endowment Fund, and the Communication Ethics Center in the Department of Communication & Rhetorical Studies at Duquesne University. The contributions of Leeanne M. Bell, Assistant Director of the conference, were invaluable.

My deepest appreciation is extended to the interviewees who generously shared their time and insights about communication ethics: Kenneth E. Andersen, Ronald C. Arnett, Sharon L. Bracci, Clifford G. Christians, Michael J. Hyde, Richard L. Johannesen, Christopher Lyle Johnstone, Josina M. Makau, and Julia T. Wood. I am grateful to the conference participants for taking part in the discussion of these ideas.

Thank you to Taylor & Francis Group for granting permission to reproduce "Communication Ethics: The Dialogic Turn," which was previously published in *The Review of Communication* (January-April 2006).

I would like to thank the students at Duquesne University who make teaching such a wonderful learning experience; my research assistants, Celeste Grayson, Reneé Stanton, and Andrew Bergstrom; the work study students who transcribed audiotapes; Todd Russell and Dennis Woytek for their help with technology; Vasil Tsarev for sharing his graphic design skills; and Annette Holba for her preliminary reading and ongoing encouragement of this manuscript.

I would also like to thank Peter Lang Publishing Senior Editor Damon Zucca, Production Coordinator Brittany Schwartz, and Production Manager Bernadette Shade for your patient support and commitment to this project. I extend my appreciation to the entire staff at Peter Lang Publishing for their work bringing these ideas to fruition.

Thanks to my friends for your ongoing encouragement and support. And always, my family—you're my heart.

Introduction

Pat Arneson

Exploring Communication Ethics: Interviews with Influential Scholars in the Field holds as its center a discussion about ethics in human communication. From the rhetorical theories and practices of the ancient Greeks to the present, ethics has long been recognized as an integral dimension of communication theory and practice. In "A History of Communication Ethics," Kenneth E. Andersen explained that people have emphasized ethical concerns to a greater or lesser extent in various historical moments. The surviving ancient writings recognize ethics as essential for effective persuasion in the governance of the polis. That view lost dominance as writings on communication moved to emphasize communication by the clergy and other learned professions. More recently, ethics has received limited treatment as simply one of many elements that comprise communication. The advent of postmodernity—marked by an awareness of competing narrative structures that resonate from various forms of diversity made visible through global media and international commerce—has once again heightened people's attention to ethics in human communication.

While scholars recognize the importance of truthfulness and the ethical obligations of persons involved in interaction, contemporary everyday events threaten to diminish people's confidence in "the word." People increasingly accept lies and deception as the norm across the spectrum of communication, including interpersonal relationships, organizational life, and marketing campaigns. James A. Jaksa's "Initiation of the Communication Ethics Commission" reminds us that meaningful interaction and the survival of society require that ethical communication be the norm in all areas of human interaction. However, an awareness of and emphasis on ethics varies between people and across different communication contexts. This project invites readers to consider ethics in the theory and practice of daily communicative life.

Introducing Communication Ethics

Generally, an introduction to the study of a topic area begins by delineating definitions and providing a history of the field. However, as Kenneth E. Andersen in "A History of Communication Ethics" explains, a "history of communication ethics" has not yet been written. He notes that even an overview "limited to the rhetorical tradition from ancient Greece to contemporary American, English, and European communication theorists does not exist" (4). To provide a commonplace to begin our conversation, this exploration begins with a brief discussion of ethics and outlines the study of ethics in human communication.

Ethics

Ethics is one of the four main branches of philosophy—along with logic, metaphysics, and epistemology. In *The Cambridge Dictionary of Philosophy*, John Deigh instructs that ethics can be divided into "the general study of goodness, the general study of right action, applied ethics, metaethics, moral psychology, and the metaphysics of moral responsibility" (284). These subdivisions are not sharply defined and many ethical studies overlap these divisions. The "main business" of ethics involves (i) the general study of goodness and (ii) the general study of right action. The study of goodness examines "what general ends we ought, as fully rational human beings, to choose and pursue." The study of right action considers "what moral principles should govern our choices and pursuits" (285).

The term "moral" is often used interchangeably with the term "ethical." The etymology of these terms helps explain their similarity of use:

> Alasdair MacIntyre points out that *moral* is the descendent of the Latin word *moralis*. However, *moralis* was a term invented by the ancient Roman philosopher Cicero to translate the ancient Greek word *ethikos*. Both terms meant, roughly and very broadly, 'pertaining to character.' English renderings of these terms have been associated with matters other than character, but no clear, consistent pattern of difference between *moral* and *ethical* seem to have developed. (Jaksa and Pritchard 5-6)

Although the term "ethics" may be "used more narrowly to mean the moral principles of a particular tradition, group, or individual" (Deigh 284), no systematic differences between the two terms have emerged.

Ethics is the study of morality. The study of ethics examines our "basic moral attitudes, dispositions, beliefs, standards, principles, ideals, and practices" (Jaksa and Pritchard 4). Ethics concerns judgments about "goodness" and the quality of our communicative actions in their capacity to either harm or benefit others.

Communication Ethics

Ethics are an integral dimension of human communication. Richard L. Johannesen explains that ethical issues may arise in communication whenever one's behavior (i) could have "significant impact on other persons," (ii) "involves conscious choice of means and ends," and/or (iii) "can be judged by standards of right and wrong" (2002, 1). Engaging in thoughtful communication that positively contributes to interactions and relationships requires the exercise of critical thinking. Thinking before one speaks enables a person to consider the place of ethics in one's communication. Ethical communication concerns itself beyond one's right to free speech to consider the responsibility one holds toward others in communication.

Ethics in Human Communication

In general, "ethics" is concerned with how one should live one's life. Ethics addresses questions about what is right or wrong, good or bad, fair or unfair, and so forth. Addressing *Ethical Issues in the Communication Process*, J. Vernon Jensen recognized that bipolar phrasing such as "right or wrong," "good or bad," and "ethical or unethical" is problematic. He suggests that one can more usefully think in terms of degrees of ethicality—asking the question, "How ethical is a given communicative behavior?"

James A. Jaksa and Michael S. Pritchard note that ethics is concerned with both one's character and one's conduct. The area of character considers human vices and virtues. The area of conduct addresses the basic principles and rules one may use to guide and evaluate one's behavior. Human conduct and symbolic action fall within the purview of the communication discipline. As such, numerous points of ethical contact exist in human communication, including considerations related to the domain in which communication occurs; the type of relationship communicators have with one another; characteristics of each interactant in the communicative exchange; and the purpose, form, and content of message. Further, there are numerous ways to engage communication ethics in varying situations.

There are several fundamental *domains* of communication that deserve ethical consideration. These include interpersonal communication; small group discussion; communication in organizations; rhetorical communication; advertising, public relations, and/or marketing campaigns; and the news media. Each area is distinct but the categories can overlap and also be further subdivided into additional areas of inquiry.

Various kinds of *relationships* are possible in any domain. For example, interpersonal communication could occur with an intimate partner in a personal context, a friend in a social context, a professional colleague in a work context, a patron in a business transaction, or as a conversation between two citizens addressing civic issues. In addition, one must consider the *characteristics of each interactant* in the communication. People bring their full range of experiences with them into interaction which informs their understanding of an issue. Considerations such as gender diversity, cultural diversity, sexual orientation, religious differences, age differences, and whether one is able-bodied or physically disabled must be considered when engaging in ethical communication.

Ethical issues are potentially relevant in any aspect of *communication*: "the source or sender; the message or content; channels of communication; receivers; the effects; and the situation, environment, or context of communication" (Jaksa and Pritchard 7). Ethics are present whether human communication takes an oral or written form. In addition, ethical considerations are woven throughout the function of a message, such as "whether a communicator seeks to present information, increase someone's level of understanding, facilitate independent decision in another person, persuade about important values, demonstrate the existence and relevance of a societal problem, advocate a solution or program of action, or stimulate conflict" (Johannesen 2002, 2).

Communication scholars have delineated various *categories of human communication ethics* which may be used in different interactions. Ronald C. Arnett, Pat Arneson, and Leeanne M. Bell discuss these categories in "Communication Ethics: The Dialogic Turn" within this volume. Scholarly bearings include: democratic communication ethics; universal-humanitarian communication ethics; codes, procedures, and standards in communication ethics; contextual communication ethics; narrative communication ethics; and dialogic communication ethics.

A multiplicity of issues exists for consideration in one's communicative choices. In human communication, "standards such as honesty, promise-keeping, truthfulness, fairness, and humaneness usually are used in making ethical judgments of rightness and wrongness in human behavior" (Johannesen 2002, 1). One must consider the domain; type of relationship; characteristics of each interactant; and the form, function, and content of the message. Ethical human communication requires critical reflection about one's

Introduction

communication with others before, during, and after the communicative exchange.

Critical Thinking

Communication is a complex and multi-faceted act requiring thoughtful reflection to sustain and enhance one's relationships with others. James A. Anderson and Elaine E. Englehardt explain that ethical decisions ultimately rest on the power of reason to justify beliefs and actions. While reason is not the only guide to "truth," ethicists advocate reason as providing the best avenue for arriving at "truth."

> Ethics involves our analysis of and reflection on moral choices and judgments. When we ask individuals why they believe an action is ethical, we expect more than the answer, 'Cuz.' Within ethics and the rubric of rational justification, it is not enough to justify a point by replying, 'I feel that way,' or 'I don't know, but I'm doing it anyway.' (7)

Communication is a purposeful activity. A person can not simply say his or her behavior is "right" and leave it at that—a person must be able and willing to justify one's communication to others.

Great thinkers have, for centuries, tried to define the best way to live a moral life. James A. Anderson and Elaine E. Englehardt note that the practice of thinking typically begins with an act of questioning. In the *Apology*, Socrates asserted "the unexamined life is not worth living." He insisted on the importance of examining one's basic values and the assumptions underlying them to contribute significantly to the moral quality of our lives. However, "contemplation is not enough; contemplation must ... [build] a platform for action" (Anderson and Englehardt 27). One's actions must imbue questioning and reflection. Critical thinking—one's capacity for sound deliberation—is an important aspect of understanding and applying ethics in one's human communication (Makau and Marty 2001). This involves reflection about how one "ought" to communicate with different people in different settings for different purposes.

Following Socrates, ethical communication requires evaluating the moral values that a person or group of people accept as a guide for "right" living. Discussing *Ethics in Human Communication*, Richard L. Johannesen notes that a tension potentially exists between what "*is*" occurring (the actual) and what "*ought*" to occur (the ideal). What a person "is" doing and what one judges they "ought" to do—or what the majority says "is" ethical and what a minority would argue "ought" to be ethical—may differ. As communicators, "we should examine not only how to, but also *whether we ethically ought to*" employ various communication methods and appeals (2-3). "Oughtness" is at the heart of ethics. We "ought" to maintain the highest ethical standards in each situation, recognizing we are all only human, negotiating the tension between freedom and responsibility in our communication behavior.

Rights and Responsibilities

In ethical communication, one has both rights and responsibilities. Richard L. Johannesen, in "Diversity, Freedom, and Responsibility in Tension," acknowledges a tension between one's constitutional right to free speech and one's ethical responsibility in exercising that freedom. "Freedom and responsibility are in tension in varied communication arenas, in public and private spheres, and between persons at the centers and those at the margins of power" (182).

Freedom of expression is at the center of a democratic society. J. Vernon Jensen explained "human beings' freedom of expression [is] considered desirable and necessary for personal self-fulfillment and for a safe, healthier society" (1997, 36). The right to free expression is articulated in the First Amendment of the Bill of Rights to the U.S. Constitution, ratified in 1789, which states: "Congress shall make no law respecting an establishment of religion, or prohibiting the free exercise thereof; or abridging the freedom of speech, or of the press; or the right of the people peaceably to assemble, and to petition the government for a redress of grievance." This amendment is affirmed in Articles 18 and 19 of the United Nations General Assembly's "Universal Declaration of Human Rights" adopted in 1948:

> Everyone has the right to freedom of thought, conscience and religion; this right includes freedom to change his [or her] religion or belief, either alone or in community with others and in public or private, to manifest his [or her] religion or belief in teaching, practice, worship and observance. Everyone has the right to freedom of opinion and expression; this right includes freedom to hold opinions without interference and to seek, receive and impart information and ideas through any media and regardless of frontiers.

Ethical communicators must manage the tension between freedom and responsibility "in humane and fair ways" (Johannesen 1997, 182).

Introduction

Thomas Szasz identifies the dual experience of freedom of the will and personal responsibility as "the crucial moral characteristic of the human condition" (qtd. in Johannesen 2002, 6). J. Vernon Jensen explains that rights and responsibilities are not separate entities. The metaphor "two sides of the same coin" does not adequately "depict their intimate enmeshing. The two words characterize the yin and yang in Eastern cultures, the supposed opposites that are really complementary, each contributing to the other's fulfillment, much like inhalation and exhalation, night and day, male and female" (1997, 10). Szasz notes that people "like freedom because it gives them mastery over things and people" and "dislike responsibility because it constrains them from satisfying their wants." Yet because "rights" and "responsibilities" are interlocked, "each increase in human freedom brings with it a proportionate increase in responsibility" (qtd. in Johannesen 2002, 6). The right to free speech must be negotiated in tension with the range of one's communicative responsibilities.

J. Vernon Jensen (1997) cautions that the right to speak and be heard does not ensure that a person will be taken seriously. One must earn respect from others. In addition to logos and pathos, the ancient Greeks stressed the role of ethos. Ethos refers to the credibility and reputation of the communicator. To persuade others, one should be trustworthy and strive to lead an exemplary life. One accomplishes this through self-discipline.

James A. Anderson and Elaine E. Englehardt identify a primary goal of ethics being "to establish appropriate constraints on ourselves. We are asked to curb our inclination to always do what pleases us" (7). One can find guidance in making decisions about ethics in communication from a variety of sources. J. Vernon Jensen notes that a person can look to one's religious roots, personal role models of integrity, upright group loyalties, society's positive values, legal statutes, a desire to enhance human nature, the embodiment of a dialogical spirit, and other points of reference to aid ethical decision-making (1997, 19-35). In contemporary North American culture, Richard L. Johannesen suggests that "[c]oncepts such as material success, individualism, efficiency, thrift, freedom, courage, hard work, competition, patriotism, compromise, and punctuality" (2002, 1) can function as criteria in making choices and judgments about human communication.

A first step to enacting ethics is to communicate integrity in one's interactions with others. For Stephen Carter, "a person of integrity takes time and effort to deliberate about the right thing to do, actually does the right thing despite personal hardship, and is willing to explain what was done and to justify it" (qtd. in Johannesen 2002, 11). James A. Anderson and Elaine E. Englehardt explain that people live their lives in relationships that "overlap, intersect, interact in a complex interplay of discourse and action" (6). Communication ethics concerns the rights and responsibilities of our conduct in those relationships. The study of ethics will not tell a person what is "right" or "wrong." Instead ethics provides the methods one can use to arrive at such decisions through critical thinking. The study of ethics in communication begins with what one has already learned about "right" behavior and is continually augmented by what one learns from others.

A Beginning: Learning from Others

The editor of this volume served as the Director of the 8th National Communication Ethics Conference, held at Duquesne University in Pittsburgh, PA in 2004. A central feature of that conference was interviews with nationally recognized scholars whose work engages the study of communication ethics. Each person was purposefully selected because of his or her longstanding scholarship and influence in the area of communication ethics. While the rhetorical tradition has a long history, contemporary scholars have only recently foregrounded ethics as a major component in communication studies. This collection interviews scholars who were central in moving communication ethics to a position of prominence in the communication discipline.

The intent of these interviews was to provide a forum in which participants could hear and learn from nationally recognized scholars of communication. These scholars shared their personal experiences and trajectory of scholarship, which inspired and energized listeners in their own study of ethics in human communication. This project records scholars' authentic witness to the development of communication ethics as an area of scholarly pursuit, important for the regeneration of a healthy society.

The interview process was selected to open up the rich advantages of orality. Walter Ong explained in *Orality and Literacy* that orality, an alternative to the written approach to knowledge, relies on voice and sound. Orality recognizes that knowledge emerges in dialogue. In orality, "our most immediate contact is through voices and persons rather than through observation and objects" (Farrell 29-30). In oral cultures, "the feeling/valuing function usually dominates. As writing and reading came to play a more central role in Western culture, they contributed to the development and

Introduction xix

dominance of the thinking function" (Farrell 30). This project seeks to wed the "feeling/valuing function" of oral discourse with the "thinking" function of written discourse. Rather than privileging "information" as the central metaphor, this book privileges the metaphor of "narrative." This shifts the reader's task from an emphasis on absorbing informational content to experiencing the revelation of ideas, inviting the reader into the interviewee's lived world.

The interviews invite each scholar to function as a community storyteller, sharing his or her understanding of communication ethics with others. Walter R. Fisher explained that *Human Communication as Narration* assumes "that all forms of human communication can be seen fundamentally as stories, as interpretations of aspects of the world occurring in time and shaped by history, culture, and character" (xii). He noted that regardless of the genre engaged by the communicator, discourse communicates a story, inviting the listener to assess and act on its narrative rationality. Some communication does not fulfill requirements for narrative rationality, instead taking on the qualities of a "prenarrative," illustrated in discourse that may not progress in time or reveal the storyteller's insight and interpretations (Herman qtd. in Riessman 4). Both prenarrative and narrative qualities of discourse function to exhibit communication as a reasoning art.

During the time of Socrates, philosophy, poetic, and rhetoric were unified in the Greek *paideia*. Following Socrates's death, Plato advocated the separation of these three disciplines. Aristotle promoted this separation—which was even further advanced by the literacy revolution. The separation of these three areas (philosophy, poetic, and rhetoric) is experiencing an "extraordinary convergence of social, technological, and theoretical pressures: that, in effect, reverses the literacy revolution that separated the reasoning arts" (Lanham qtd. in Langsdorf 110). The narrative approach responds to the postmodern call to once again join *theoria-poiesis-praxis* as a way to more fully engage one's lived experience.

D. Jean Clandinin and F. Michael Connelly explain how listening to (reading) another's narratives can enhance one's own understanding of the world:

> [J]ust as painters learn to paint by adopting a painter's style so, too, one of the ways a person may experiment with narrative form is by adopting the signature of a favorite ... [speaker]. Just as painters often develop their own styles as an outgrowth of experimentation with the signatures of well-known, accomplished painters, so, too,

this experimentation eventually may lead to an individual ... [adapting another's narrative form]. In this process of adaptation and the creation of signature, we are well advised to listen to the remnants of narrative form handed down to us. (425)

Lifelong learning, necessary in a postmodern age, occurs as one strives to comprehend themes or underlying patterns in a narrative to adapt and potentially adopt in one's own life and research.

In the interviews, readers learn how scholars create order out of the flow of experience and make sense of life as an ethical process. The personal stories along with the philosophical and theoretical interpretations offered by the interviewees provide insight into their individual observations about how to claim one's identity as an ethical communicator and use that knowledge to construct one's life. This book enlivens the study of communication ethics by presenting theory in the voice of each interviewee. The work harmonizes the interviewee as an embedded agent with his or her philosophical and theoretical knowledge of communication ethics.

Selected Scholars

The following nine interviews invite readers into a conversation with widely recognized communication ethics scholars. Each interview follows a similar course of questions, inviting the scholar to broadly express her or his ideas. Scholars were invited to discuss their interest and understanding of communication ethics, provide thoughts about communication ethics in a postmodern age of narrative contention, and address areas for reading and further research in communication ethics. Readers will observe that in the interviews scholars reveal *questioning* as the first step in their thinking, which also provides rich heuristic opportunities for others interested in communication ethics. These communication scholars are featured because their body of scholarship provides insight that contributes to transforming the study of communication ethics.

Christopher Lyle Johnstone introduces us to Greek conceptions of wisdom and their relation to speech and language. He notes that various sets of ethical standards may be applied to communication and also that different systems and/or ways of looking at ethical issues in human communication are available to scholars. Sharon L. Bracci's research situates communication ethics in the broad category of public moral argument and democratic deliberation. She synoptically addresses how communication ethics are manifest across historical periods. Richard L. Johannesen draws upon

Introduction xxi

classical and contemporary literature to enrich an understanding of how content informs various starting points. Ronald C. Arnett explains that in a postmodern age of competing narratives, communication ethics is first and foremost an act of learning that guides oneself, the other, and the historical moment. Josina M. Makau's interest in ethical deliberation explores the need to recognize and connect two interdependent facets of communication ethics: developing guidelines for reasoned deliberations and fostering conditions for living well together. Clifford G. Christians discusses his interest in communitarian ethics and considers challenges that new technologies present for engaging communication ethics in one's personal life. Michael J. Hyde looks to everyday existence to determine how research in communication ethics might help us improve human living. Julia T. Wood addresses the role of "difference" (e.g., gender, power, privilege) in relational ethics as they are developed and negotiated between people who experience the world differently. Kenneth E. Andersen's interest in *ethos* and the development of good moral character emphasizes the ongoing need for educators to prepare students for ethical communication, which is necessary for reinvigorating civic culture.

The closing essay, "Communication Ethics: The Dialogic Turn" by Ronald C. Arnett, Pat Arneson, and Leeanne M. Bell provides a state-of-the-art review of scholarly literature in communication ethics. Arnett, Arneson, and Bell draw upon Immanuel Kant's metaphor of "ought" to understand communication ethics as a "good." They identified six scholarly themes present in communication ethics literature published in 1985–2004, each of which emerged according to how the interplay of theory, action, and contextual discernment (Schrag 1986) was approached. A significant scholarly work was selected to serve as a standard-bearer for each theme: democratic communication ethics; universal-humanitarian communication ethics; codes, procedures, and standards in communication ethics; contextual communication ethics; narrative communication ethics; and dialogic communication ethics. Communication ethics is central to the dialogic process of negotiating contending social goods in a postmodern society, an era of narrative and virtue contention.

Taken together, the scholarly interviews and state-of-the-art literature review mirror the evolution of contemporary communication ethics. The interviewees' intellectual biographies are, in effect, the intellectual biography of contemporary communication ethics. The scholars' impetus for developing this area of study provides historical documentation of their involvement and perpetuates the generation of scholarship.

This edited book presents voices and echoes of voices in a way that stirs the imagination to consider communication ethics anew. The interviews, like all good conversation, J. Vernon Jensen notes, take us "over a broad terrain, showing us various scenes and the same scene from various places of view.... [The conversations] are part advocacy, part exposition, and part inquiry fed by insights and information not only from communication, but also from history, philosophy, religion, literature, psychology, and media studies" (1991, x). The scholars' intellectual generosity "leaves us with heightened ethical sensitivities and an enlarged storehouse of information"; their conversation leaves us with the tasks "of synthesizing, reconciling, deciding, and action. But that is what a good conversation should do" (1991, xii). One way to keep the conversation going is to ask questions of the other.

During the interviews, scholars pose numerous questions about communication ethics for consideration and further research. The art of "open questioning" recognizes that "[e]verything else, in a sense, flows from the questions that we're curious about or courageous enough to ask" (Anderson and Ross 15). Questioning interrogates one's experience from one's standpoint and opens up vistas of understanding and ways of negotiating one's experiences in the world in ways one may not otherwise attend. Conversations that ask questions and seek response are a necessary process for regenerating our social communities. *Exploring Communication Ethics* is a "good" place to begin that conversation.

Works Cited

Andersen, Kenneth E. "Developments in Communication Ethics: The Ethics Commission, Code of Professional Responsibilities, Credo for Ethical Communication." *Journal of the Association for Communication Administration* 29 (2000): 131-144.

———. "A History of Communication Ethics." *Conversations on Communication Ethics.* Ed. Karen Joy Greenberg. Norwood, NJ: Ablex, 1991. 3-19.

Anderson, James A., and Elaine E. Englehardt. *The Organizational Self and Ethical Conduct: Sunlit Virtue and Shadowed Resistance.* Fort Worth, TX: Harcourt College, 2001.

Anderson, Rob, and Veronica Ross. *Questions of Communication: A Practical Introduction to Theory.* 2nd ed. New York: St. Martin's, 1998.

Bill of Rights. http://www.archives.gov/national-archives-experience/charters/ bill_of_rights _transcript.html. Accessed July 1, 2006.

Clandinin, D. Jean, and F. Michael Connelly. "Personal Experience Methods." *Handbook of Qualitative Research*. Eds. Norman K. Denzin and Yvonna S. Lincoln. Thousand Oaks, CA: Sage, 1994. 413-427.

Deigh, John. "Ethics." *The Cambridge Dictionary of Philosophy*. Ed. Robert Audi. 2nd ed. Cambridge, UK: Cambridge UP, 1999. 284-289.

Farrell, Thomas J. *Walter Ong's Contributions to Cultural Studies: The Phenomenology of the Word and I-Thou Communication*. Cresskill, NJ: Hampton P, 2000.

Fisher, Walter R. *Human Communication as Narration: Toward a Philosophy of Reason, Value, and Action*. 1987. Columbia: U of South Carolina P, 1989.

Jaksa, James A. "Initiation of the Communication Ethics Commission." Speech Communication Association Convention. New Orleans, LA. November 1994.

Jaksa, James A., and Michael S. Pritchard. *Communication Ethics: Methods of Analysis*. 2nd ed. Belmont, CA: Wadsworth, 1994.

Jensen, J. Vernon. Foreword. *Conversations on Communication Ethics*. Ed. Karen Joy Greenberg. Norwood, NJ: Ablex, 1991. x-xii.

———. *Ethical Issues in the Communication Process*. Mahwah, NJ: Lawrence Erlbaum, 1997.

Johannesen, Richard L. "Diversity, Freedom, and Responsibility in Tension." *Communication Ethics in an Age of Diversity*. Eds. Josina M. Makau and Ronald C. Arnett. Urbana: U of Illinois P, 1997. 157-186.

———. *Ethics in Human Communication*. 5th ed. Prospect, IL: Waveland, 2002.

Kant, Immanuel. *Grounding for the Metaphysics of Morals*. Trans. James W. Ellington. 3rd ed. Indianapolis, IN: Hackett, 1993.

Langsdorf, Lenore. "The Homecoming of Rhetoric." *The Philosophy of Communication: Volume II*. Eds. Konstantine Boudouris and Takis Poulakos. Alimos, Greece: International Center for Greek Philosophy and Culture, 2002. 104-119.

Makau, Josina M., and Debian L. Marty. *Cooperative Argumentation: A Model for Deliberative Community*. Prospect Heights, IL: Waveland, 2001.

Ong, Walter J. *Orality and Literacy: The Technologizing of the Word*. New York: Routledge, 1982.

Riessman, Catherine Kohler. *Narrative Analysis*. Qualitative Research Methods Series: Volume 30. Newbury Park, CA: Sage, 1993.

Schrag, Calvin O. *Communicative Praxis and the Space of Subjectivity*. Bloomington: Indiana UP, 1986.

Universal Declaration of Human Rights. http://www.un.org/Overview/rights.html. Accessed July 1, 2006.

A Conversation about Communication Ethics with Christopher Lyle Johnstone

How did you become interested in studying communication ethics?

As an undergraduate student at UC Davis in the late 1960s, I was originally drawn to both rhetoric and those fields in philosophy that dealt with "ultimate questions" of existence—metaphysics and ontology. After several years and much study, I realized that my metaphysical questions didn't really have answers—or, at least, they didn't have answers that satisfied me. That realization, though, turned my attention to more practical matters. Even if I could never be sure what "reality" was, I recognized that all of us still have to make choices every day about what to do and not do. This is where my interest in ethics originated—in my awareness that we all need some means of deciding how to behave. So, in graduate school at the University of Wisconsin, my outside course work gravitated toward moral philosophy. Whereas my earlier reading in Aristotle, for example, had concentrated on his *Metaphysics*, I was now drawn to his *Nichomachean Ethics*. I also read other moral philosophers—Francis Bacon, Thomas Hobbes, John Stuart Mill, and Jeremy Bentham, for example. Sometime during my first few years in graduate school, I was encouraged to read John Dewey, and more than anyone else, he really engaged my thinking about ethics. Out of all this came my doctoral dissertation, which was entitled "Communication and Morality." In it, I examined the connections between rhetoric and ethics in the writings of Aristotle, Bacon, and Dewey. My teaching and scholarship in communication ethics ever since have been an outgrowth of that study. In fact, two of my first publications on ethics and rhetoric—one on Aristotle and one on Dewey, both appearing in *Philosophy and Rhetoric*—were based on chapters of the dissertation. Even now, my interest in Greek conceptions of wisdom and their relation to speech and language is a manifestation of the work I started doing in graduate school.

How do you define communication ethics?

I'm fairly literal in how I frame things, starting with ethics, for example. The word "ethics" is basically a direct translation from the Greek *ta ethika*. *Ta ethika* is a plural noun, and it translates roughly as "things having to do with character." Ethics, by its origin, is plural rather than singular, so I think that there are multiple "ethics" that might be applied to human communication.

Let's go back to the meaning of the term and this notion of things having to do with character. Obviously ethics is related to *ethos*. The term *ethos* itself derives from an older term that appears in Homer, referring to the "customary dwelling place of animals," their "haunts" or "abodes." For example, the *ethos* of the sheep, so to speak, is the place where the sheep are accustomed to hanging out. If you go there, you would expect to find your sheep. If you've lost your sheep, you go to their customary place—down by the water hole, for example.

This notion of the "customary dwelling place" got metaphorically "stretched" over time. I'm borrowing an expression here from Eric Havelock, who talks about the "stretching" of the old Greek language to do the work of philosophy. One of the things I've been studying over the last twenty years or so is how the older terms from the mythopoeic tradition—from Homer and Hesiod and the other poets—were extended by the earliest Greek philosophers, like Thales and Anaximander and their successors, to express abstract concepts that hadn't existed before their time. They took the language that was there and put it to their own use. Thus, the term *kosmos*, which was used by Aristotle to refer to the "ordered universe," was derived from an earlier, Homeric term (*kosmeô*) that denoted the act of "ordering" or "arranging" an army into ranks. Likewise, as I mentioned earlier, the notion of *ethos* as "customary dwelling place" or "abode" morphed into the notion of "custom" or "habit," and then into "character."

Certainly by the time we get to Aristotle, *ethos* as "character" refers to a person's habitual or customary way of acting—to her or his "characteristic" modes of conduct. We come back to the notion of ethics as "things having to do with character." Ethics has to do with character, and character can be conceived as what John Dewey, another influential thinker in my own intellectual development, called the "interpenetration of habits." What he called "the moral self" or "self" in general—or what we would call "character"—is defined by the acquired tendencies, habits, predispositions, and so on, that lead one to act in particular ways rather than in others. What defines a person as a person is, by this conception, the things that one tends to do. "How does one tend to behave in various kinds of circumstances?" "What can I count on you to do?" "What kind of person are you?"

That led me, finally, to an interest in the processes by which conduct is chosen. When I think of ethics, and again I'm looking at starting points here, I can't conceive of a meaningful sense of ethics without presupposing the phenomenon of choice. My starting point is this event. We are all confronted numerous times each day with decisions that we have to make: "Should I get up or stay in bed?" "Should I have cereal or toast?" Granting all the things about the de-centeredness and instability of the self, the problems with agency, and the whole postmodernist critique of the Enlightenment project—nonetheless, we have the experience of deciding what to do. I have the experience of having to make up my mind on what to do. To me, ethics kicks in when that process is at work.

When we are studying ethics, what we are studying, it seems to me, is those factors—psychological, conceptual, emotional, and philosophical—that bear on the process of choosing conduct. To me, it has to do with the ways in which we make our deliberate choices. When I think about the process of choosing an action, I think of the experience of deliberating, of thinking something through. "Should I do A or B?" We make those kinds of decisions in different ways, but nonetheless there is some sort of thought. If we're acting purely on impulse or reflex, where there is no opportunity for reflection, then I'm not sure that ethics is an issue. Also, if I'm in a situation where I have literally no choice—or only one choice—I'm not sure ethics applies there, either. There must be the operation of some sort of choice making, of some deliberate selection of action from among realistic alternatives. Aristotle discusses this in his *Nichomachean Ethics* (Bk. III) when he distinguishes merely "voluntary" action from action that is "deliberately chosen."

The very idea of human moral experience is very complicated; there are no simple answers. It's full of irresolvable tensions. There is just no way around them. John Dewey said it really well, too. He said that the fundamental fact of moral life is uncertainty. We can never be sure that we're doing the right thing. He wrote a book called *The Quest for Certainty*, and his basic position was that, in the moral realm, there is no such thing as certainty. We act always, we decide always, we choose always in the face of uncertainty, always with a risk and always with an awareness that we might be wrong.

Decision-making is a conscious process; it involves cognitive and affective elements. Some people obviously do act impulsively, even when they have the opportunity for reflection. I would want to say that raises ethical problems. I think that people ought to reflect when circumstances permit, that they ought to consider the potential ethical aspects of the various alternatives for action that lie before them. For me the central ethical question when I'm trying to decide what to do is ask, "What are my obligations here?" The process of ethical or moral decision making as the manifestation of moral selfhood is discussed in John Dewey's *Ethics* and in his *Human Nature and Conduct*. There are some discussions in these books on the moral life and the concept of moral selfhood. It seems to me that the most appropriate and ethically necessary move for me to make is to think about what my obligations are.

There's an article by Ralph Eubanks called the "Reflections on the Moral Dimension of Communication" in the *Southern Speech Communication Journal* that I use in my communication ethics course. He opens this up with a quote from W. D. Faulk, which goes as follows: "There is one commitment whose ground is intimately personal and which comes before any other personal or social commitment whatsoever: The commitment to the principled mode of life as such. One is tempted to call this the supreme moral commitment." That, to me, is a really important starting point, because it suggests that the first ethical choice we have is the choice of whether or not to try to be ethical. This is indeed a moral choice that reflects who we are and how we approach the task of living and decision-making and choice-making. That decision, about the commitment to the principled mode of life, is another way of saying the first ethical choice I have to make is, "What sorts of things should I be thinking about when I'm making up my mind about whether to act one way or another?" The most important central ethical question to raise, for me, is, "What are my obligations to myself, to the Other, to the earth, to God, to Being?" and so on. "What ought I to be trying to do? What am I bound to do in my actions?"

There are, of course, questions that are logically prior to "What are my obligations?" For example, "Do I have *any* obligations?" If so, "Why? What creates obligation?" John Caputo, in his book *Against Ethics*, asserts that "obligation exists," but he doesn't want to answer the question, *why* is this so? Caputo's position isn't philosophically satisfying to me. I want to know why. This curiosity is what led me on to my philosophical track, on to the line of inquiry I've been pursuing for almost 30 years: "What is the source of obligation?" "Why do we have obligations?" "Where do they come from?" One of the things I've done in my reading and writing and teaching is to explore various approaches to the sources of obligation and of principles. This has been part of my ethical project. I've tried to examine various ways of understanding the grounds of obligation, of understanding why I ought to do one thing rather than something else.

Would you talk about the themes in your scholarship related to communication ethics?

My own sense is that there are various sets of ethical standards that may be applied to communication and different systems and/or ways of looking at ethical issues in human communication. We have multiple approaches to identifying those issues and to resolving ethical questions in communication activities. In fact, a lot of my work has really been devoted to exploring different approaches to communication ethics, as opposed to coming up with "the ethic" for communication. I do think about it pluralistically: "What happens if we start here?"

In 1980 I had an article published in *Philosophy and Rhetoric* that examined connections among ethics, politics, and rhetoric in Aristotle's thinking. I was interested in seeing how one of the first Western thinkers who taught and wrote systematically about these subjects might have viewed such connections. Among the things I found that were interesting to me were, first, that for Aristotle the idea that humans are "political animals," designed by nature to live in communities, was the foundation of morality. I also discovered that, in Aristotle's view, the essential activity of moral decision making is deliberation—excellence in deliberation is the essence of *phronêsis* or "practical wisdom"—and since rhetoric is used when we deliberate about practical actions, it seemed to me that moral deliberation and the operation of *phronêsis* are fundamentally rhetorical. Beyond this, Aristotle stipulates certain moral or ethical constraints in his theory of rhetoric, so I was able to perceive some important linkages between rhetoric and ethics.

A few years later, I wrote an article on John Dewey (also published in *Philosophy and Rhetoric*) called "Dewey, Ethics, and Rhetoric," where I tried to look at communication ethics and indeed at rhetorical ethics from a Deweyan perspective. I found that there's a certain amount of overlap among his conceptions of selfhood, habit, and the instrumental uses of communication. In fact, the central feature of what I found in Dewey's thought had to do with what he called "practical intelligence" but what I aligned with *phronêsis*, "practical wisdom." This is what I had also seen as a central feature in Aristotle's thinking about ethics, rhetoric, and politics in the "Aristotelian Trilogy" essay. In the end, these two studies led me to many of the same conclusions—for example, that ethics is concerned with human conduct insofar as it is chosen or deliberate; that rhetoric, both as a form of deliberate conduct and as a form of conduct concerned with deliberation, is intimately connected with ethics; and that public deliberation in the service of democratic decision making is the process by which individual members of society construct the shared moral visions that are supposed to guide our communal life.

I also looked at the ethical implications for communication of other conceptions of human nature. Whereas Aristotle and Dewey both emphasize our "communal" or "political" nature as starting points for their treatments of ethics and rhetoric, I wondered what would happen if one began with a definition of being human in terms of our species-designation, *homo sapiens*. I wrote an article titled "Ethics, Wisdom, and the Mission of Contemporary Rhetoric" that addressed the question, "What happens if we start with the idea of fulfilling our nature as human as the ground of obligation?" On this view, we are obliged in our communicative and other behavior to enrich and cultivate our humanness, whatever that is. I took the notion of *homo sapiens*—in fact, we are *homo sapiens sapiens*, as distinct from *homo sapiens neanderthalensis*—to see how it might lead to some ethical principles or guidelines that could be applied to our communication. *Homo sapiens* means, literally, the human that knows, or the "wise" hominid. *Sapientia* or *sapienza*, if you look at the Latin and the Italian, has to do with wisdom. We are the "wise" human, in contrast to the upright-walking human, *homo erectus*, or *homo habilus,* the tool-using human. What is distinctive about our particular form of humanity is our capacity for sapience, for wisdom. I traced that out in the article, and I tried to explain how a commitment to pursue "wisdom" might shape our thinking about what is ethical and unethical in how we communicate with each other.

Another of my essays came out in a European journal called *Dialogue and Universalism* that tried to situate the grounds of obligation in yet another conception of "humanness." Here I asked, "What happens if we start our understanding of ethics with our existence as a living creature, with the fact that we are a life form on the planet Earth?" If we start with the assumption that our first obligation is to sustain the existence of our own species, what obligations flow from that and what are the implications for how we should communicate? In some ways, this essay integrated insights I had drawn from both Aristotle and Dewey, and I was able to develop and argue for a set of fairly specific ethical principles that can guide both our personal decisions about how to communicate with others and our judgments of others' communication with us.

I published another article in the *Southern Communication Journal* that took a somewhat different tack. Instead of looking to some conception of "human nature" as a source of groundings for ethical principles, I tried to develop a set of such principles for evaluating political discourse by starting with the basic tenets of democracy as a mode of governance and of political decision making. I looked at ethical issues in the 1984 presidential campaign between Ronald Reagan and Walter Mondale. I wanted to come up with an ethic that would be used appropriately to evaluate campaign discourse. What I did there was to situate ethics within the values of democracy as a mode of political association. What strikes me now, as I think back on that particular effort, is that the ethical guidelines I articulated there could be applied to *any* political campaign, and indeed to other modes of public, political discourse, including current debates about the war in Iraq and the limits of presidential power in time of war. I think the principles I argued for in that essay would permit us to make meaningful, justifiable ethical assessments of the discourse we now see coming from the Administration and from members of Congress.

In none of this work have I said that "this is *the* one, *the* only, *the* best" starting place. Rather, because I am basically a pluralist at heart, I have been interested in exploring the ethical implications of different starting points. I like asking, "What happens if we begin considering ethics here? What happens if we start there?"

Do you understand philosophical ethics as distinct from communication ethics?

To me, ethics comes to bear on communication insofar as communication involves choices. We choose when to talk and when not to talk, what to say and whether to say it, to whom to say it, whether to say it to this person or somebody else, whether to tell the truth or not to tell the truth, how to frame it, how to structure it. We choose message content. We choose message structure. It's hard for me to think about communication without there existing the opportunity for decision. In ordinary life, you can't make me talk. Now, you can torture me and force me talk, but these are extreme circumstances. Under ordinary circumstances, when I'm not forced to talk, when you're not torturing me, I make choices. All communication of the normal sort, in everyday life, involves choice-making and is covered by ethics. I would say that all communicative choices are covered by ethical theory and by moral philosophy.

Communication ethics is a subset of ethics generally, because not all my actions are necessarily communicative. For instance, I grow organic vegetables in my garden. Unless we are really going to stretch the notion of communication, I'm not going to talk about that as being a communicative event. I do that for the health of my family, myself, and for the earth. But it's not a communicative choice in the sense that I normally think of communication as symbolic action. The sort of ethical considerations that govern my choices about what to plant in my garden are not necessarily going to govern my communication behavior. To say that communication ethics is a subset of ethics does not mean that that all human conduct is governed necessarily by the same principles, which is why I believe ethics—in the plural—involve multiple approaches. Insofar as our communication activity involves choice-making or decision-making, it involves ethical issues. That's true whether it's direct or mediated communication. Advertisers, public relations specialists, speechwriters for the President—they are all making ethical choices just as we do in our conversation with each other.

Another element of our communicative behavior that invites ethical consideration is the fact that words have consequences. How and whether we speak can have an impact on the development and well-being of others, and because our speech is ordinarily a "chosen" form of activity, we can be held responsible for that impact. So, both in its nature as "chosen" and because it affects others' lives and happiness, our ordinary communication is an appropriate object for ethical appraisal.

How is communication ethics similar to or different from rhetorical ethics?

The question of rhetoric is an interesting one, depending on one's point of view. I hold a fairly broad conception of rhetoric. Of course, the term *rhetoric* comes from the Greek and it derives from a term that had to do with public speakers. The *rhêtôr* is the person who stands up in front of the group and speaks to them. So there was a form of the word (I think it's *rhêtêr* in Homer) used to describe the role of addressing an assemblage of people as when Odysseus, Achilles, and Agamemnon and some of the others are addressing the Greek troops in their encampment outside the walls of Troy. The term *rhetoric*, which first appears in Plato's dialogue, *Gorgias*, is derived from this earlier noun having to do with public speaking. Literally the "art of rhetoric" is *hê rhetorikê* or *hê rhetorikê technê*, which might be translated as "the speakerly art" or "the speakerish art." It's an adjective—*rhetorikê* or "speakerish"—that became an abstract noun. So rhetoric has originally to do with the speaker's art. I certainly have that as the foundation of my understanding of the concept.

Rhetoric involves the selection, the choice, of message content, structure, language, opportunity—all those things—with a view toward producing certain psychological effects in specific hearers. What we do is produce effects, and any communication that is chosen with a view to producing particular kinds of psychological effects is at least nominally subsumable under the notion of rhetoric. Generally, the effects with which rhetoric is concerned have to do with what's involved in forming judgments or in coming to decisions about practical matters—about practical actions. So, we might want to distinguish between rhetoric and, say, poetics on the basis of these sought-after effects. While poetics aims at producing aesthetic effects for their own sake, rhetoric aims at producing psychological effects (including, at times, aesthetic effects) that will lead an auditor finally to a practical judgment of some kind.

To go back to ethics and rhetoric—yes, I think that the ethics of communication in which I'm interested have their principal application in rhetoric, but I would also say that ethics is fundamentally rhetorical insofar as ethics involves making principled choices, and making principled choices involves being able to provide a coherent justification for action or belief in terms of some sort of principles. Principled action is action for which a coherent justification can be given—you have to be able to provide some kind of a *logos* or a "reasoned account" of it. Without such an account, we don't have an intellectually defensible basis for acting. There is an art to inventing justifications. I'll use Aristotle's definition of rhetoric here—rhetoric is the capacity for seeing in a given case the available means of persuasion. If I tweak it just a bit, we might consider rhetoric as the ability to identify the available justifications that can be advanced in support of a particular judgment. Thus, if ethical action involves being able to discern and compare the justifications that can be given for alternative courses of action, then doing ethics is rhetorical. That's not a major change in Aristotle's definition of rhetoric. It's a matter of being able to come up with arguments. "What are the arguments for and against this?" "What are the principles that are involved here?" "What are justifications for those principles?" "How far back can I go?" "What are the first principles from which I'm arguing?" One has to be able to think that through and talk about one's first principles. In the end, for ethical decision-making, you have to start somewhere. I'm going to start with the preservation of human life, for instance, and then I'm going to go from there. Or I'm going to start with the preservation of the ecosystem and then I'm going to go from there. Circumstances vary, and I'm going to have to have some starting points that are appropriate to a given set of circumstances and to the particular form of communication involved. This is why I start with that notion of commitment. When I want to think about what my communicative obligations are with respect, say, to my role as a teacher, or as a parent, or as a husband, or as a citizen, I have to ask, "What are the relevant ethical principles here to which I choose to dedicate myself?"

In any case, and to return to your original question, I see the term "communication" as being broader than the term "rhetoric," so that, while all rhetorical acts are communicative, not all communicative acts are necessarily rhetorical. Insofar as rhetoric is principally concerned with the practical, strategic uses of communication techniques, the ethical principles that apply to it may not be equally applicable to other instances of communication—to the sort of "aimless" talk that can occur between friends, for example.

What are your thoughts about a universal communication ethic?

My thinking in general has been that there is not a single right way, a single meta-ethical or meta-philosophical approach to thinking about communication ethics. There are multiple ways, each of which leads to different kind of insights and each of which might be applicable to different kinds of communication situations. Within an ethics of teaching, for example, which is a distinctively communicative and, I would say, rhetorical enterprise, I'm not sure that an Aristotelian or a Deweyan or an evolutionary approach to ethics is the best way to proceed. Their work has emerged for me as kind of a starting point in a lot of my thinking about ethics, but I don't hold any of these approaches to be "universally valid" for all communication situations.

When I set out to identify a set of ethical principles that might be appropriate to a certain kind of communicative activity, I start by looking at the nature and end of the activity itself. If I want to consider, for example, what my obligations are as a teacher, I start by asking, "What's teaching supposed to accomplish? What is the function or *telos* of teaching?" If I can come up with a conception of what teaching is supposed to be about and of what education is, then I'm obliged to do as a teacher whatever it is that advances the goals of education. I start with trying to find a definition or coherent conception of the activity. In the case of teaching, for instance, I might begin by maintaining that the function of teaching is to educate. "What does it mean to be an educator?" "What is education?" "What does the term 'educate' mean?" I'm not a philologist, but I like looking at that kind of stuff. The word *educate* comes from the Latin root, *educare*, which has to do with "rearing" or "raising something up." I understand this both in terms of rearing children and raising vegetables. That allows me to think metaphorically about education as a process of nurturing, cultivating, and stimulating the growth of human beings and minds. Then I can ask myself, "What conditions are necessary for human minds to be nurtured and cultivated and grown?" This permits me to begin identifying specific guidelines for teaching that, in the end, are ethical principles that can guide my actions insofar as I seek to be a "good" or "ethically sound" teacher. What are my obligations to my students? Well, they are to foster those conditions that are necessary for my students to grow, expand their thinking, become more mature as human beings. Given enough time, I could probably identify those conditions, and then articulate some ethical principles that ought to guide my teaching. I have actually published a couple of small essays on this matter—"Communication and Responsibility" and "Academic Freedom"—so I have put my mind to these sorts of questions before.

Part of my project, as I mentioned earlier, has been to explore ethics from different sorts of perspectives. The thread of continuity that has recurred for me and has really occupied my thinking and my research over the last decade and a half has been the notion of wisdom. "What is the wise human?" If I start with the premise that my first obligation, in all of my conduct, is to cultivate humanness, then my first obligation given this starting point is to do what I can in all of my conduct—communicative and otherwise—to nurture, cultivate, enhance, and augment the essence of our humanness. There is such a thing as a proper life for a human being, given at least the Western humanistic tradition, going back to the Greeks—not just to Socrates, but also his predecessors. We should enhance our humanity through what we do and say. I'll start with the assumption that, in its essence, humanness is a good thing. This sort of essentialist thinking is problematic and I understand that, but this is kind of how I approach it anyway. Keep in mind that this premise, to cultivate humanness, doesn't have to be a starting point, but it is one that speaks to me.

If the thing that distinguishes us most conspicuously from other life forms is our capacity for a certain kind of wisdom, human wisdom, then what we need in our behavior—communicative and otherwise—is to do all we can to help us grow in wisdom. That's led me, of course, to the more fundamental question: "What is wisdom?" That's what I've been working on for about the last 15 years, exploring the idea of wisdom and its relationship to speech and language in early Greek thought. I've been thinking about what it means to be wise. This has allowed me to develop my thinking about the grounds of obligation.

Let me then digress for a moment on this notion of obligation. "Do we have any obligations and if we do what are they?" So we're starting with that primary question: "Do we have obligations, and if so, what is it that creates obligation?" I recently read John Caputo's *Against Ethics*. He asserts that "obligation exists," and I want to say, "Why?" For me, that simple assertion isn't philosophically satisfying. "What is it that creates that obligation?" It seems to me that in one aspect my being here creates a ground for obligation, my decision to be here, now, rather than to leave my society or to leave life altogether. What really creates obligation is, again, a choice that we make. We make certain commitments in our lives when we make choices, including the choice to keep on living. In the making of those commitments, we create obligations.

For example, when I decide to get married and I take wedding vows, I commit myself in that overt act to love and to cherish and all the rest of it. I have created an obligation for myself. I have made a commitment. I have, by that choice, created a set of obligations. I'm obliged to communicate in ways that will nurture and sustain that relationship. So, to go back to the choice to live, to the bare fact of one's existence, we are born into the world and we are born into a society. I can't say that by this very fact of being born we take on obligations—that obligations are created—though Caputo asserts that "obligation always already exists" when we enter the world. But if I make the choice to continue living, and to live in a given society, I am obliged to conduct myself in ways that are consistent with my continued presence on the earth and with membership in that society. If I don't want to have any obligations to anybody, I have two choices: leave society and go somewhere where there won't be any other people and I will have no obligations to others, or commit suicide and free myself from all obligation (including whatever obligations I may have to the earth itself). By deciding to stay alive and not to exile myself, I have certainly obliged myself to live in such a way that I fulfill my obligations to where I'm living. If I decide to live in this particular society rather than another society such as Greece or France or somewhere like that, I incur by that choice the obligation to behave in such a way that I advance the fundamental values of this particular society. I am obliged to play the "game of life" according to the rules that govern the game in the society of which I'm a member.

I think this "game" metaphor can be helpful, and it has certainly been employed usefully by proponents of game-theory. Our existence is like being involved in a game and there are rules to it. If we decide to stay in the game, then we are obliged to understand what those rules are, and then to play by them. If I'm going to play poker with you, then I oblige myself to not cheat at cards. We're obliged to play by the rules of the game. What creates an obligation for me is the choice to stay in the game. The obligations then are embedded in those rules and I have to figure out what the rules are.

"What are the rules of living in a democratic society?" one might ask. Well, we can identify what some of those things are. These would then function as obligations, insofar as I choose to continue living in such a society. Another question might be, "What are the rules that govern politicking, as in running for office in a democratic society?" Or, "If one chooses to run for public office, what are the moral rules—the obligations—that one acquires by this very act?" This is what my article on Ronald Reagan investigated. What about the larger game, the game of existence? The game of, "Here I am." Here I am, a self-conscious creature plopped down in the middle of the universe, and I've decided to stay in it. I want to do right by it. So, "What is the game and what are the rules? How am I supposed to play this?" That is what the moral quest in life is about, trying to figure out what the rules of the game are. It seems to me that wisdom ultimately is understanding the rules of the game. Insofar as there are rules to govern the game of life, the game of one's own existence, then understanding what the rules are constitutes wisdom. The way in which that wisdom manifests itself is in guiding the decisions we make about how to act, both generally and with respect to communication in particular. It's a game that came along before I was here. According to Kenneth Burke, it's like coming into a conversation that started before you got here and will keep on going. For all of us, our ultimate obligation is trying to figure out what those rules are and then abiding by them.

I've been interested in looking in particular at the "wisdom of the West." I'm a Westerner. I'm not trying to privilege the Western over other cultural traditions—over African, or South Asian, or East Asian, or aboriginal North American cultural traditions—but for better and for worse we are products of Western civilization. Our language system and conceptual categories, academic institutions, social institutions of all various kinds bear the stamp of the Western world. I go back to the Greeks to get some insight into it, because that's where we started. I'm an archeologist at heart, and I like to go back to "first things," to origins. I started with that, and one of the things that I've learned is that, among other things, many of the earliest Greek thinkers, in their love of wisdom—their *philo-sophia*—were trying to understand the rules according to which the cosmos works. It involves the laws, if you will, the principles according to which the world itself, the whole process, is unfolding. Insofar as we can understand what those principles and rules are and live by them, then we're playing by the rules and are living a "moral life."

What do you think is the biggest challenge for communication ethics in a time of postmodernity?

What postmodernism has done, of course, is to challenge the whole universalist way of thinking about doing ethics. That whole rational paradigm, the notion of arguments, of reasoning, of logical coherence, of avoiding self-contradiction, all that good stuff. That is to me a very significant intellectual challenge and in some respects a practical challenge, too. It's a healthy one because it, again, invites us not to take anything for granted—including the very method or technology of inquiry that we bring to bear on our thinking about ethics.

In some respects the challenges of postmodernity and of globalism are the same; that is, dealing with an enhanced awareness of difference, of disparity, of fragmentation, of the pre-eminence or predominance of perceptions of disunity and disharmony. The problem is that we are talking about "ethics" while trying to respect different folks and different cultures, and there's a lot in me that's relativistic. The ethics that function appropriately in another society won't necessarily apply here, and vice-versa. If I push that far enough, who are we to say that democracy is the best for everyone in the world? I think that one of the things that postmodernism has done is to encourage us to ask those questions, to challenge the givens. I'm teaching a graduate seminar next semester on rhetoric and ethics, and in addition to reading Aristotle and John Dewey, we're going to read John Caputo's book, and Alasdair MacIntyre's *After Virtue*, and Zygmunt Bauman's *Postmodern Ethics*. I am including these works because I want us to interrogate "traditional" conceptions of ethics and moral philosophy. I want us to challenge our assumptions, what we take for granted. This sort of interrogation and challenge, I think, is important, and I think that "postmodernism" (whatever that term actually means) provides for a very useful critique of our traditional ways of thinking about ethics.

I don't think that these questions are new with people like Zygmunt Bauman, or Michel Foucault, or Jacques Derrida. I think that Protagoras and Gorgias were asking essentially the same questions in the fifth century BCE: "Let's question received tradition, let's question received opinion, and let's challenge the very notion that there is such a thing as objective reality, that there really is a physical and a moral universe out there." That's what the Pythagoreans were about for example, trying to grasp the "ultimate realities" of the universe and trying to have their own personal conduct in tune with the sort of the proportions and numerical relationships that they saw governing the cosmos. There's a single principle I think that runs through Greek cosmological thinking—the notion of equilibrium, balance, proportion. The term *logos* actually means "proportion," and to live morally for Greek thinkers such as Pythagoras, Heraclitus, and even Aristotle is to live in harmony with the principle of balance and proportion that governs the cosmos. That's what Aristotle's doctrine of the Mean in moral virtue was all about.

Then the Greeks also give us this other, sophistical stance, which says, "Wait a minute. How do you know there's a universe out there? Even if there is a universe, how do you know that what you know about it is the way it really is? Even if you could know it the way it really is, how could you possibly communicate that to other people?" These questions are basically restatements of Gorgias' "three theses," and I think they foreshadow and anticipate the kinds of challenges to tradition and accepted terminological categories that have been raised again in the last half-century or so. I don't think it's a new thing. I think it's a re-emergence of sophistical thinking, actually. That brings us back to raising these kinds of fundamental questions. I think that's a significant challenge. I think that the challenges of globalism and postmodernism have to do with recognizing difference, disparity, particularity, fragmentation, the instability of the self, the problem of identity, and so on. There are multiple cultural groundings for different kinds of ethics; different cultures have different kinds of approaches.

Relativism allows us to respect difference and not to assume that our way of looking at ethics is the best way, the right way, or the only way. However, "What do you do about genocide?" for example. "What do you do about Rwanda?" You say, "well, you know, that's their thing and in their culture that's acceptable." "What about the Holocaust?" "What about the imposition of fundamentalist Islamic law on women?" "What about the caste system in Hinduism?" "What do we do about what the universalists want to say is a violation of fundamental human rights?" There's this tension in there. I think, indeed, this is one of the fundamental issues in our time that has to be dealt with. Yes, we want to respect difference and multiple approaches and ethics in the plural. Yet what happens when, in the name of cultural tradition, female genital mutilation—which is an ethnically biased way of putting it—occurs? When you call it "mutilation" there's a culturally biased slant on it. There's a more neutral term, female circumcision. I was called on that in class one time. An African-American female student said, "You have already taken a moral position on this issue by that very language. What it's called by those who practice it is female circumcision." What about these kinds of things? There's an ongoing tension with all that.

What that leads me to think about, going back to your earlier question, is, "Is there something that would function as a universal ground that allows us to transcend culture in developing a ground of obligation?" You have to respect difference, but are there things that we have in common? I think that one of the things that has been submerged or marginalized by the recent interest over the last 20 or so years in postmodernist and post-colonialist approaches, is an interest in what we have in common rather than what distinguishes us. I think we have to look back at what we have in common. One of the things we have in common is, of course, our humanity. If we can agree on that, we may not agree what it means to be human yet, but at least we've got humanity in common and we might agree that our most fundamental ethical obligation is to respect one another's humanity.

We've come as close as it's possible to come, I suppose, to embracing that as a universal ground in the Geneva Conventions and the United Nations' *Declaration of Human Rights*. These things are "universals" by consensus. Not everybody signed on to these documents, but there is a consensus across many cultures and among people in societies around the world—not all people in all societies, but by some people—that there are such things as human rights. By virtue of our very humanity, we deserve to be respected as humans, and so even in a time of war we can treat each other with a certain amount of dignity. There is a fundamental human rights question at issue there. It's the same thing with female circumcision, or the caste system in India, or genocide in Rwanda or in Bosnia, or the oppression of women under the Taliban and in other Islamic states. We're all human and we have to treat each other with our own kind of individual dignity and autonomy. That is a possible guide to, or portal on, some kind of a universal grounding.

Things have been tried sporadically through the United Nations, which is the closest we have to a global "community center," to stop genocide, to stop oppression. Again, the United Nations is trying to secure the agreement of our fellow members in the community of nations. In any case, we agree to abide by these rules, that the rules of this game of living as societies on the face of the Earth are going to involve respect for each other's cultural traditions but at the same time to respect human life and autonomy. When a particular cultural tradition comes into conflict with this generally agreed upon sense of what basic human rights are, then something has got to give. What ought to give is the cultural tradition. We, not as the result of international pressure, but as a result of internal pressure, did away with slavery, which was an abomination in terms of human rights. We changed cultural traditions.

The other thing I would say in looking for first principles and groundings, while still trying to be responsive to the challenge of multiculturalism and to the postmodern critique, you have to have first principles. You've got to have some place to stand, but we have to recognize that those places we stand are always open to challenge and that we can be called upon to justify those. I once presented a paper called "Between a Rock and a Hard Place." The subtitle is "Searching for Groundless Grounds of Communication Ethics." There is a discussion in that paper which may end up in a chapter in the next book I'm going to write. It talks about the necessity of having an anchor by which to attach or on which to ground our justificatory apparatus. If I'm going to justify "X" action, it's going to be finally justifiable in terms of some first principle, but recognizing at the same time that those principles are not set in concrete. They are open to challenge and they are not quite themselves stable.

In Caputo's introduction to *Against Ethics*, he talks about his sense that he's on an island adrift in a sea on a starless night with nothing to navigate by. At the same time, though it's a floating island, it's the only place you have. You have to hook in somewhere. Otherwise, everything is adrift and you have nothing to stand on. As Archimedes said, "If you give me a place to stand and a lever, I can move the Earth." You have to have that place to stand in order to go forward and act. If you don't have a place to stand, you can't move outward. The ground sinks away. You try to thrust upward in quicksand and you go downward. So there has got to be a place that you can stand for the moment, recognizing that it's slowly, slowly sinking below and you have to get to this other stone, some other relatively firm place. In that respect, ethics is kind of an ongoing search for points of relative stability from which we can act, recognizing that those points of stability are transitory. This, again, goes back to the Sophists, and for that matter back to Heraclitus—everything is in flow, everything is in flux.

Another challenge that postmodernism has raised is that it calls into question our traditional ways of thinking about ethics. My sense of ethics involves the experience of agency or choice or volition. That is, I do feel like I've got a choice to make here. I can think about a problem and solve it. To be principled is to think about my actions and ask myself, "What are my obligations here and what justifies my choice?" If I can't justify this moral judgment then what basis do I have for acting on the problem? That's a very Aristotelian, very rationalistic, approach. If I can't come up with a rationale for my choices, then I have no rational basis for making them. Therefore, I have no actual ground. I can throw it to chance basically. "Let's see how the dice come out," as opposed to making up our minds and thinking it through, or looking in a sacred book such as the *Bible* or *Koran*. We've got to make up our own minds and to ask, "How do I know what I think is the right thing to do is really the right thing to do?" I have to see if I can make an argument for it. I have to see if I can indeed provide justifications for my choice.

One of the gifts of postmodernism is that it has put back to the forefront this challenge to confidence in our own thinking. It challenges the very notion of agency, of choice, of the self as an origin of action. The postmodernist critique is directed at a legacy of modernity, and specifically of the Enlightenment project and the scientific revolution going back to Francis Bacon and his successors, which held that we can be the masters of nature. I think there is an arrogance there, and I think that's why the postmodernist critique is so important, because it has debunked that conceit.

Works Cited

Aristotle. *Metaphysics*. Trans. Hugh Lawson-Tancred. New York: Penguin, 1998.

———. *Nichomachean Ethics*. Trans. K. A. K. Thomson. New York: Penguin, 2004.

———. *Rhetoric*. Trans. W. Rhys Roberts. New York: Modern Library, 1954.

Bacon, Francis. *Collected Works of Francis Bacon* (12 vols.). London, UK: Routledge Thoemmes, 1996.

Bauman, Zygmunt. *Postmodern Ethics*. Oxford: Blackwell, 1993.

Bentham, Jeremy. *An Introduction to the Principles of Morals and Legislation*. Eds. J. H. Burns and H. L. A. Hart. New York: Oxford UP, 1996.

Burke, Kenneth. *The Philosophy of Literary Form: Studies in Symbolic Action*. Berkeley: U of California P, 1974.

Caputo, John D. *Against Ethics: Contributions to a Poetics of Obligation with Constant Reference to Deconstruction*. Bloomington: Indiana UP, 1993.

Derrida, Jacques. *Of Grammatology*. Trans. Gayatri Chakravorty Spivak. Baltimore, MD: Johns Hopkins UP, 1976.

Dewey, John, and James H. Tufts. *Ethics*. New York: H. Holt and Co., 1908.

Dewey, John. *Human Nature and Conduct: An Introduction to Social Psychology*. New York: H. Holt and Co., 1922.

———. *The Quest for Certainty: A Study of the Relation of Knowledge and Action*. New York: Putnam, 1929.

Eubanks, Ralph. "Reflections on the Moral Dimension of Communication." *Southern Speech Communication Journal* 45 (1980): 297-312.

Foucault, Michel. *The Archaeology of Knowledge*. Trans. A. M. Sheridan Smith. New York: Pantheon, 1972.

Gorman, Peter. *Pythagoras, A Life*. Boston, MA: Routledge and Kegan Paul, 1979.

Guthrie, William Keith Chambers. *The Greek Philosophers from Thales to Aristotle*. London, UK: Methuen, 1967.

Havelock, Eric. "The Linguistic Task of the Presocratics." *Language and Thought in Early Greek Philosophy*. Ed. Kevin Robb. LaSalle, IL: The Monist Library of Philosophy, 1983. 7-82.

Hesiod. *The Poems of Hesiod*. Trans. R. M. Frazer. Norman: U of Oklahoma P, 1983.

Hobbes, Thomas. *The Collected Works of Thomas Hobbes*. Ed. Sir William Molesworth. London, UK: Routledge Thoemmes P, 1992.

Homer. *Iliad: Books I-XII*. Oxford, UK: Clarendon P, 1884–1893.

Johnstone, Christopher L. "An Aristotelian Trilogy: Ethics, Rhetoric, Politics, and the Search for Moral Truth." *Philosophy and Rhetoric* 13 (1980): 1-24.

———. "Ethics, Wisdom, and the Mission of Contemporary Rhetoric: The Realization of Human Being." *Central States Speech Journal* 32 (1981): 177-188.

———. "Dewey, Ethics, and Rhetoric: Toward a Contemporary Conception of Practical Wisdom." *Philosophy and Rhetoric* 16 (1983): 185-207.

———. "Communication and Responsibility: Teaching Ethics in Human Communication." *Texas Speech Communication Journal* 8 (1983): 3-8.

———. "Academic Freedom in the Speech Communication Classroom: Toward an Ethics for Teaching." *ACA Bulletin* (1990): 63-70.

———. "Evolution, Speech, and Morality: Toward a Rhetoric of Survival." *Dialogue and Universalism* 5 (1995): 85-104.

———. "Reagan, Rhetoric and the Public Philosophy: Ethics and Politics in the 1984 Campaign." *Southern Communication Journal* 60 (1995): 93-108.

———. "Between a Rock and A Hard Place: Groundless Grounds for Communication Ethics." Eastern Communication Association. New York, NY. 1996.

Kahn, Charles H. *Anaximander and the Origins of Greek Cosmology*. Indianapolis, IN: Hackett, 1994.

———. *The Art and Thought of Heraclitus: An Edition of the Fragments with Translation and Commentary*. Cambridge, UK: Cambridge UP, 1979.

MacIntyre, Alasdair. *After Virtue*. 2nd edition. South Bend, IN: Notre Dame UP, 1981.

Mill, John Stuart. *The Ethics of John Stuart Mill*. Ed. Charles Douglas. London, UK: Blackwood, 1897.

Plato. *Gorgias*. Trans. W. C. Helmhold. Indianapolis, IN: Bobbs-Merrill, 1952.

A Conversation about Communication Ethics with Sharon L. Bracci

How did you become interested in studying communication ethics?

My initial interest in communication ethics emerged out of my rhetorical studies, especially Aristotle's *On Rhetoric, Nichomachean Ethics*, and his theory of *phronesis*, a kind of practical wisdom honed through experience. The classical version of language, language as an instrument of persuasion, was both exciting and frightening. "How far can I go in trying to persuade someone? Is it even right to try to do so?" I suppose we could say that the power of the word is what led me to try to find some legitimate constraints on my enthusiasm to convince any hapless soul who has the misfortune to appear before me. I really loved to argue. Then, "How does one argue ethically? How does one argue in good faith?" These seemed the more interesting questions.

A second prompt was practical and pedagogical. At Ohio State I supervised the basic course in argumentation under Josina Makau's direction. Frankly, if I was fretful about the ethical use of argument for myself, I felt even greater pressure to do right by the hundreds of students that took these courses. Over time, dovetailing effective and ethical use of communication in the classroom just became a natural combination that has never left me.

I think that the third prompt was this growing interest in bioethical discourse. I see it as an exemplar of public moral reasoning over value-laden issues. I committed myself to understanding the rhetorical and ethical dimensions in this discourse. I pursued it in my scholarship, of course, in Communication Studies, and then made a more formal commitment to it by taking a second master's degree in bioethics at Case Western when I left Ohio State.

What drew me to bioethics from a communication ethics perspective was a need in bioethical discourse to talk across disciplines. What norms are going to guide philosophers, physicians, legal scholars, religious ethicists, social scientists, and communication scholars to hear one another out?

It's been instructive to study how this discourse engages the postmodern critique. If there is ever an ethics with a view toward contingent action, medicine is it. In the research lab and at the bedside, one simply can't avoid evaluating issues and courses of action in which the stakes are sometimes enormously high. I think my initial interest in communication ethics parallels the bioethics angst. I am trying to learn to "speak postmodern" in healthcare contexts, as David Morris joked in an insightful article in a recent *Hasting*

Center Report. In sum, I think rhetoric, argumentation, and bioethics would be my three impulses.

How do you define communication ethics?

This is a difficult question because any definition I give you is going to reveal a set of assumptions and biases, points of emphasis. Having conceded that, the short answer that comes to mind is that communication ethics is moral argumentation. That's basically how I've approached it. On the other hand, I think we could probably tease it out more. Let's call communication ethics an inquiry into the range of other-regarding communication patterns that engage difference and, at the same time, uncover a common humanity—human commonalities—in ways that contribute to our willingness to live peaceably among one another. There is a lot more to say, of course, in terms of understanding, evaluation, judgment in interpersonal and public contexts, but I think if we focus on key notions of other-regardedness—difference within commonality—then we can capture an interest in ethics as both social and as action-oriented. Then those actions can arise out of this common ground we discover together, through language.

I prefer the term "communication ethics" rather than "communication ethic." Communication ethics seems to capture a plurality of theories, principles, norms, and language patterns we invoke to justify our behavior. This plurality, in turn, reflects the plural methods and goals of communication itself. So, communication ethics examines better and worse reason-giving with a view toward action. Communication ethics is a mode of moral argumentation, from my perspective.

Do you understand philosophical ethics as distinct from communication ethics?

I used to think of communication ethics as a kind of a subset of moral philosophy. I don't think quite that way anymore. I think that communication ethics differs in scope and focus. Moral philosophy is a broader category. It is a systematic inquiry into the nature of the good life: "How do I know it?" "How do I live it?" "Where are the intellectual resources to help me justify my version of it?" There are some broad metaphysical and epistemological issues embedded in moral philosophy because they relate to claims about human nature and truth claims.

Communication ethics, on the other hand, is a more focused inquiry into what it means to be an ethical dialogical self in terms of the communicative process itself and the dialogical virtues required to participate well in that process. We ask "Who can speak?" and then, "How are specific patterns going to do a better or worse job of building understanding and, importantly, developing the will to engage difference, not only respectfully, but critically?" So, the questions focus on access, the quality of the language once that access is gained, and the dialogical virtues required to sustain engagement throughout deliberation.

Having said that, communication ethics has historically sought to defend a view of ethical communication by looking to moral philosophy for intellectual support. We pretty much tied our fortunes to moral philosophy and so we now face the same crisis in credibility that philosophers face. As philosophical assumptions are challenged, so are ours. We need to think about how to answer the critiques of classical theory and look to our own field for some theoretical support. My own view is to take my support where I can find it. I believe there is much in both philosophy and communication theory to help us address serious challenges to the ability to do ethics.

How is communication ethics similar to or different from rhetorical ethics?

Historically, rhetorical ethics has been concerned with legitimate constraints on efforts to persuade or convince an audience: "What are the ethical limits of what I can say in my efforts to win others over to my view?" "What are the limits of my willingness to adapt to audiences?" "How much do I want to manipulate their beliefs, their values, their sensibilities, their fears, to pursue what I think is a common end for both of us?" The common perception that rhetors adapt and manipulate shamelessly for their own purposes is, of course, what gives rhetoric its bad name among some philosophers and the public today.

But I don't want to make too much of the difference between rhetorical and communication ethics—there are too many overlapping issues with respect to the nature of selves, the grounds for truth claims, the possibility of moral autonomy, the ideal of checked power. The lines are blurred, so perhaps it is a question of emphasis rather than substance.

How would you characterize the integration of dialogic ethics and moral argument in your work?

My research situates communication ethics in the broad category of public moral argument and democratic deliberation. My work is much more in public case studies than in small group or dyad patterns. So, my focus is on public deliberation with a view toward action.

If you want to tie it back to moral philosophy, there are some basic themes here. Obviously, an inquiry into what it means to deliberate well. This is a broad category of current interest across disciplines, including political philosophy, political science, and sociology. Each looks at what it means to engage in effective and ethical deliberation, what justifies policy-making. These intersect traditional communication concerns about "Who has access to deliberative space?" Once concepts of power, liberation, and empowerment are engaged, questions about the limits of moral autonomy and agency remain. Finally, students of public deliberation wrestle with the problem of potentially incommensurable ends. Arguably, this constellation of concerns never came up in quite the same way, historically.

A second theme that really is interesting is the interplay, if you will, between cognitive and emotional appeals in deliberation: "What is the role of emotion in public moral argument?" "What are some guidelines for evaluating the appropriate argumentative force of some specific emotions?" "What is the cognitive force of something like righteous anger? moral outrage? compassion? guilt? fear?"

Another theme centers on media. In the United States, let's face it, most of us live with the proliferation of mediated images and texts. Young people, especially, are exposed to a stunning amount every day. I think questions in ethics arise here: "Does this proliferation of exposure help shape our moral sensibilities, particularly of children in their formative phase?" "Do media influences mean that we need to take formal account of them when we theorize and practice communication ethics?" Maybe what I'm asking is "Do theories of moral education, now, need to build in an account of mediated moral sensibilities?" I think this is a very interesting question.

A final theme relates to what we might call the moral burden of knowledge. I think most of us would concede that once we know something with some potentially powerful ethical implications in a context, we're obliged to take account of it. We can't "un-know" it or wish it away. This knowledge is going to become the eventual springs of action for some of us. So, the question arises: "What are the limits of our moral burden to find out, to turn knowledge into an understanding that can lead to wisdom and action?" These days are ethically challenging for the uninformed, the unreflective, the unknowing in an information-rich culture such as the United States: "Are we just merely naïve?" "Do we practice a kind of willful ignorance?" "Given all of our resources, do information-rich societies have an increased moral burden to know?" Perhaps ignorance is no longer a morally neutral standpoint. With respect to issues that guide my scholarship, I would say those are the main themes.

If a person has information, that implies an obligation.

Right. Cases of distant suffering are the ones that come up all the time in media. Zygmunt Bauman talked about this in *Postmodern Ethics* and *Life in Fragments*. In the past, communication traveled so slowly; many were ignorant of distant horrors. We don't have that excuse anymore. We *know*. On some level, even glancing at a headline, we know something. How we react to headlines says something about moral sensibilities. "What do we say about the compassionate and altruistic aspects of human nature that are getting rattled in an information-rich environment?" I'm dancing around the debate over compassion fatigue here. We see, we hear, horrors of distant suffering. We freeze in a kind of impotence; we don't know quite what to do and often we do nothing. The thesis of compassion fatigue assumes that at one time readers and viewers of distant suffering did not disengage, but now the constant onslaught of images overwhelms us, jades us, and we turn the page.

I just finished reading Susan Sontag's *Regarding the Pain of Others*. She's written a marvelous monograph in which she conducts a wide sweep of visual depictions of war, terror, et cetera. She concludes that there is an unbridgeable difference between being there and getting the mediated image. The mediated image will never have the same impact and that's why there is such a disconnect with the photojournalist who is trying hard to get us to see what he or she sees. Yet, viewers can't, the distance is too great. It doesn't mean we can't act and be compassionate, but there is a basic disconnect in the experience of horror and the mediated visual representation of it. Her book is a provocative contribution to discussions over the role of art to stimulate the moral imagination and strengthen our compassionate sensibilities.

In addressing themes in your scholarship, you've mentioned several writers. Are there others who have influenced your work in communication ethics?

Definitely. Early on as I was trained in rhetorical theory and criticism, Aristotle and to a lesser degree Cicero, were strong influences. I was very much interested to understand prudential reasoning, *phronesis* as a kind of experiential wisdom that was "close to the ground," as they say, always attending to the contextual constraints in decision making. This is very useful, of course in bioethics. Stephen Toulmin was very influential to me as I began to read the bioethical literature. I read his challenge to universalist reasoning in *Cosmopolis* and in his work on bioethics with Al Jonsen in *The Abuse of Casuistry*. These were marvelous defenses of particularistic reasoning that was very refreshing to see take hold in bioethical decision-making.

Also, early on, the philosopher Isaiah Berlin, in *The Crooked Timber of Humanity*, influenced me. He offered a lucid and eloquent defense of pluralism. He was absolutely poetic, I think, in castigating the evils of monistic schemes and universalism gone awry. Berlin also wrote an insightful essay on Machiavelli that was a turning point in my thinking about prudential reasoning and pluralism. Then, of course, in our own field, scholars in communication ethics have challenged me to extend my thinking in ways that more seriously engage the postmodern critique of several classical thinkers.

Outside of the field, scholars who study the discursive or communicative turn in public deliberation are many. Most begin from Jürgen Habermas's challenge, especially to Aristotelian reasoning in the public sphere. Partly in response to Habermas, there is a wide literature in deliberative democracy that is trying to theorize dialogical interactivity as a kind of democratic rationality. John Dryzek's early text on this is actually called *Discursive Democracy*. There are lots of people working on this: Dryzek, Amy Gutmann and Dennis Thompson, among others.

Of course, Seyla Benhabib is the most enduring for me. She reworks Jürgen Habermas in a way that answers a lot of serious challenges to discourse theory. She puts these challenges in conversation with feminists, postmodernists, communitarians, and theorizes her version of interactive universalism. In doing so, she manages to make plausible what seems impossible. She defends a dialogical process that attends to particulars and contexts and gender differences and the formation of identity in narrative. At the same time, she rethinks the normative constraints of conversation and defends principles that transcend context to develop ways to reason, post-conventionally, beyond kin and culture. In this scheme, all norms are negotiable once deliberation is underway. I think a key insight of interactive universalism is its potential formative power. There's a modest but real hope that participants can develop this kind of enlarged thinking that eventually takes more people into their circle of concern.

You've mentioned the contributions of scholars from Aristotle and Cicero to Jürgen Habermas and Seyla Benhabib. What differences emerge in communication ethics across different historical periods?

If we want to approach communication ethics in a traditional mode, we're going to proceed from a very different set of assumptions about the nature of human selves, our place in the cosmos, the nature of rationality and emotions, the capacity for moral autonomy, and certainly gender relations. Having said that, I don't really think that Greek, Roman, and Stoic styles are interchangeable. Let's just mention a few commonalities and differences and leave it at that.

With respect to human nature, I think Platonic, Aristotelian, and Stoic ethics share a pretty high regard for humans as rational—well, men anyway. The cultivation of our rational capacity is the surest way to self-control. This is important for the kind of self-mastery that Charles Taylor talks about in *Sources of the Self*. In any event, our self-control is going to be in sync with broader harmonies. The self desires an orderly harmonious life that reflects the larger cosmic order. Emotions don't work very well here because they are perceived as chaotic. They are certainly not trustworthy. Our desires can lead us astray into disorder, chaos; worse, for the Stoics, emotional desires lead to perpetual dissatisfaction. We can't ever really satisfy our emotional wants. So some level of detachment is called for, and I think that's why the life of contemplation is so highly valued in this tradition.

If I want to engage communication ethics in the Platonic mode, I'm going to focus on objective detachment. I'm on this monistic mission to find the Good and the True. But, I'm also going to value some kind of Socratic dialogue in which assumptions are rigorously examined, all the time. Plato is just not going to let me get away with some self-satisfying complacent life, and call myself ethically engaged. That's a marvelous legacy, I believe. Aristotle obviously valued rationality, the contemplative life, but I think he made a bigger space for emotions in ethical deliberation. You couldn't call him an emotivist, as we understand that term today. Certainly Aristotelian ethics is about much more than preferences, but I think we can see it's rigorously focused on proportionality. Doing the right thing at the right time and doing it in accord with this virtuous balance is the goal (and the way to happiness), which is why Aristotle's doctrine of the Mean is so important.

I think that both Aristotle and Plato would agree that character formation, a kind of habituation of virtue, is important and it happens early. If I want to engage communication ethics in an Aristotelian mode, I'm going to be much more focused on those communication patterns that habituate the dialogical virtues I want to champion. *Phronesis* keeps me in a position where I need to respect other opinions. I need to have this reciprocal engagement and I have to have some hope that the process is formative, wherever we go. If nothing else, Aristotelian ethics is practice, always attending, always close to particulars.

Let me just leave it with one example. I'm going to see good in the world, perhaps small pockets of peacemaking in a violent environment, but will reject the Platonic model of contemplating an ideal of peace. Let's say if Aristotle were around right now, I think he'd nudge us to study virtuous behavior in the midst of vice, people who choose not to participate in wrongdoing. I think he'd want us to pay particular attention to whistleblowers, for example. That would be my varied approach, in a classical mode.

The modernist mode is going to continue rational pursuits with a vengeance, striving toward rational control of the problem before me. René Descartes and Immanuel Kant make this pretty explicit. If I'm in the modernist mode, I place great faith in the power of reason to solve all problems, not just ethical problems, but also social and political problems. If I'm doing ethics in the modernist mode, I am relatively isolated in this task. Importantly, let's not forget what emerges now is a concept of inherent human dignity that's very important. I don't think that's left us. Modernist ethics necessarily counts on the sameness of humans in its deliberations, whether it is in considering if I would be willing to universalize the norms of my actions for everyone, or in considering how everyone counts for one and no more when I consider the consequences of some speech in action. In the end it's individualistic. It's rational. It's disembodied. I'll be attempting objectivity, but I'm also going to be focused on sameness. We may talk a lot about justice claims and what rights and obligations are going to flow from those claims.

The postmodern challenge is pretty much turning all of this on its head. So if I'm going to engage it in the postmodern tradition, I'm really taking a very different approach in terms of my ability to exercise rational control over anything. I'm going to give up the notion of consensus on what counts as a binding mode of reasoning or even on ends. I'm going to be very concerned about epistemological claims: "What constitutes truth?" "What methods are legitimate ways of knowing it?" I'm going to be very focused on power, and power for people to distort communication, because they're also controlling access. I'm going to be much more focused on the mediated nature of human experience. Prior to this period the assumption was that humans can know from experience and can learn from experience. The postmodernists want to remind us that our experience is itself a set of mediated values and cultural beliefs that shape us. So, teaching in this mode will assume more awareness of the cultural horizon from which we deliberate. This is very difficult. It's impossible to escape these confrontations in our reasoning since we can't move out of where we are.

As a consequence, communication ethicists have some options in their approach. I'll mention just three. First, communication ethicists can reject some or all of these contemporary challenges and work to rehabilitate classical or universalist theories in *toto*, as they were originally thought, on the view that they have not been seriously discredited to the point of moral irrelevance. Second, communication ethicists can accept these challenges to rationality, autonomy, consensus making, and so forth, and respond by shifting the grounds of their efforts. This would involve a move away from grounding communication ethics in discredited theories and justifying it instead in the virtues of the communicative process itself. This approach would also form common cause with postmodern concerns and regard communication ethics as an engagement with issues related to gender, empowerment, decentered selves, multiple narratives, and ethical pluralism. A third way would try to engage the various challenges of postmodernism with respect to rationality, consensus, the nature of selves, et cetera, by asking if existing ethical theories can be fitted or refitted to meet some of the demands of contemporary ethical life. In my own thinking, this third way has merit. Let me say, however, that I am mindful of Susan Moller Okin's insight in *Justice, Gender and the Family* that we cannot just add women and stir—for example, to classical theory—because a whole edifice, a way of life is predicated on the patriarchal assumptions of some theories.

What is the biggest challenge for communication ethics in a time of postmodernity?

Well, I think we've been talking around this a little bit. The greatest challenge of course to any universalist claim today is going to be in the realm of the epistemological or the metaphysical: "How much knowledge do we have?" "What rendering of human selves makes knowledge possible?" From the postmodernist view, any prior understanding of human nature and autonomy is not only misguided, it is repressive. Human subjects are not similarly focused on self-mastery. We do not all share a desire to hold domination over nature. We do not all embrace an instrumental rationality that is so technologically focused that any experiential wisdom is lost. The postmodern is going to challenge reason and discourse that's purely instrumental. Sometimes discourse just wants to celebrate a playful enjoyment of otherness. The critique is that modernism and classicism destroy any hope of doing that, destroy any kind of discourse that permits the non-instrumental use of otherness. This is a harsh critique, and I'm not sure that it's entirely warranted. Even so, I think we need to listen to it.

Joseph Dunne noted that his project in *Back to the Rough Ground* was to approach Aristotelian *phronesis* carefully, to show that it is a complex, subtle process. Before we trash it, let's understand it, he cautioned, and maybe the same could be said in present circumstances. The task for us I think is to approach discourse and dialogue among radically situated and contextualized selves, selves who are not fully autonomous and individualistic with subtlety and a view toward understanding the ways identity is both formed and reformed in language. We might not have to jettison the past entirely to grapple with the ethical implications of identity formation. I think the problem for us is that communication ethics, like ethics in general, has to assume some level of accountability and has to assume some level of autonomy and even intentionality. After all, "ought" implies "can." We cannot speculate about ethical dialogical selves outside some understanding of what human selves can do.

We need to address this challenge and preserve some varying degrees of accountability, motivation, intentionality, and ability to grow. I think that's the key idea: growing moral autonomy. This involves developing an ethical mind of one's own. One doesn't say "Well, we do it this way because we've always done it this way." Or, "Well, that's how we do things in the United States." Or, "My grandparents voted that way, of course I'm voting that way." One must think through the reasons for speaking in a particular way and assume responsibility for it. Ethics can still be interested in how humans can develop ethical minds of their own beyond conventions or traditions even as we take account of the constraints of those conventions and constraints.

We are contingently formed in narrative—some of which we're not the author of, but some of which we can be. Every person who's decided to reinvent herself knows what that's all about. Sociological evidence supports Seyla Benhabib's view that individuals weave an identity of themselves out of conflicting narratives over time. Accountability and a fragile autonomy also emerge in this process. So, "If there is evidence that humans can do this, can we then join the minimalist perspective on universals?" I think we can as long as we emphasize "minimalist." Not so minimalist that all discourse uncovers is a range of empty platitudes and commonplaces that are so general they're meaningless. Conversely, if we're going to put too many normative constraints into the process, well then we've lost most of our ethical credibility. Here again is how Benhabib's interactive universalism is a valuable contribution. She's trying to stay in the Kantian tradition of universalizing something that speaks to the common ground of human dignity. She's very focused on trying to get people to engage in kind of an enlarged thinking. Benhabib's project isn't really to critique universalism as being wrong-headed. Neither is she challenging the contingent and contextual nature of moral reasoning. She's just trying to theorize a conversational model that accepts the critique but sets in place formative conversational norms that help us develop this capacity for enlarged thinking that's both culturally embedded and culturally transcendent. It's a huge task.

Seyla Benhabib recently talked about the so-called "scarf affair" in France. A Muslim girl was told not to wear her scarf in school because doing so made an explicit religious statement. This was a situation in which we had a lot of institutional debate going on. We had a lot of religious speakers come in and say, "We're preserving this and that." What we never engaged were the opinions of the girls themselves. They were never part of the conversation. Later, in private conversation, girls noted that they were wearing the scarves after conversation with their Jewish and Christian friends who were wearing modest displays of their religious symbols. Scarf wearers were reframing their actions as a political statement, or a statement of individualism. They were not wearing scarves as a mode of oppression or strict party line in terms of religious sensibility. They were re-signing it, making the semiotic move. A girl could now assert that she was making a change in what it means to her and asserting that meaning and, in the process, re-identifying herself. A process that's formative allows all that to come out; allows other girls to hear that; respects and allows people to reverse their perspective and think beyond the traditional norm. So you'd start with these basic normative constraints, namely universal moral respect and egalitarian reciprocity, by allowing anybody who can speak to the affair and has a stake in the outcomes to join the conversation. All can question. All can challenge the norms and points of relevance as they relate to the topic of religious symbols.

This is tentative work, but Martha Nussbaum and some others have done really interesting work on theorizing what she calls the "human capabilities approach." She's not the only one working here, but this is another movement in universalism that I think holds promise. As a classicist, Nussbaum is an insightful interpreter of Aristotle's work. What she and others are theorizing now is a normative theory of human flourishing. On some level it is, unapologetically essentialist, to the degree that the theory posits components of what it takes for any human to flourish. Now we can debate the range of this or that component, but if we begin from some set of basic human capabilities we have a workable framework for universal human rights. Obviously, that dialogue's already going on in the United Nations and other places, but she's bringing some philosophical weight to it that I find extremely promising. It's tentative, but it's a real start. Nussbaum practices an admirable kind of engaged philosophy. She's done some terrific work in the emotions, in the upheavals of thought, and intelligence of emotions in an edited volume with Jonathan Glover called *Women, Culture, and Development*. She's no armchair philosopher. She travels the world. She participates in international forums, and she's increasingly aware that the push for human rights is very vibrant today. So, why not theorize some grounds for those rights in the nature of selves, or at least try?

What are some of the elements that would inhibit or enhance the possibility of a globalizing vision of ethical discourse?

Oh, lots of things! The inhibiting forces are some of the tensions we've been talking about—philosophical risks and theoretical hurdles that have to be addressed. My bias is that we have to circumscribe our definition of universalism. Otherwise, cross-cultural conversations feed the perception that

Westerners are only and always ready to run up the flag of cultural imperialism. It is too easy to see strong claims as disingenuous attempts to impose one's cultural bias on another.

Another force these days includes the various identity movements—gender, race, ethnicity, and sexual identity. There's such a plurality of goals within these movements and there is a legitimate call for recognition. So, identity politics will clash pretty fiercely with some other cultural goals and make common goals of ethical discourse very difficult. Sometimes there's a perception that there's not enough shared ground to begin the conversation. At other times, I might be so passionately focused on my legitimate goals, I'm just not going to have the energy or the will to engage serious difference in a deliberative forum. Identity politics right now is a serious barrier to any universalizing vision.

I think an enabling possibility is one that lets us look at cultures as much more contested. They're narrative sites of identity, yes, but they're also narrative sites of reforming that identity. If the problem is the huge tension between post-Soviet and post-colonial cultures trying to find their own identity, and alternatively this globalization push, if you will, then maybe we need to take a closer look at what cultures are like. Here again, I think Seyla Benhabib can help us. In her recent book, *The Claims of Culture*, she shifts her lens of focus from gender, as she did in some of the work we talked about before, to a complex view of culture. Let's go back to the scarf affair. When I look into a culture, I might mistakenly see an essentialism that isn't there. If I'm inside, I know that participants are looking at their shared stories, but they're contesting their stories as well.

We have an enabling possibility if we reject the view of cultures as homogenous, as holistic. This rejection helps us to engage specific claims for truth and validity in specific contexts. If we restrict our universalism to an accommodation of this plurality and the contested nature of cultures, I think we have a better chance to have a good dialogue. Benhabib calls this a dual-track of democratic deliberation, because it permits the widest amount of contestation within and among groups. The dual track continues to embrace the normative components of interactive universalism—respect and reciprocity—but it adds the notion of voluntary self-ascription: citizens self-identify in these tracks and retain the freedom to exit. This track encompasses social movements, kitchen-counter conversations, probably cyberspace chat rooms, and any place we get together in a non-institutional public space. This track parallels a wider space of legislative and judicial bodies, longstanding institutions. Between the two, of course, we're trying to deliberate what we can do. Working to make the dual track more vibrant will widen public space and encourage a broader agenda. "What should be on the public agenda as opposed to determining justice issues in advance?" To answer that, we must attend to the plural and contested nature of cultural groups themselves.

Again, the key for Benhabib is that the process itself is formative. I wouldn't say that she's not interested in consensus, but that's not her focus. Her focus is on a formative process that has enough normative constraints to encourage participation with less fear. Participants become more willing to risk their views. Participants slowly expand, not only their ability to think beyond their traditional norms, but also to widen the circle of their concern. Over time, this becomes a discursive way of life. This is a utopian vision, of course it is, but it's a vision of the process as formative in ways that people will want to know another view and will want to think more expansively. They will want to live peaceably with one another.

Our lives seem to move much more quickly with advancing technologies. Do you think people may lose the will to make an ethical choice in a moment of fatigue?

Sometimes it's more than lack of will. Sometimes it's hatred born of fear, and the violence that this fear unleashes today, both in the perpetrators and in the victims. Technology speeds up the process by which we discover that we all have dirty hands.

We can engage in the historical cycle of retaliation much more quickly now. Historically, the cycle of retaliation attached to the revenge model of justice has worked against any global vision of how to talk about peaceful solutions. Also, historically, deliberations over global violence have not been inclusive enough to legitimate the use of state power to address violence with more violence. When we examine who's doing the deliberating, it hasn't been very inclusive, because it is focused on maintaining power. Global discussions at the nation-state level assume that the protection of sovereign power is key. If I'm going to engage in a truly inclusive process on the international level, I've got to be willing to share and not hoard this power. I'm at risk here, because if I engage in this deliberation, I'm going to be bound by the outcome and maybe I don't want to be. This diminishes good faith negotiations.

How can we engage communication ethics in our relationships with others to accomplish pragmatic outcomes toward social change?

I'm back to communication ethics as a form of moral argumentation. How do we encourage that view of it? The biggest fear of argumentation that many have is the worry that cherished beliefs and values will be lost forever. Conversely, I may not want to argue with my friends or acquaintances because I'm afraid I'm going to destroy these relationships. Pragmatically, our task is to show people communication ethics as moral argumentation can be fun, is not necessarily destructive of relationships and is not necessarily going to mean the end of all we hold dear.

Yes, argumentation is a risk, and I think we'd be disingenuous to say otherwise. Many people want to live peaceably, and if we're going to live peaceably, we not only have to be willing to engage difference, we are well served to locate a few kernels of common humanity. There are some things humans share and many find a great deal of joy when they discover some shared concerns and aspirations. This might partially account for the pleasure many find in reading history—for that shock of recognition that somebody 5000 years ago thought like you did, shared your current hopes and dreams and fears. If we can cultivate our dialogical courage to enter the conversation, to risk both comforting and surprising outcomes, then the potential outcomes are valuable.

For me, the primary ethical commitment arises in the view that we are made, at least in part, in discourse. If we can continue to theorize communication patterns that enable people in conversation and in debate to reflect carefully on how narratives form identity, and to open a space for reforming that identity, then we have done good work as teachers and scholars.

Works Cited

Aristotle. *Nichomachean Ethics*. Trans. H. Rackham. Cambridge, MA: Harvard UP, 1934.

———. *On Rhetoric: A Theory of Civic Discourse*. Trans. George A. Kennedy. New York: Oxford UP, 1991.

Bauman, Zygmunt. *Postmodern Ethics*. Oxford, UK: Blackwell, 1993.

———. *Life in Fragments: Essays in Postmodern Morality*. Oxford, UK: Blackwell, 1995.

Benhabib, Seyla. *Situating the Self: Gender, Community, and Postmodernism in Contemporary Ethics*. New York: Routledge, 1992.

———. *The Rights of Others: Aliens, Residents, and Citizens*. Oxford, UK: Cambridge UP, 2004.

———. *The Claims of Culture: Equality and Diversity in the Global Era*. Princeton, NJ: Princeton UP, 2002.

Berlin, Isaiah. *The Crooked Timber of Humanity*. Princeton, NJ: Princeton UP, 1998.

Cicero, Marcus Tullius. *Cicero: De Oratore*. Trans. E. W. Sutton. Cambridge: Harvard UP, 1942.

Descartes, René. *Meditations on First Philosophy: With Selections from the Objections and Replies*. Ed. John Cottingham. Cambridge, UK: Cambridge UP, 1996.

Dryzek, John S. *Discursive Democracy: Politics, Policy, and Political Science*. Cambridge, UK: Cambridge UP, 1994.

Dunne, Joseph. *Back to the Rough Ground: 'Phronesis' and 'Techne' in Modern Philosophy and in Aristotle*. Notre Dame, IN: U of Notre Dame P, 1993.

Glover, Jonathan, and Martha Nussbaum, eds. *Women, Culture, and Development: A Study of Human Capabilities*. Oxford, UK: Oxford UP, 1996.

Gutmann, Amy, and Dennis Thompson. *Why Deliberative Democracy?* Princeton, NJ: Princeton UP, 2004.

Habermas, Jürgen. *Between Facts and Norms: Contributions to a Discourse Theory of Law and Democracy*. Trans. William Rehg. Cambridge, MA: MIT P, 1996.

Jonsen, Albert R., and Stephen Toulmin. *The Abuse of Casuistry: A History of Moral Reasoning*. Berkeley: U of California P, 1990.

Kant, Immanuel. "Foundations of the Metaphysics of Morals." *Kant Selections*. Ed. L. W. Beck. Englewood Cliffs, NJ: Prentice Hall, 1988. 237-298.

Morris, David B. "How to Speak Postmodern: Medicine, Illness, and Cultural Change." *The Hastings Center Report* 30 (Nov/Dec 2000). 7-16.

Nussbaum, Martha. "Human Capabilities: Female Human Beings." *Women, Culture, and Development: A Study of Human Capabilities*. Eds. Jonathan Glover and Martha Nussbaum. Oxford, UK: Oxford UP, 1996. 61-104.

Okin, Susan Moller. *Justice, Gender and the Family*. New York: Basic Books, 1989.

Plato. *Plato in Twelve Volumes*. Cambridge, MA: Harvard UP, 1980.

Sontag, Susan. *Regarding the Pain of Others*. New York: Farrar, Straus, and Giroux, 2002.

Taylor, Charles. *Sources of the Self: The Making of the Modern Identity*. Boston, MA: Harvard UP, 1989.

Toulmin, Stephen. *Cosmopolis: The Hidden Agenda of Modernity*. Chicago: U of Chicago P, 1992.

A Conversation about Communication Ethics with Richard L. Johannesen

How did you become interested in studying communication ethics?

It has become very clear to me that the starting point was somewhere toward the end of my doctoral work. It occurred to me that in the coursework that I had taken in Speech/Speech Communication, now Communication, in the late 1950s and early 1960s, that virtually all of what we were taught or were teaching in those courses was "how to": how the communication process worked, how the techniques functioned, which processes were most effective and successful with which audiences and under what conditions. At the same time it occurred to me that very seldom did we ask or were we asked "whether to" questions. Even if we knew that something would work, even if we knew how something would work, ought we to do it in terms of ethical responsibility?

As I best recall, the only places in the late 1950s and early 1960s where communication ethics was focused in textbooks were persuasion textbooks: one by Robert Oliver and one by Wayne Minnick. And there was an argumentation and debate and discussion book by Henry Eubank and J. Jeffrey Auer that included a solid chapter on ethics. As I recall that's about it. Unless you were taking a persuasion course that used one of those texts or an argumentation and group discussion course that used the Eubank and Auer book, you probably weren't forced by many teachers to ask questions about ethical responsibility.

For some reason, that bothered me. I guess it was a nagging realization that there was something missing in my education and perhaps the education of others that was really important. That puzzled me and it bothered me. I think that was the initial "click" moment that made me decide to include communication ethics as part of my professional life—even though most of my training in doctoral work was in the history and criticism of American public address, with a minor in American history. If I had to do it over again I would minor in philosophy, but you know, you can't do it over again. That really was the motivational force.

Do you prefer the term "communication ethic" or "communication ethics"?

Over time I've become more comfortable with the phrase "communication ethics" to designate what I'm working in or about, rather than a communication ethic. I think the phrase communication ethics is broad enough, flexible enough in scope, to include a variety of issues and contexts. It can still allow anyone working in the field to propose and argue for a communication ethic as most appropriate as they see it, or the best that we can do at this point. I don't start out by thinking that there is a communication ethic and that it is out there somewhere, like a Platonic ideal, and I can intuit it. It'll be constructed by us collectively over time. So I'm very comfortable with the phrase "communication ethics."

I also don't differentiate much between rhetorical ethics and communication ethics. I guess I would have coming out of graduate school, but I don't anymore. I think both of them have a communicator with the intent or purpose to influence others in some way to some degree. Both involve choices among communicative means to achieve whatever the communicative end might be, and we're responsible for those choices. Sometimes, even in my texts, I'll use rhetorical ethics or communication ethics more or less interchangeably. Others may not feel comfortable in doing that, but I have tended to. I like the phrase "communication ethics" because it is comfortable for me to designate a field of study, not a formal traditional discipline, but an interdisciplinary field of study. Also I see communication ethics, in one sense, clearly as applied philosophy of ethics. Practical ethics, but not just any old practical ethics, because I think we've become collectively more and more convinced that communication is central to what it means to be human. If that's the case, then we can't avoid communication ethics playing a central role in the exploration of ethical issues generally.

To be human is to be a communicator in an essential way, in my mind at least. We should be asking questions about groundings of our communication ethics, underpinnings, basic principles, and not just be about applied ethics. I think we have an obligation to also do philosophical theory and critique. Over time a lot of this has evolved. I know I wouldn't have answered some questions the same way fresh out of graduate school that I do now or even at midpoint, but two years into retirement, that's the way I think.

Would you talk about the themes in your scholarship related to communication ethics?

I would describe it by who influenced me, and I can describe it by themes that I think are typical of my work over time. At the end of my doctoral work and very early in my career, I was clearly influenced by the writings of three people whom I consider within our field as founders of the study of communication ethics. Namely Karl Wallace at University of Illinois, Franklyn Haiman at Northwestern University and, often neglected, Tom Nilsen at the University of Washington. All of them were actively publishing in the 1950s in national and regional journals on communication ethics. I think of Karl Wallace's article that appeared in *The Speech Teacher* on an ethical basis for communication. I would warrant it is one of the most reprinted and commented on pieces in communication ethics during the 1950s and '60s. Franklyn Haiman, who we identify with massive and solid work on freedom of speech, started out early writing about communication ethics and persuasive ethics, and he's always worried about both. An early article of his reexamining the ethics of persuasion appeared in the *Central States Speech Journal* in 1952, and more predominate was his article on democratic ethics and the hidden persuaders in the *Quarterly Journal of Speech* in 1958. I suppose that Tom Nilsen's work was most influential to me early on. One journal article, of which he published a number, that I found most helpful was "Free Speech, Persuasion, and the Democratic Process," also published in the *Quarterly Journal of Speech* in 1958. Nilsen's textbook, the first textbook in communication ethics, *Ethics in Speech Communication*, went through two editions and was very influential. I always admired it because, unlike mine, although my bias has become apparent in it, his was a book written from a standpoint about democracy and reason and discussed the implications for a communication ethic. His wasn't a survey of various approaches or emerging trends or issues, but it was a very valuable book, I think, both for students and teachers. Admittedly, the writings of those three people were very influential on me.

Then, over time, my interest in Martin Buber has also been a major influence on my writing and on my life, especially his three major books: (i) *I and Thou*, (ii) *Between Man and Man*, and (iii) *The Knowledge of Man*. Those three books collectively capture the heart of his philosophy of dialogic communication. So you'll find that clearly reflected in a lot of my work. More recently I would point to the books and articles of Ron Arnett, particularly his books (i) *Dwell in Peace*, (ii) *Communication and Community*, and (iii) *Dialogic Education*. He has influenced me interpersonally as well as through his writings. Two people who have not been directly active in the work of this conference or the National Communication Association Communication Ethics Division, but who were influential in writing about Martin Buber and ethical implications, are Rob Anderson and Ken Cissna. Their books and writings have been influential on my understanding of not only

Buber's approach to dialogue, but also other conceptions of dialogue including Mikhail Bakhtin's work. Their books hold fascinating content, especially the critical analysis of *The Martin Buber–Carl Rogers Dialogue*—how it is or is not Buberian dialogue, or another of their books entitled *Moments of Meeting*. A third book of theirs, *The Reach of Dialogue*, was done in conjunction with Ron Arnett. And most recently, a fascinating book simply called *Dialogue: Theorizing Difference in Communication Studies*, edited along with Leslie Baxter. I think they've moved the discussion about the nature of dialogue forward through all of their work.

Then, admittedly, Cliff Christians and his writing and example have influenced me with his books, his articles, and the broad range of concerns that he presses upon us. First, the notion of looking for some kind of minimal universal ethical norm for communication. This is perhaps best reflected in the book of original essays that he edited with Michael Traber called *Communication Ethics and Universal Values*. Along with that is a continuing concern of his for not just worrying about personal ethics—individual ethics—but really worrying more about institutional ethics, systemic ethics, and organizational ethics. That's reflected in part in his book with John Ferré and Mark Fackler called *Good News: Social Ethics and the Press*, and particularly crystallized in a very recent article of his with Kaarle Nordenstreng called "Social Responsibility Worldwide" in the 2004 *Journal of Mass Media Ethics*. Also influential has been his openness to exploring diverse approaches to communication ethics. He attends to non-major traditions of ethical theorizing, and to theorists that may be a little on the periphery of what we've been used to, or to at least what formal ethics and philosophy departments have been used to. That's pulled together, I think brilliantly, in the edited volume that he did with Sharon Bracci, that was published a few years ago called *Moral Engagement in Public Life*. Those kinds of themes in his work, in both books and articles, have caught my attention and generally I've agreed with much of what he's argued. So those are some of the kinds of influences that I guess I would look back on.

I do think that there are some themes in my work. I guess, since I preach about it in my classes and writings, one of the major themes has to be the ongoing tension between freedom and responsibility. We can't avoid that tension in what we're teaching about communication. We have to make students understand that, yes, at least in our political system, we have certain maximum freedoms of communication. At least in theory we do and we need to understand what they are. We also need to understand that you can exercise those freedoms in more or less responsible or ethical ways. Freedom and responsibility are related but separate issues: "What are my constitutional rights?" "What is the tension between legality and ethicality?" "Should we make them synonymous—that which is legal is ethical—and try to disabuse students of that tension?" That has, I think, been a theme in my text *Ethics in Human Communication* through all five editions.

The one time I had to really pull that together was for a chapter in a book edited by Ron Arnett and Josina Makau, *Communication Ethics in an Age of Diversity*. It was a chapter entitled "Diversity, Freedom, and Responsibility in Tension." I tried to talk about the tension between ethics and freedom in three contexts—allegedly obscene rap lyrics, pornography, and hate speech—and explore how that tension works itself out.

A second theme has become more and more important in my work; the role of what I call formed ethical character in ethical decision making. This entails who we are at a given moment, in terms of our formed ethical character, and has a lot to say about our sensitivity to ethical issues. Depending on who we are at that moment, we will either recognize or not recognize that there is an ethical issue at all. Who we are in terms of ethical character at that moment will determine how motivated we are to do anything at all about an ethical issue, and whether to worry about it at all. As several people have pointed out, there may be time constraints where we don't have the luxury of reflection: deadlines, pressure, and crisis. In those moments who we are, our ethical character, will more or less determine whether we do the right thing or not, rather than applying some formal ethical framework in a more leisurely fashion. My argument would be that a healthily developed ethical character would allow a person more times than not to do the right thing in those kinds of situations. Not invariably, not absolutely, but given the uncertain circumstances that you're in, a person of sound formal moral character will probably do the right thing. That's been at least in the last couple of editions of my text. I had the opportunity to really focus on that topic in a book chapter called "Virtue Ethics, Character, and Political Communication" published in an anthology called *Ethical Dimensions of Political Communication* edited by Robert Denton.

I guess the third theme that I have become more interested with and about in the last couple of editions of my text are the various versions of the feminine or feminist ethic of care as it has developed somewhat similarly but somewhat differently in various authors, starting with Carol Gilligan, and Nel Noddings, but including Rita Manning, and Joan Tronto, and our own

Julia Wood. They all approach this topic in slightly different ways. I had the chance to look at some connections between Martin Buber and Nel Noddings's work in an article published in the *Southern Communication Journal* entitled "Nel Noddings's Uses of Martin Buber's Philosophy of Dialogue."

I've been fortunate to be able to play out those themes in textbook form for students but also in book chapters where you can really approach it in more detail with more examples and see how it works. I'm comfortable with identifying those as three really important themes for me over time in work on communication ethics. There may be other themes that people would detect in my work, and that's probably true.

The inclusion of feminist communication ethics attests to a change in the way we understand and study communication ethics. What are your thoughts about communication ethics and the historical shift to postmodernity?

Well, I've tried to grapple with the issue of postmodern ethics and include some of that in my my text. From my point of view, I don't think there is any one universally accepted definition of postmodernism. I've tried through a series of questions with my students and in print to capture the contrast between what went before postmodernism, whether it's called traditional or modern or whatever, and the postmodern critique itself.

Let me suggest these kinds of questions as my way of thinking about some of the essential elements of the postmodern critique: "What would be the result for communication ethics if truth, reality, is contextual, contingent, and constructed in discourse rather than universal, absolute, and discovered?" "What if there is no individual moral agent, no autonomous unencumbered individual self, deciding ethical questions impersonally about abstract others apart from the social, economic, and institutional contexts in which the self is embedded and constructed?" "What if there are no personal speakers in communication with attendant ethical responsibilities for choice, but only interchangeable role players, whose communication is dictated by the discourse rules of a dominant culture?" "What if there are no grand master narratives or absolute universal values that warrant general allegiance across groups and cultures?" "What if probing the nature of human nature is but a delusion or an exercise in political power?" "What if the alternative to absolutism and universalism is nothing but fragmentation and alienation?" "What if there can no longer be ethics as we know it?" That set of questions and discussion about them have served to crystallize for me, and hopefully for students, what the postmodern critique is about, in terms of contrasting former assumptions and postmodern assumptions.

I think a good example of that has to do with debate over the self as an ethical agent, whether there can be an ethical agent or not. "Can we devise a viable concept of the self as an ethical agent?" I think of a journal article by Lynn O'Brien Hallstein in the *Western Journal of Communication*. She argued for a postmodern perspective of self within a feminist context of an ethic of care. She comes fairly close to trying to grapple with melding some concerns about postmodernism with the need for some sense of self—not an unencumbered self but an embedded self, and an interrelationally developed self. This is just one example, and there are others, of not going all the way as some postmodernists do to say that the self is completely fragmented, alienated, impotent, and determined—and doesn't really have any choice at all and has no responsibility at all.

If we were to ponder the issue of what's the next development, where to go after postmodernism—is there a post-postmodernism, in terms of communication ethics—I don't know. I don't know how I would venture guesses about it. What I do know, however, is I think we shouldn't jump too quickly to some notion of post-postmodern ethics until again we further explore more carefully and in-depth some of the attempts that have been made to develop a postmodern communication ethic. There have not been many, but there have been some in the English Department's version of rhetoric. I think the book by James Porter called *Rhetorical Ethics and Internetworked Writing: An Ethic For the Computer Age* is an interesting attempt to blend Aristotle and Kenneth Burke on the one hand with Michel Foucault, François Lyotard, Seyla Benhabib, and Luce Irigaray on the other. A book that blew me away in some senses, puzzled me in others, was a recent book by James Anderson and Elaine Englehardt titled *The Organizational Self and Ethical Conduct*. To my knowledge it's the first flat-out thorough postmodern organizational communication ethics book: "Modernist writing is objective, its authorship is concealed, and its claims are essentialist. Postmodernist writing declares its standpoint, reveals its authorship, and reflexively analyzes the constructed character of the claims." That's not the only place they heighten their devotion to postmodernism in their writing. I'll be interested to see what the people working in organizational communication make of the book.

Of course, I would urge reexamination of the work of my late colleague Martha Cooper, particularly two of her book chapters. The first, now a decade or so old, is called "Ethical Dimensions of Political Advocacy from a

Postmodern Perspective," and that appeared in the book titled *Ethical Dimensions of Political Communication* that Robert Denton edited. Then more recently, and it's reprinted in the 5th edition of my text, her chapter titled "Decentering: Judgment: Toward a Postmodern Communication Ethic." It's a serious attempt to construct a postmodern communication ethic. It's in the book *Judgment Calls*, edited by John Sloop and James McDaniel, and she draws in varying ways on Jürgen Habermas, Michel Foucault, Nancy Fraser, and the feminist ethic of care.

I also think of the work of another colleague in my department, David Gunkel, who may not be well known yet but he will be, writing about cyberspace ethics. He finds traditional modern standards really not workable. He doesn't always know where to go from there and that's part of his project. Starting with his book called *Hacking Cyberspace*, but more recently and more provocatively in a journal article that he co-authored with Debra Hawhee titled "Virtual Alterity and the Reformatting of Ethics" in the *Journal of Mass Media Ethics*. I haven't quite come to grips with some of his conclusions yet. Part of his worry about traditional approaches not applying to cyberspace ethics is that they are too human centered and don't work that well in cyberspace for an ethic. He's questioning, really, the humanist centeredness of ethics generally: "Does alterity have to be human to involve us in ethical issues?"

Before we jump to post-postmodernism we need to carefully and thoroughly consider at least some of the attempts that have been made toward a postmodern ethic, whether we agree with or disagree with parts of it. I think perhaps these attempts at a communication postmodern ethic have been passed over or haven't been noticed. We worry about postmodernism generally, what it is and what impact it has, but I'd urge that we reconsider these specific attempts at a postmodern communication ethic.

I've been fascinated by Cliff Christians's emphasis on a minimalist universal ethic. I puzzle over that a lot and read a lot in that area. Some of that is reflected in my textbook now, finally. I think that a lack of commitment solely to some kind of invariable and universal absolute ethical principles doesn't mean we can't be committed to a minimalist set of some universal norms that can be transcultural. This minimalist set of norms, it seems to me, could readily acknowledge that ethical standards within a culture or among co-cultures within a culture can be more relative to their specific cultural, ethnic, gender, or class context.

The minimalist set of universal norms that we've committed to, whatever they are, can be used then to critique practices within these more relative applications of ethics. To put it another way, relativistic, culturally bound, situationally bound ethics always should be open to critique by that minimalist set of transcultural norms—such as those that Cliff and others have been searching for.

"If there are transcultural values considered universal, in what sense do we mean universal or should we mean universal?" Here I found most helpful a book by Robert Kane, called *Through the Moral Maze: Searching for Absolute Values in a Pluralistic World*. He tries to voice his view about what we could mean by universal. Universal, he says, "does not have to mean that we are absolutely certain about values or that we have the right to impose them on others through fanaticism or authoritarianism. Universal simply means that we believe these values are valid for all persons, times, and viewpoints." The real issue, he says, "is whether we have good reasons for believing in at least some universal values despite not being certain." Kane also argues we "need not require that the ethically relevant human traits that we seek be completely universal traits and provably so." Merely that they are common human traits. It's enough, he feels, "to know that human beings commonly need certain things. . . . We can reason that since we are human, there is a high probability that we need these things as well for a fulfilling human life." Cliff Christians, Michael Traber, Sissela Bok and others have worked in the direction of trying to figure out people's universal ethical standards—their universal, but not absolutely certain, commitment to values that are highly probable and defensible as transcultural norms.

I would urge you to look at Sissela Bok's book called *Common Values*. It is a fairly brief book but was very influential on me. She's well known for her book *Lying* and her book *Secrets*, but this is well worth reading also, because she presents her argument for a minimalist starting point for the search for transcultural values. She "seeks out the values that are in fact broadly shared without requiring either absolute guarantees of them or unanimity regarding them." Such minimalist values, she says, "can serve as a basis for communication and cooperation across cultures and for discussion of how they might be applied or extended in scope." In addition such common values "provide criteria and a broadly comprehensible language for a critique of existing practices both within a particular society or culture and across societal boundaries." She identifies a small cluster of minimalist moral values that are held in common by most human beings that had to be worked by all human societies, at least in her viewpoint. Namely, she suggests the positive duties of mutual support, care, loyalty and reciprocity; the negative duties of refraining from hurtful actions of deceit, betrayal and violence; and the standards for rudimentary fairness and procedural justice when conflicts arise.

I find her attempt resonates with the work of Cliff Christians and Michael Traber in their book *Communication Ethics and Universal Values*. Their search for universal values is rooted not solely in anthropological sameness but is rooted in philosophical assumptions about human nature. The ethical values that they identify, from their viewpoint, are not foundational assumed certainties. They are commitments open to reexamination. The universality of these values, they believe, is beyond culture. It's "rooted ontologically in the nature of human beings"; these values are universal by virtue of what it means to be human. Furthermore, they say, no matter the cultural differences that focus either on individualism or the community, communitarianism, there is a "growing consensus that certain universal standards for social accordance of human dignity must be upheld regardless of cultural differences." The protonorm or foundational value underlying most cultures, and at the heart of what it means to be human, is the sacredness of life—the "irrevocable status" of respecting human life. From that, they identify some guides for our uniquely human capacity to use language, namely truth telling, human dignity, no harm to the innocent, unconditional acceptance of the other as a person, and solidarity with the weak and the vulnerable. They call their approach "world view pluralism," in which ethical beliefs are held in good faith and debated openly and a commitment to universals does not eliminate differences of viewpoint. The only question for them "is whether our world views and community formations contribute in the long run to truth telling, human dignity, and nonmaleficence."

Sissela Bok seems to agree. She says "cultural diversity can and should be honored, but only within the context of respect for common values. Any claim to diversity that violates minimalist values…can be critiqued on cross-cultural grounds involving the basic respect due all human beings." That's one answer to the notion of where do we go if there aren't absolutely certain lists of values we must abide transculturally and not go all the way to extreme relativism, be it cultural or ethical relativism at the other end. I'm comfortable, so far, with this kind of a project that they seem to be working out for a minimalist set of universal values.

What are some of the significant areas for future communication ethics research?

Well there are many that could be suggested. The first one that I view as important, in a sense, is one that's been with us throughout the development of communication ethics as a field. It's an important one continually: that in our work on communication ethics we balance, not in some precise way, but we balance our research on and teaching about both individual personal ethics on the one hand and institutional systemic, organizational ethics on the other. We can't view communication ethics as wholly dealing with individual standards and responsibilities or think that the only really important question is how the social system influences ethical decisions and constructs, constrains, and restrains them. I think you've got to consider both continually.

I hope we don't ignore individualism and individual responsibility and forget about that; lose the sense of personal responsibility. I just can't buy, "I was just following orders," as the reason for some of the abuse in the prison in Iraq. It didn't wash in Nuremberg, and I don't think it should wash here. Now that's not to say that the system of which the soldiers were a part also didn't have causal influence on what happened, but I don't think the soldiers were just automatons in the grip of a system.

My worrying about the continuing concern for individual ethical responsibility was best captured two years ago in my keynote address at the 7th National Communication Ethics Conference on a role for shame in communication ethics. It's a controversial topic, examining in what contexts it manifests itself and how we can too often be just satisfied with the work of psychologists and psychiatrists who are against shame—by which they mean kind of a pervasive and debilitating shame that influences our entire life. I think we need to also to consider a role for what I, and others, call "situational shame." Situational shame is what Michael Hyde, in the beginning of his book *The Call of Conscience*, indirectly sees as an element of conscience. Without conscience, shame goes out the door. My views on shame aren't all worked out, but it illustrates my concern for individual responsibility issues.

At the same time we need to continue to work out how the structures, norms, rules, regulations, and expectations of a given organization, system, or institution either helps or hinders ethical development within the organization: "What's acceptable and why?" "How are decisions made?" "Are there very many systems and organizations where for virtually every decision ethical questions are asked right alongside questions about costs, efficiency, implementation, legality, and so on? And if not, why not?" "How do elements of the system retard people's ability to act ethically, perhaps forcing them to act unethically to save their job, or allow them to think that ethics aren't important in that institution or organization?"

There have been a number of explorations of organizational communication ethics, certainly. For example, looking at the role of formal codes of ethics in organizations. I've been doing that in print for a while. There are serious pros and cons of formal codes. Codes can be just public relations puff pieces to fend off government regulation: "Yeah, we're self-regulated. We've got a code; government you don't need to tell us what to do." A code can be self-serving in the sense that it's very carefully written to give approval to existing ethically suspect practices by excluding certain things, thereby sanctioning existing ethically suspect practices. I think there are legitimate uses for codes. A code of ethics can depict in words the ideal ethical character expected in that organization. Not so much a list of rules and regulations but a word picture of the ethical character of an employee. It can be very practical as a source of argument. At least it gives something to everybody to which they can turn to make arguments about ethicality. Just because a behavior is either in the code or not in the code doesn't mean it's ethical or unethical, but it gives a starting point for talk in the organization about ethics and judgments about ethics.

I agree also that codes alone won't do it. They are very ineffective. Codes have to be integrated with many other efforts within the system, within the organization—top down leadership by example as role models of ethical behavior: "What resources is the organization willing to commit to the organization and the employee's thinking about ethics?" "Is there an ethics officer to whom people can turn for advice?" "Is there an ethics office?" "Is there an ethics training program at all levels?" If a code is integrated along with those kinds of things it might be a little more effective. In any case, I think we need to continue to balance our concern both for issues of individual ethical responsibility and institutional ethical responsibility. We shouldn't forget about this topic simply because it has already been addressed.

The other area, ethics for nonverbal communication, may seem old hat, too, but I've thought about it in print for about two decades. We talk about ethics for visual communication. This presents the whole issue of where to go for advice about ethical nonverbal communication. You can't go to a nonverbal communication textbook. You won't find it there. For example, silence is a dimension of nonverbal communication. "What are the ethics of silence?" I don't know where I would go for ethical advice on that. "Can we assume that ethical norms for verbal communication apply equally well to nonverbal?" I don't think so in every case, but I don't think it's an issue that we've looked at enough. There are elements of it that people are writing about, but we should have some more sustained analysis by people trained in communication ethics.

For example, images in commercial advertising, such as in the video that many people use in class called *Killing Us Softly*. Or images in music television: some people expose their students to a video entitled *Dream Worlds*, which includes perfect examples for ethical analysis. The people producing the videos don't put it in quite those terms, but they are golden opportunities to raise the issues or for a scholar who studies some of the instances appearing in such videos: "What do we make of this in terms of ethical responsibility?" "Who's responsible directly or indirectly?" Another area is documentaries and documentary images. Larry Gross and his colleagues consider that in their book *Image Ethics*, but beyond that there has not been a lot done recently in terms of the responsibilities of the documentary video or filmmaker: "What are their responsibilities to their subjects? To the art in general?"

Probably the area that catches our attention and makes us think that people have been worrying about visual communication ethics is journalistic ethical images—the images captured by photographers and videographers. I think of an image, a photograph of 9/11 of the person who jumped from one of the burning towers and was caught in a still photo as he plunged to his death. In some versions, that photo was enhanced enough that the person's face could be recognized: How does the family feel about that? What's the impact on friends that knew this person? The photograph is no longer just an abstract representation of the tragedy, it's personal and it invades privacy. Then we have the issue of the photos from the prison in Iraq. In this instance, it's not the ethical issue of what they did. Now it's the issue of journalists deciding which images to disseminate to us out all of those they have available: "Are any of the images ethically questionable?" "What standards do they use?" I agree that Tom Wheeler's book *Phototruth or Photofiction* is a good stab in the right direction of trying to figure out some guidelines for that, but there aren't a lot of books that I know of in photojournalism that worry about the ethical issues. There's the "how to," still not enough of the "whether to." So the issue of ethical standards of nonverbal communication is still one I think worthy of further exploration. Those are the two major ones I'd suggest as we continue our scholarship on communication ethics.

Works Cited

Anderson, James, and Elaine Englehardt. *The Organizational Self and Ethical Conduct: Sunlit Virtue and Shadowed Resistance.* Fort Worth, TX: Harcourt College, 2001.

Anderson, Rob, Leslie A. Baxter, and Kenneth N. Cissna, eds. *Dialogue: Theorizing Difference in Communication Studies.* Thousand Oaks, CA: Sage, 2004.

Anderson, Rob, and Kenneth N. Cissna. *The Martin Buber–Carl Rogers Dialogue: A New Transcript with Commentary.* Albany: State U of New York P, 1997.

Anderson, Rob, Kenneth N. Cissna, and Ronald C. Arnett, eds. *The Reach of Dialogue: Confirmation, Voice, and Community.* Cresskill, NJ: Hampton, 1994.

Arnett, Ronald C. *Dwell in Peace: Applying Nonviolence to Everyday Relationships.* Elgin, IL: Brethren P, 1980.

———. *Communication and Community: Implications of Martin Buber's Dialogue.* Carbondale: Southern Illinois UP, 1986.

———. *Dialogic Education: Conversation About Ideas and Between Persons.* Carbondale: Southern Illinois UP, 1992.

Bok, Sissela. *Lying: Moral Choice in Public and Private Life.* New York: Vintage, 1979.

———. *Secrets: On the Ethics of Concealment and Revelation.* New York: Pantheon, 1983.

———. *Common Values.* Columbia: U of Missouri P, 1995.

Bracci, Sharon L., and Clifford G. Christians, eds. *Moral Engagement in Public Life: Theorists for Contemporary Ethics.* New York: Peter Lang, 2002.

Buber, Martin. *Between Man and Man.* Trans. Ronald Gregor Smith. New York: Macmillan, 1965.

———. *I and Thou.* Trans. Walter Kaufmann. New York: Scribner, 1970.

———. *The Knowledge of Man: A Philosophy of the Interhuman.* Trans. Maurice Friedman and Ronald Gregor Smith. Ed. Maurice Friedman. New York: Harper and Row, 1965.

Christians, Clifford G., John P. Ferré, and P. Mark Fackler. *Good News: Social Ethics and the Press.* New York: Oxford UP, 1993.

Christians, Clifford, and Kaarle Nordenstreng. "Social Responsibility Worldwide." *Journal of Mass Media Ethics* 19.1 (2004): 3-28.

Christians, Clifford, and Michael Traber, eds. *Communication Ethics and Universal Values.* Thousand Oaks, CA: Sage, 1997.

Cissna, Kenneth N., and Rob Anderson. *Moments of Meeting: Buber, Rogers, and the Potential for Public Dialogue*. Albany: State U of New York P, 2002.

Cooper, Martha. "Covering Tragedy: Media Ethics and TWA Flight 800." *Ethics in Human Communication* by Richard L. Johannesen. 5th ed. Prospect Heights, IL: Waveland, 2002. 319-331.

———. "Decentering Judgment: Toward a Postmodern Communication Ethic." *Judgment Calls: Rhetoric, Politics, and Indeterminacy*. Eds. John Sloop and James P. McDaniel. Boulder, CO: Westview, 1998. 63-83.

———. "Ethical Dimensions of Political Advocacy from a Postmodern Perspective." *Ethical Dimensions of Political Communication*. Ed. Robert E. Denton, Jr. New York: Praeger, 1991. 23-47.

Dreamworlds II. Media Education Foundation, 1995. [55 min., www.mediaed.org]

Eubank, Henry Lee, and J. Jeffrey Auer. *Discussion and Debate: Tools of a Democracy*. New York: F. S. Crofts, 1941.

Gilligan, Carol. *In a Different Voice: Psychological Theory and Women's Development*. Cambridge: Harvard UP, 1978.

Gross, Larry, John Stuart Katz, and Jay Roby, eds. *Image Ethics: The Moral Rights of Subjects in Photographs, Film, and Television*. New York: Oxford UP, 1988.

Gunkel, David. *Hacking Cyberspace*. Boulder, CO: Westview, 2001.

Gunkel, David, and Debra Hawhee. "Virtual Alterity and the Reformatting of Ethics." *Journal of Mass Media Ethics* 18.3/4 (2003): 173-193.

Haiman, Franklyn S. "Democratic Ethics and the Hidden Persuaders." *Quarterly Journal of Speech* 44 (1958): 385-392.

———. "A Re-examination of the Ethics of Persuasion." *Central States Speech Journal* 3 (1952): 4-9.

Hallstein, D. Lynn O'Brien. "A Postmodern Caring: Feminist Standpoint Theories, Revisioned Caring, and Communication Ethics." *Western Journal of Communication* 63 (Winter 1999): 32-56.

Hyde, Michael J. *The Call of Conscience: Heidegger and Levinas, Rhetoric and the Euthanasia Debate*. Columbia: U of South Carolina P, 2001.

Johannesen, Richard L. "Diversity, Freedom, and Responsibility in Tension." *Communication Ethics in an Age of Diversity*. Eds. Josina M. Makau and Ronald C. Arnett. Urbana: U of Illinois P, 1997. 155-186.

———. *Ethics in Human Communication*. 5th ed. Prospect Heights, IL: Waveland, 2002.

———. "Nel Noddings's Uses of Martin Buber's Philosophy of Dialogue." *Southern Communication Journal* 65 (2000): 151-160.

———. "Virtue Ethics, Character, and Political Communication." *Ethical Dimensions of Political Communication.* Ed. Robert E. Denton, Jr. New York: Praeger, 1991. 69-90.

Kane, Robert. *Through the Moral Maze: Searching for Absolute Values in a Pluralistic World.* New York: Longman, 1994.

Killing Us Softly III. Media Education Foundation, 2000. [30 min. www.mediaed.org]

Manning, Rita C. *Speaking from the Heart: A Feminist Perspective on Ethics.* Lanham, MD: Rowman and Littlefield, 1992.

Minnick, Wayne. *The Art of Persuasion.* 2nd ed. Boston: Houghton Mifflin, 1968. [1st ed. 1957]

Nilsen, Thomas R. *Ethics in Speech Communication.* 2nd ed. Indianapolis: Bobbs-Merrill, 1974.

———. "Free Speech, Persuasion, and the Democratic Process." *Quarterly Journal of Speech* 44 (1958): 235-243.

Noddings, Nel. *Caring: A Feminine Approach to Ethics and Moral Education.* Berkeley: U of California P, 1984.

Oliver, Robert T. *Persuasive Speaking: Principles and Methods.* New York: Longmans, Green, 1950.

Porter, James. *Rhetorical Ethics and Internetworked Writing: An Ethic for the Computer Age.* Greenwich, CT: Ablex, 1998.

Tronto, Joan C. *Moral Boundaries: A Political Argument for an Ethic of Care.* New York: Routledge, 1993.

Wallace, Karl. "An Ethical Basis of Communication." *The Speech Teacher* 4 (1955): 1-9.

Wheeler, Tom. *Phototruth or Photofiction?: Ethics and Media Imagery in the Digital Age.* Mahway, NJ: Lawrence Erlbaum, 2002.

Wood, Julia T. *Who Cares? Women, Care, and Culture.* Carbondale: Southern Illinois UP, 1994.

A Conversation about Communication Ethics with Ronald C. Arnett

How did you become interested in studying communication ethics?

I have two answers, with one being more personally interesting. I completed my Ph.D. at the age of 24 and as I sat in my first faculty meeting, the faculty seemed incredibly old. They were all around 45 or 50. At that moment, Don Sikkink, who is a wonderful man and who had just turned 50 that day, made me think: "I can't believe I'm sitting in this room with this person who is twice my age plus." (Now I am 52—God's revenge.)

Don began talking about a course he was teaching that dealt with ethics and free speech. His comment was, "You know, the course is just not going very well. I prefer not to teach it. Who could teach that course instead of me? Perhaps, ah … the youngest." He pointed at me and I responded, "Oh, what a wonderful opportunity!" My introduction to communication ethics came from Don Sikkink. Only later did I know the care and wisdom of that call to responsibility. I am grateful.

The more serious answer is that out of the turmoil of the 1970s, I was involved in the anti-war movement. I worked with students at St. Cloud State University to start a group called NOVA, "Non-Violent Alternatives." My first book was *Dwell in Peace: Applying Nonviolence to Everyday Relationships*. Much of my work at that particular time engaged questions of nonviolence. At that point, the major work in nonviolence was by Gene Sharp who was doing strategic nonviolence as a way to deal with military defense. We brought him to campus and began a "Nonviolent Alternatives" week of speakers and events.

In addition to that, I was interested in the work of Mahatma Gandhi and the notion of *satyagraha*, differentiated from *duragraha*. *Duragraha* is stubborn persistence. *Satyagraha* is dialogic nonviolent change. In *Dwell in Peace,* I examined connections between Martin Buber and Gandhi, knowing that the letter exchanges they had were somewhat contentious. At one point, Gandhi was asking Buber to utilize nonviolence against the Nazis and received the comment from Buber that such action was impossible. However, there are important connections between their callings, including the fact that neither *satyagraha* nor dialogue are possible as unreflective techniques unresponsive to the historical moment.

I had a great deal of interest in the area of communication ethics and very little formal education. My impulse was to go in and look at what Albert Schweitzer called the sanctity of human life, or the sacredness of life, which was one of the major themes of *Dwell in Peace*. I began teaching that ethics and free speech course, pretty much like the majority of my courses, as a learner beginning with questions and seeking temporal answers. I center learning as an "ironical foundation" of a postmodern age of narrative and virtue contention. Learning is the central communication ethics principle in such an era, with engagement of difference becoming a postmodern barometer of "common sense."

Who are some of the key figures who influenced your work in communication ethics?

There are many; the lineage begins with Bobby Kennedy when I campaigned for him locally in Fort Wayne, Indiana. I witnessed in him what Aristotle called "a commitment to the 'good.'" Postmodernity reminds us of the complexity of "goods," but this is does not reject, nor de-privilege, the importance of temporal discernment of a given "good." Postmodernity assumes the loss of one universal "good" and lives within the tapestry of multiple social "goods." The second major influence was Martin Luther King, Jr. He united the narratives of a faith story and democracy, reminding us of a call to responsibility to the Other, not just to me or my kind.

The third major influence was people in the anti-war movement. The most important person to me, philosophically, in the anti-war movement was John Howard Yoder. John Howard Yoder was a Mennonite who eventually taught philosophy at Notre Dame. Another person of great importance was Dale Brown, who wrote the foreword to my first book, *Dwell in Peace*. He was director of a peace studies program at Bethany Theological Seminary. I have a Master's of Divinity from Church of the Brethren seminary in peace studies. Additionally, my friend Tom Hurst, who was the director of a group called On Earth Peace, has been an important influence. Tom has been an inspiration since our undergraduate work at Manchester College.

Another influential person was our campus minister at Manchester College, Robert Kuneckle. During the summers of my undergraduate experience, I visited and discussed books on peace that we read together. We went through numerous books during one summer and more the next. He provided a safe place to read and study. Perhaps I actually began my scholarly career in his office.

From that sense of welcome, I stumbled from the work of Mahatma Gandhi to that of Martin Buber simply because I was at Manchester College, where the oldest peace studies program in the world was established, and sitting in the classroom with one of the founders of interpersonal communication connected to dialogue, Paul Keller. He was just a wonderful and patient human being; he introduced me to the connections between Buber and Gandhi and to the importance of communication students' reading literature. Much of my career direction lives within his care and guidance.

Then I went to graduate school at Ohio University. I just talked to a colleague today, and I've never thought about one fact until today—my dissertation committee was composed of three Manchester College graduates. Ray Wagner directed my thesis and dissertation; he is one of the finest educators I have ever known. Paul Boase, the director of the School of Interpersonal Communication, was on my committee; I later roomed with him at conferences for over 20 years. We also asked Paul Keller to join as an external person who was not at Ohio University to be on that committee. In short, I had a committee composed of only Manchester College graduates, two of whom were conscientious objectors, and the dissertation was, of course, on nonviolence. I was too young and naïve to recognize how incredibly unusual it was to have those three people from the same undergraduate campus on my committee. They were simply wonderful. Ray Wagner's thoughtful care kept me in the field, and his friendship, along with that of Paul Boase, provided a sanctuary for me for many years. NCA was a return to a sense of home when I roomed with them. They were simply gracious to me.

My work received a jump start in a conversation with Stan Deetz (another Manchester College and Ohio University graduate). Stan said, "Do you want to be known as a Buber scholar?" I said, "No." He then said, "Then you can never stop reading." I am still reading and learning …as I tell students, there is much joy in not knowing and in seeking temporal answers. Since that moment, Hans-Georg Gadamer has guided me in reflecting on dialogue as ground with bias and prejudice. I returned to Aristotle because of Gadamer. I stumbled my way into critique of agency through the work of Christopher Lasch. Recently I finished a book on Dietrich Bonhoeffer that assisted in bringing the question of conviction to a world of difference.

Now my conversation turns to Albert Camus, Hannah Arendt, and Emmanuel Levinas. Albert Camus permits me to investigate anew the importance of existentialism in times of narrative fragmentation. Hannah Arendt opens the question of public and private, differentiating public and private space. She gives us insight into the "banality of evil" in taken-for-granted assumptions that accompany modernity: the blurring of public and private and the presupposition of progress. Once you give up the presupposition of the inevitability of progress, then you need to reclaim public and private space as a natural dialectic that calls into account the undisputed authority of the "social" or popular consensus. This dialectic guided Dietrich Bonhoeffer in his writing and struggles against the Third Reich. As a genuine aristocrat, Bonhoeffer had a private life that permitted him to critique the public framework that sustained Nazi Germany. His life and work provided me with a tempered read of an aristocratic upbringing. The differentiation of public and private space is essential in an era of contention and difference.

The most important read for me currently is Emmanuel Levinas. I have written a couple of essays on Levinas. I am not ready to write a book on Levinas; his work represents a major conceptual and cultural leap. I consider him the scholar who most strongly critiques the West's mistaken view of identity. Levinas is the most important philosopher I have ever encountered in my professional career. The reason is the issue of agency. He has the strongest sense of self, the most powerful view of agency of any author I have ever read. The "otherwise than convention" question is, "How does he get there?" His understanding of agency is derivative, not originative. He offers a responsive "I" rather than the agency of an "I" that imposes willfulness upon the world. The notion of "call" is fundamental to Levinas; his ethics begins with a voice other than our own. Additionally, the work of Alasdair MacIntyre, Charles Taylor, Seyla Benhabib, and on a personal level the work of Dorothy Day, keep me in conversation and attentive to temporal moments of insight in an era of confusion and wonderful opportunity for learning.

How do you define communication ethics?

In the field of communication, communication ethics centers around one major action metaphor: choice. I would suggest that the notion of choice begins with a given "good" we want to protect and promote. We choose a philosophical standpoint that privileges a given sense of the "good." For instance, a democratic ethic protects individual input and influence and a narrative understanding of communication ethics protects a given story. The work of James Chesebro and, later, my own work point to differing communicative categories that protect and promote a given sense of the "good." Chesebro's work addresses democratic, universal, and contextual communication ethics, along with codes and procedures, with my work adding narrative and, in a current project co-authored with Pat Arneson and Leeanne Bell, adding dialogic ethics. Communication ethics is the carrying of a given sense of the "good" into personal and professional life; it impacts what we see and do and, most importantly, what we privilege.

Do you prefer the term "communication ethic" or "communication ethics"?

Only recently did I begin to differentiate between the terms "communication ethics" and "communication ethic." In an essay I wrote for Sharon Bracci and Cliff Christians, I differentiated "a communication ethic" from "communication ethics." Communication ethics is a multiplicity of communication ethic positions, each of which recognizes a bias or ground that promotes a given sense of the "good." In my work, there is no such entity as "the communication ethic" with the power of a universal claim; each ethic presupposes what Jürgen Habermas outlines as a bias of "interests."

In my most recent book on Dietrich Bonhoeffer, I look at the interplay of rhetoric, dialogue, and dialectic in a communication ethic. Dialectic takes us to texture missed by modernity, as Hannah Arendt penned in her rejection of the "social," the blurring of public and private communicative life. Dialectic is the first check on communication ethics. Checked confidence permits one to make a dialogic move, which requires one to understand the ground upon which one stands and then to learn and understand the ground of another. Emergent insight comes from the "between" of ground or narrative bias. The prescriptive move of communicative ethics is rhetorical. Calvin Schrag outlines the inevitable nature of a rhetorical turn. I do not discuss these in linear fashion, however, because our very first choice of a "good" that we seek to protect and promote is a rhetorical move. Emmanuel Levinas reminds us that ethics are descriptive and prescriptive. He thought "otherwise" than the modern project of universal truth.

I work with the assumption that the 21st century is tied to the metaphor of "learning," not to the metaphor of "knowledge"—the notion of knowledge is a 20th century metaphor. The 21st century metaphor of "learning" means that whatever I know must engage and risk being reshaped in a given moment. My interest in dialogue ties to the importance of "learning" that is historically engaged. However, as stated earlier, dialogue begins with narrative ground that has bias and prescriptive vision that both sharpen and limit our insight.

Emmanuel Levinas's emphasis on the descriptive and prescriptive required me to stress "dialogic confession" as a postmodern metaphor attentive to communication ethics. To confess one's ground carries with it a dialectical responsibility to texture understanding, to continue to learn, and to acknowledge one's bias and prejudice. There is no way that I can work out of a communication ethic that does not have a persuasive framework. Once you leave modernity and the presupposition that I can stand above history and look down upon another or an event, as if somehow I am a non-biased objective agent, confession takes on pragmatic currency in a communication ethic.

This privileged view of one's own insight contrasts with Alasdair MacIntyre's disdain for emotivism, decision making by personal preference. In her interview with you, Julia Wood talked about Sandra Harding's view of standpoint theory. This socio-cultural insight confronts us with difference. Together the insights of emotivism and standpoint inform communication ethics. Emotivism is a modern temptation when the demand for constant learning from differing standpoints, narrative structures, and encounters with a given historical moment gives way to the fatigue of the familiar.

Perhaps the philosophical movement to understanding each communication ethic as protecting and promoting a sense of the "good" started with existentialism. I view existentialism as a philosophical juncture connecting modernity and postmodernity in that it both reflects the postmodern issue of the multiplicity of ground (rejecting a universal sense of ground) and yet depends upon the modern solution of the communicative agent. In all deference to Albert Camus, who stated that he was not an existentialist, the metaphor of "stranger" assumes a sense of detachment central to modernity that is unresponsive to the postmodern agent embedded within a multiplicity of possibilities of ground. Postmodern scholarship does not reject agency, but situates and embeds it in what Martin Buber called the mud of everyday life; one cannot stand above history. The ultimate element is what agency is embedded in—it is embedded in multiplicity of ground or what François Lyotard would call "petits récits" or "little narratives." That multiplicity of ground makes all the difference. So in communicating, we seek to understand "What is the story or ground that guides self, other, and historical moment?" without falling prey to psychologism that ascribes motives to another person. The danger of psychologism is that it embraces three modern fictions: first, the autonomous self; second, the ability to stand above history and figure out the motives of another; and third, narrative amnesia about the power and bias of the ground or narrative that shapes communicative life.

Can you explain the difference or similarities between "ground" and "narrative"?

I use the term "narrative" because it comes from ethics scholars such as Alasdair MacIntyre and Stanley Hauerwas. The term also guides Robert Bellah, who is indebted to MacIntyre. The notion of "ground" connects to Martin Buber and Dietrich Bonhoeffer. Buber reminded us that life is akin to walking in the mud, not in pristine clarity. Think about mud up to your ankles, to your knees, to your hips, to your shoulders, to the tips of your earlobes—that is the ground of everyday life of an embedded communicative agent. I have talked so long about the issue of "narrative" that I worry at times that it becomes a kind of floating cloud-like framework. With the issue of ground, literally your feet are in the ground; as an embedded agent you are saying, "I can't stand above anything. I am so confused; I do not know what to do. But I'm still going to act." The notion of ground is more concrete for me. As Buber stated, the ground is the mud of everyday life. Sometimes we have mud up to our eyebrows. I have not worked out all the connections between narrative and ground, but I am partial to the image and texture of mud! As Bonhoeffer said, the most immoral thing to do to another is to destroy the ground of another person.

Ground is not individual turf; from an existential phenomenological standpoint, I can stand on ground and attend to the ground of another, allowing persons to be co-informed by ground that emerges "between" persons. The ground is not fragile and is, ironically, capable of becoming invisible as one focuses too much upon its existence. Phenomenology presupposes that ground evaporates upon too much concentrated reflection. It is like lecturing in the classroom when all is going well, only to be disrupted by the reflection: "Yes! I am good today!" Something happens, and that moment of undue refection makes it impossible to reclaim the moment.

Phenomenologically, ground is not fragile; it is, however, temporal and tempted to seek cover in moments of undue light. To turn a phrase, ground seeks cover when too much artificial light focuses attention. Such is the reason I stress that we can only glimpse the face of the Other. In the Old Testament, we never see the face of God, only a glimpse. Dialogically, we never see or grasp the face of the Other. As I remind nontraditional students who are in my class, "It does not matter why you are here. It does not matter if your Mom on her deathbed said, 'Please get an education.' It does not matter if somehow you are here because you love knowledge. It does not matter if you are here because the bus dropped you off with nowhere else to go. I do not care why you are here—it not my business. The only thing I have a right to ask is that we seek to learn together." "Come and learn, no matter what the reason" rests within the insight of Dietrich Bonhoeffer—do not unmask another. Such a move invites the danger of expecting another to engage a task with the same motives as my own. Life simply needs to be bigger than such provincial impulses of attribution.

It's not my right to unmask the ground of another. The Old Testament reminds us of the importance of a glimpse of the face of God and no more. The face of God, I think, for the 21st century is a human face situated on real ground. The glimpses of the human face come as a derivative of learning the ground of another; we are a people situated and embedded in ground, the mud of everyday life.

I remember being in a different administrative position in which a student came in and was in tears. He was in a class with a theology professor who kept ridiculing and making fun of this person's very conservative "me and Jesus" theology. I met with the professor over coffee. I said, "It seems important that you tell each student everything you can about contemporary scholarship. But why do you ridicule the student's personal faith?" This professor said, "I need to rid this student of these really unsophisticated ideas." I said, "You know, you are not in print about your 'sophisticated ideas.' You have not published a book; is it possible that your ideas have not stood the test of peer review? Yet, with untested ideas, you seek to destroy another's faith life. Why don't you work from an additive framework and begin a class with, 'Where you stand on a personal level in your faith is your decision. Now I am going to tell you everything that I know from my bias of my scholarship, my ground. Some of my ideas are true and some will not stand the test of time.'" Such is the reason that Dietrich Bonhoeffer worked as a scholar in the day and hit his knees in common prayer at night. A glimpse, not a grasp, guides communication ethics that protects the ground of another.

I now have been a scholar long enough that I am in print critiquing what I wrote at an earlier stage in my work. It is not only ethical, but also prudent to be careful about destroying another's ground. One may find, as all have in a long life, moments of regret, even academics, about what is or is not in print. Dietrich Bonhoeffer, while writing a novel in prison, stated it is immoral to destroy someone's ground. I think the primary thing that we need to do is to say as teachers, as educators, that my task is not to destroy someone's ground but to question with my own admitted limitations. That is why I made the move to a constructive hermeneutic that seeks implications; such a position is not naïve but is reluctant to assume the modern premise that I can stand above history and proclaim truth for the misinformed. I am not opposed to a deconstructive hermeneutic when engaged with Søren Kierkegaard's call of "fear and trembling." It is bravado and undue confidence, however, that makes me tremble in my soul.

What are your thoughts about communication ethics and the historical shift to postmodernity?

The term "postmodernity" explicitly announces the rejection of modernity as a failed experiment. In a traditional culture there is a universal agreement; the practices are embedded in life together. In modernity, there is an expectation that one can assume the universals of progress, efficiency, and the autonomous agent.

As I talk to students about the move from modernity to postmodernity, I ask questions such as, "How many of your parents expected to keep their jobs forever and how many have not?" "How many parents and friends do you know who are divorced?" Our daily encounter with fragmentation reveals the world of "Leave it to Beaver" as now pragmatically untrue for many. Such a world personifies, in the words of Jean-Paul Sartre, "bad faith." Postmodernity acknowledges the fib of modernity. Interestingly, postmodernity is more akin to traditional life than to modernity. I encourage students interested in postmodern issues to study medieval life, not modern life. Medieval life gives us a greater insight into a postmodern world; both deal with narrative contention and struggle, with the difference being that the conversation no longer revolves around the Church. Postmodernity opens narrative dispute to all walks of life. This postmodern moment is a juncture, a pause, a rhetorical interruption. The assumptions of universal agreement are gone and the temporal assumptions in the stage after postmodernity not yet in place. In short, postmodernity is not forever, but it is a glorious moment of learning; it is a call to learn and to give up leaning on universal assumptions. This is a learning moment, not a teaching moment, in human history.

Postmodernity is a moment that makes discussion of religion possible; all ideas have a place at the table of conversation and dispute. Such is the reason Jürgen Habermas reminds us of the importance of religion in this historical moment. We live in a time of shaken foundations, a rhetorical interruption that reminds us that we do not know all. Learning is the demand of this historical moment.

Scholarship is now moving beyond the celebration of postmodernity to figuring out what might be temporal universals that will guide us in a time of recognized difference. Cliff Christians and Michael Traber are insightful on this count. The demand for learning, however, is the ethical first principle of this historical moment. I am studying French, and if my fluency ever reaches beyond a modest level, I will turn to another language. The key is not what we know, but a commitment to what a colleague called "non-stop learning." In an era of recognized difference, it is unethical to stop learning—it is inadequate to say, "Gee, I know something about Judaism and I'm a Christian." Religious complexity is great within the worlds of both Judaism and Christianity, and now no one can exclude an Islamic faith perspective from the conversation. No matter what we know, it is simply not adequate or enough.

Learning as an ethical first principle requires us to figure out, "What are the differing places or ground upon which people stand?" I am an educator. I am not a politician. My first task is to learn and to be careful about premature solutions to the complexity of the world before us. My deepest hope is that we may learn about one another and enjoy the incredible texture of difference. Emmanuel Levinas is right in beginning with the face of the Other that reminds us that I am my brother's keeper. At this moment, the "keeper" is the person of "non-stop learning."

Postmodernity has a lot of energy left, even as we move in differing directions. Postmodernity is first a questioning of modernist bravado and then a call to conversation and learning. We must fight the impulse of fear of the demand for constant learning accompanied by a retreat back to the comfort of modernity and its universal assurances. I have priests and friends in religious life that I encourage to embrace this moment. Modernity took much off the table, including religious conversation. Postmodernity is the era of welcome—a welcome to learning and difference. We cannot fall prey to the temptation to return to modern familiar assumptions of progress, efficiency, and the autonomous agent. Postmodernity opens the conversation by offering an invitation to enter the conversation. If one is to engage communication ethics in this era, the first principle is learning.

How does the work of philosophers, social theorists, and theologians inform communication ethics?

My engagement with communication ethics begins with the assumption that all discourse rests within what Jürgen Habermas calls "interests." There is no neutral view of communication—philosophers, social theorists, and theologians point us to presuppositions, interests that contain a given view of the "good" that is protected and promoted. Communication ethics requires informative investigation; I turn to such scholarly venues for insight. In modernity, the primary question is implementation; there is paradigmatic agreement. I assume that paradigms are in conflict and require analysis of differences.

I was asked by an assistant superintendent in the Pittsburgh area to assist with communication problems among parents, students, and teachers. I asked him to ask the parents, students, and teachers to define basic communication concepts such as empathy and acts of active listening. The next phone call revealed the following: "Sure, they know how to define these terms and many more related to communication." I then said, "Then the issue isn't one of knowledge and implementation. The issue is situated in the question of 'why'—'Why' work with and care for another human being?" The fundamental communication ethics question for me is no longer "How do we help people to resolve conflict?" The fundamental communication ethics question is "Why one should care about and desire to work with another human being and learn from difference?" The fulcrum points of discourse in communication ethics for the 21st century are more closely linked to background questions of "why" learn than to foreground questions of paradigmatic implementation of "how" to fix.

I find it interesting to go back to Mahatma Gandhi and his engagement with Kantian philosophy—the ends are the means in the making. Essentially, foreground implementation happens to be the end of the means that were in the making; the background shapes the foreground. The foreground is, in a sense, the end, but the means in the making is the background in which we live, situated in what makes all the difference. Keeping "means" as primary privileges learning over knowledge. The example I share with students is that sometimes when a person meets another and the two people become incredibly good friends very quickly, only later to become archenemies, one asks, why? Friendship based upon implementation agreement is different from friendship based upon learning about changing means and paradigmatic changes. As the world of implementation changes, we connect through learning, through questions of "means" that engage and shape the world of tomorrow. Communication ethics rests in learning more than in telling and implementation.

How would you characterize the integration of dialogue and communication ethics in your work?

Initially Mahatma Gandhi propelled me with a pragmatic understanding of "truth." When Gandhi was asked, "How do you find truth?" his comment was, "You follow a path, and you have the courage to follow that path. You also have an appreciation that others follow different paths. If at some point you find that you stumble and fall, you are thankful that others have followed a path other than your own. If you find out that another path is better than yours, you need to have the courage to change your direction." I began to work with ethics with this pragmatic Gandhian framework, which foreshadows a postmodern pragmatism.

The dialogic component in my work embraced a continental understanding of dialogue based upon ground and narrative, contrasted with an American understanding of dialogue situated in conversation between autonomous communicative agents. The substantial reason I connected dialogue to Martin Buber and Hans-Georg Gadamer and not to Carl Rogers rests in the emphasis on ground or narrative as *a priori*—dialogue begins before people in conversation meet; we carry a ground-laden, a story-laden, bias into the discourse. With a Rogerian or an American understanding of dialogue, we presuppose the dialogue begins when the conversation begins. That kind of American dialogue presupposes, in a sense, narrative agreement. It presupposes that interlocutors have similar ground. The primary difference for Buber is that the ground makes a difference. Ground is the bias, or what Gadamer would call the fundamental prejudice, with which one enters the interpretive act of dialogue.

As time evolved, I understood the importance of ground more and more thoroughly. Without an understanding of ground, an American understanding of dialogue presupposes that universal understanding will emerge out of the discourse. If, indeed, we work from that kind of position, we will never resolve the problems in the Middle East, nor issues related to race, ethnicity, gender, religion, and affectivity. The American view of dialogue is philosophically malnourished. If you look at Martin Buber and his dialogic work that came out of World War II, after there were eight to ten million people killed in concentration camps, and one acknowledges the extreme anguish and pain and human suffering, it is clear that narrative agreement is a modern fiction.

The notion of ground or narrative differences moves communication ethics to a non-humanistic position. The issue is not that I am in dialogue with you; I am in dialogue with the ground upon which you stand—which is the issue of embedded agents in discourse. The power of this dialogic understanding of communication ethics announced itself in Martin Buber's meeting with a student at Union Theological Seminary. A Protestant seminarian asks Buber, "What is it like to be a Jew?" Buber's eyes began to glare with incredible intensity as he looked at the man and asked, "Do you really want to know?" The student then said, "No." This was a dialogic act in which Buber was saying, "Do you want to meet this ground, this narrative land of the Jew?" That exchange was not the kind of dialogue we talk about in the United States. Buber was not Mr. Rogers; he was not Carl Rogers. The intensity of Buber's view of dialogue moved us from a therapeutic moral *cul de sac* situated in feeling to the pragmatic necessity of learning, narrative ground, and a conversation well underway before the discourse begins. Communication ethics and dialogue connect as one embraces the necessity of encountering and learning from differing narrative ground without falling prey to relativism. As Buber revealed, such a view of dialogue has a position that nourishes a given sense of the "good" that frames a given communication ethic.

If someone asked you to identify significant areas for future communication ethics research, what would you tell that person?

I would have to give two answers. One is that I would say, "Follow your questions. Study what does not make sense and forces you to learn." It is like writing a dissertation. You need to study what you don't understand. The key is to move from telling to learning. Someone was asking, "Why do you write?" I said, "I am propelled by ignorance." The more questions I have, the more I engage ideas and write to learn. As a scholar of the humanities, I can meet confusion and discover temporal clarity that takes me to additional questions.

If I were to give another answer, I would point to a love of ethnographic learning, discovering the difference that others offer, whether framed as encountering and learning from differing ground, narrative structures, or standpoints. All the terms point to learning as an encounter with difference. Such a view of learning is akin to the academic subject matter of "comparative religion." Communication ethics is learning of and about differing ground with comparative awareness that rests in comparative goodwill and as dialogic a first step, keeping evaluative dismissal of another's ground as a reluctant act, rather than the communicative gesture of routine.

In a postmodern age of narrative and virtue contention, communication ethics is academically and in everyday life first and foremost an act of learning about the ground, narrative, and standpoint that guides oneself, the Other, and the historical moment. Each position or ground protects and carries a sense of the "good." Using the insight of Calvin Schrag and communicative praxis, I would frame the following horizon for communication ethics. Communication ethics is learning *about* difference from ground, narrative, and standpoint. Communication ethics is *by* an embedded communicative agent situated in the historical moment, the mud of everyday life. Communication ethics from a non-humanistic framework is *for* a given sense of the "good" that calls one to act in a given direction, regardless of liking or emotive response to another. I love Emmanuel Levinas's reminder to care for another without regard for the color of another's eyes. Communication ethics lives within the mandate to learn, unabated by our own sense of whim and propelled by a power more substantial than liking—a phenomenological ground that calls us as a "responsive 'I'" to act as "my brother's keeper" not as a teller, but as a learner.

Works Cited

Arendt, Hannah. *On Revolution.* New York: Viking, 1963.

Aristotle. *Nichomachean Ethics.* Trans. Terence Irwin. Indianapolis: Hackett, 1985.

Arnett, Ronald C. *Communication and Community: Implications of Martin Buber's Dialogue.* Carbondale: Southern Illinois UP, 1986.

———. *Dialogic Confession: Bonhoeffer's Rhetoric of Responsibility.* Carbondale: Southern Illinois UP, 2005.

———. *Dialogic Education*. Carbondale: Southern Illinois UP, 1992.

———. *Dwell in Peace: Applying Nonviolence to Everyday Relationships*. Elgin, IL: The Brethren P, 1980.

———. "Hannah Arendt: Dialectical Communicative Labor." *Perspectives on Philosophy of Communication*. Ed. Pat Arneson. West Lafayette, IN: Purdue UP, in press.

———. "Paulo Freire's Revolutionary Pedagogy: From a Story-Centered to a Narrative-Centered Communication Ethic." In Sharon L. Bracci and Clifford G. Christians, eds. *Moral Engagement in Public Life: Theorists for Contemporary Ethics* (pp. 150-170). New York: Peter Lang, 2002.

———. "The Responsive 'I': Levinas's Derivative Argument." *Argumentation and Advocacy* 40 (2003): 39-50.

———. "The Status of Communication Ethics Scholarship in Speech Communication Journals from 1915-1985." *Central States Journal* 38 (1987): 44-61.

Arnett, Ronald C., and Pat Arneson. *Dialogic Civility in a Cynical Age: Hope, Community, and Interpersonal Relationships*. Albany: State U of New York P.

Arnett, Ronald C., Pat Arneson, and Leeaanne M. Bell. "Communication Ethics: The Dialogic Turn." *The Review of Communication* 6 (2006): 62-92.

Bellah, Robert N., Richard Madsen, William M. Sullivan, Ann Swidler, and Steven M. Tipton. *Habits of the Heart: Individualism and Commitment in American Life*. Berkeley: U of California P, 1985.

Benhabib, Seyla. *Situating the Self: Gender, Community, and Postmodernism in Contemporary Ethics*. New York: Routledge, 1992.

Bonhoeffer, Dietrich. *Ethics*. 1949. Harper and Row, 1954.

Brown, Charles T., and Paul Keller. *Monologue to Dialogue: An Exploration of Interpersonal Communication*. 2nd ed. Englewood Cliffs, NJ: Prentice-Hall, 1973.

Buber, Martin. *Between Man and Man*. 1947. New York: Macmillan, 1965.

Camus, Albert. *Resistance, Rebellion, and Death*. 1960. Trans. Justin O'Brien. New York: Vintage Books, 1974.

———. *The Stranger*. Trans. Matthew Ward. New York: Knopf, 1993.

Chesebro, James. "A Construct for Assessing Ethics in Communication." *Central States Speech Journal* 20 (1969): 104-114.

Christians, Clifford, and Michael Traber (Eds.). *Communication Ethics and Universal Values*. Thousand Oaks, CA: Sage. 1997.

Day, Dorothy. *Dorothy Day, Selected Writings: By Little and By Little*. Ed. Robert Ellsberg. Maryknoll, NY: Orbis, 1992.

Gadamer, Hans-Georg. *Truth and Method.* 1960. New York: Crossroad, 1986.

Gandhi, Mahatma. *Gandhi on Nonviolence.* Ed. Thomas Merton. New York: New Directions, 1965.

Habermas, Jürgen. *The Future of Human Nature.* Cambridge, UK: Polity Press, 2003.

Harding, Sandra. *Whose Science? Whose Knowledge?: Thinking from Women's Lives.* Ithaca, NY: Cornell UP, 1991.

Hauerwas, Stanley. *A Community of Character: Toward a Constructive Christian Social Ethic.* Notre Dame, IN: U of Notre Dame P, 1981.

Kierkegaard, Søren. *Fear and Trembling.* Trans. Alastair Hannay. New York: Penguin, 1985.

King, Jr., Martin Luther. *The Papers of Martin Luther King, Jr.* 4 vols. Ed. Clayborne Carson. Berkeley: U of California P, 1992.

Lasch, Christopher. *The True and Only Heaven: Progress and Its Critics.* New York: W. W. Norton, 1991.

Levinas, Emmanuel. *Time and the Other.* 1947. Trans. Richard A. Cohen. Pittsburgh, PA: Duquesne UP, 1987.

———. *Ethics and Infinity: Conversations with Philippe Nemo.* Trans. Richard A. Cohen. Pittsburgh, PA: Duquesne UP, 1985.

Lyotard, Jean-François. *The Postmodern Condition: A Report on Knowledge.* Trans. Geoff Bennington. Minneapolis: U of Minnesota P, 1984.

MacIntyre, Alasdair. *After Virtue: A Study in Moral Theory.* 1981. Notre Dame: U of Notre Dame P, 1984.

Rogers, Carl. *On Becoming a Person: A Therapist's View of Psychotherapy.* Boston: Houghton Mifflin, 1961.

Sartre, Jean-Paul. *Being and Nothingness: An Essay on Phenomenological Ontology.* Trans. Hazel E. Barnes. New York: Washington Square P, 1953.

Schrag, Calvin O. *Communicative Praxis and the Space of Subjectivity.* Bloomington: Indiana UP, 1986.

Schweitzer, Albert. *The Teaching of Reverence for Life.* Trans. Richard and Clara Winston. New York: Holt, Rinehart, and Winston, 1965.

Sharp, Gene. *Power and Struggle: Part One of The Politics of Nonviolent Action.* Boston: Porter Sargent, 1973.

Taylor, Charles. *Sources of the Self: The Making of the Modern Identity.* Boston, MA: Harvard UP, 1989.

Yoder, John Howard. *The Politics of Jesus.* Grand Rapids, MI: Eerdmans.

A Conversation about Communication Ethics with Josina M. Makau

How did you become interested in studying communication ethics?

As an undergraduate, I began an obsession with questions that still drive me: "What is required to make good decisions in everyday life?" "How do we know we've made good decisions?" "Where can we turn for reliable guidance?" And, more broadly, "What is required to live a good life?"

In using the term "good" in each of these contexts, I'm including every dimension of life, from the purely pragmatic, practical, material dimensions, to the spiritual, ethical, and philosophical. Clearly, exploration of what it means to have made a "good decision" in pursuit of a "good life" inherently encompasses all of these dimensions.

Early on, I turned to philosophy as the discipline most likely to provide the answer, or answers really, to these and related questions. I found myself attracted as well to the field of speech communication. I joined the debate team, and participated actively in forensics activities, earning a bachelor's degree in philosophy with a minor in speech communication.

From there, I went on to graduate study in philosophy. When I entered UCLA as a graduate student in 1972, the majority of nationally recognized philosophy departments embraced versions of the western analytic philosophical paradigm. Most faculty in prominent programs at that time shared René Descartes's view that, in the absence of certainty, humanity would be left with arbitrariness as our only option. Unwilling to accept arbitrariness and its grave consequences in human affairs, philosophy faculty sought pathways to certainty.

With this framework as a guide, philosophers at UCLA applied mathematical principles to a variety of contexts. For example, when studying philosophy of language and linguistics, we applied a sentential calculus. When exploring ethics, we were encouraged to pursue de-ontic logic. We studied modal logic as a resource for epistemological inquiry. This work was extraordinarily interesting and engaging. As philosophers today have become increasingly aware, however, these pursuits offer little practical guidance for ethical and effective decision making in daily life. Indeed, ironically, pursuing the path of logical positivism has a tendency to foster a sense of cynicism regarding the possibility of identifying (or developing) viable guidelines for ethical reflection and practice.

By the end of my first year of graduate study, I became acquainted with the work of Chaïm Perelman and Stephen Toulmin, philosophers who had mined ancient rhetorical and philosophical texts in pursuit of insights into *practical reasoning*. Rejecting Cartesian dualism, Perelman, Toulmin and other "New Rhetoricians" sought an alternative paradigm.

Excited by the possibilities of this work, I entered UC-Berkeley's graduate program in Rhetoric. It was wonderful to read Kenneth Burke, Wayne Booth, Stephen Toulmin, Chaïm Perelman, and others whose writing explored such practical questions as "How do we come together to solve the important questions of the day?" "How do we avoid another Holocaust?" "How do we work together as humans to resolve the complex issues confronting us as a human family?" "What are the key elements of reasonableness, and how does this differ from rationality?"

It was wonderful, in particular, to study argumentation theory because here I found a marriage between the ancient field of rhetoric, on the one hand, and contemporary philosophical inquiry on the other. Argumentation theory provided fertile ground for interdisciplinary explorations of ethical and effective decision making in practical contexts.

Stephen Toulmin and Chaïm Perelman identified legal reasoning as a particularly fruitful field of inquiry. Here, they suggested, we had the promise of finding the integration of "rule-based" reasoning applied contextually. Following their counsel, and using argumentation theory as my tool, I studied Supreme Court reasoning. As the highest court in a land which prides itself in living by the rule of law, I reasoned, the United States Supreme Court holds the promise of providing guidelines (and perhaps even principles) for making sound practical decisions. I followed this course of study for more than a decade and learned a great deal.

During the course of this study, I began to notice that most students of rhetoric appeared interested primarily in using rhetoric to its fullest potential as a means for persuasion. They embraced Aristotle's view of rhetoric as the art of finding, in any given case, all the available means of persuasion. However, they appeared to part company with Aristotle in his quest for applying rhetorical insights in pursuit of *phronesis*.

It soon became apparent to me that my focus on discerning guidelines for ethical and effective decision making fell well outside the "mainstream" of rhetorical studies. At the same time, I found myself increasingly disturbed and discouraged by the adversarial nature of scholarly work in the Academy. Colloquia with great promise for shared exploration of complex theoretical and practical issues felt more like "contests" with highly invested participants "staking ground" (intellectually and professionally). Safe and inviting spaces for scholarly exchanges were rare. Little attention, if any, was given to exploring the ethical, "real-world" consequences to others of embracing proposed perspectives.

Fortunately, the UC-Berkeley Rhetoric doctoral program included a required demonstration of competency in two selected fields outside the department. My selected outside fields—Law and Philosophy—yielded invaluable resources to address my concerns. Through extensive research into judicial reasoning, I was able to develop a deliberative model integrating the strengths of rhetorical inquiry with those of philosophical study. Berkeley's doctoral program also provided strong pedagogical training in rhetoric and composition to graduate teaching associates. Experience in this program proved invaluable to my development as an educator.

Upon completion of my doctorate, I joined the Ohio State University Communication Department faculty. Among my primary responsibilities were development of an undergraduate program in argumentation theory and practice, a pre-law program, and related graduate programming. I was responsible as well for administering the university's "Pro and Con" program. Provided nearly complete autonomy in each of these assignments, I had the opportunity to develop and implement a cooperative model of argumentation pedagogy aligned with the judicial model of reasoning I had crafted earlier.

Shortly after beginning this work, I saw an announcement in *Spectra* regarding development of a national communication ethics commission. Here, I thought, is the marriage; in the study of communication ethics, we have the opportunity to bring it all together. I responded to the ad with enthusiasm.

At about the same time, the *Journal of Communication* published a special issue on "Ferment in the Field." Articles in this provocative and insightful issue featured explorations of important differences between administrative and managerial communication programs on the one hand, and those embracing critical research and pedagogical models on the other. At my home campus, Ohio State University, the Women's Studies program was providing faculty an invaluable series of workshops exploring related issues across the humanities and social sciences. Each session introduced us to insights from feminist scholars and researchers in ethnic studies. It was an extraordinary learning opportunity, one I will always remember with gratitude.

These and related experiences nurtured in me a deep and abiding interest in communication ethics. Since then, the opportunity to engage in this study and to teach in this area has been among my greatest passions and joys. It's difficult for me to imagine a more important and worthwhile endeavor for someone driven by lifelong pursuit of guidelines for responsible and effective decision making and for living well.

How do you define communication ethics?

On the surface, this would seem a simple question. And yet so much is potentially conveyed by these terms. I don't have a singular definition. For example, I have taught courses in communication ethics for about 25 years. Some aspects of the coursework change routinely, but there are some elements that have changed very little. Among the latter is recognition that every act of communication has central to it a fundamental ethical component—or perhaps I should put that in the plural, ethical components. Even the decision to smile or not to smile when encountering a stranger on the street has an ethical dimension in the sense that the act is imbued with choice, has consequences to others, reflects our values, and supports a perspective on responsible and responsive communication. How we interact nonverbally with every person we meet, and all other acts of communication every moment of every day of our lives reflect and enact ethical choices. In this sense, all communication has an inherently ethical element. When speaking of the ethics of communication, this comes to mind for me.

Another "constant" is the fact that communication is an inherently key element of living well together. That's where what some people have called "the communicative ethic" is particularly salient, and I'm deeply interested in that as well.

Then there are institutional and structural elements implied by the words "communication ethics." In light of today's global context, for example, I'm increasingly committed to studying about and teaching media ethics and its partner, media literacy, because it strikes me that we live in an age where increasingly the narratives embraced by the public through consumption of media are instrumental to public policy. But the influence doesn't stop here.

Recently, several colleagues and I were discussing what's going on in many middle and high schools today, the way in which young people are interacting with one another, sometimes in potentially destructive ways. Following our discussion, I asked myself, where do today's youngsters learn their habits of communication? I think it would be fair to say that mass media play a significant role. On average, children in the United States spend more time "taking in" media images, sounds, and stories than interacting with their parents, teachers, friends, or classmates. In such a context, studying and teaching communication ethics must (of necessity) entail thoughtful attention to mass media production, distribution, and consumption. Similarly, fostering media literacy is an important responsibility for parents and educators in today's world.

Finally, the graduate school experiences alluded to earlier helped inform my understanding of and commitment to communication ethics. From my perspective, exploring, developing, and applying insights regarding conditions for ethical and effective dialogue are key to studying and teaching communication ethics.

I see "communication ethics" as covering a broad array of issues, questions, and ultimately, pursuit of guidelines. Included is the quest for guidelines, norms, or principles for ethical production, dissemination, and consumption of mass-mediated communication. Narrative ethics, the ethics of interpersonal communication, guidelines for intercultural and cross-cultural communication, principles for ethical uses of technology, dialogic ethics, and much more are included as well. In contrast, the term "communication ethic" is a useful shorthand for each of the many paradigms and frameworks proposed as foundational resources for these pursuits.

Do you understand philosophical ethics as distinct from communicative ethics?

The marriage of rhetoric, dialectic, and logic has been a guiding force in my work for more than three decades. While on the one hand, I appreciate and value discussions of differences between these fields and inquiries—and I have participated in such explorations throughout my academic life—I have found integrative work the most satisfying and fruitful. In terms of the relationship of philosophical ethics to communicative ethics in particular, I believe that each is interdependent upon the other.

For example, the philosopher in me is very interested in such foundational epistemological questions as: "How do we know?" "How do we know we know?" "Are there differences between opinion and knowledge, belief and fact, appearance and reality, and if so how can we discern these differences?" "What is truth?" "Is there such a thing?" "If so, what are the most reliable sources and pathways to its discovery (or invention)?" "What is wisdom?" "How does one acquire wisdom?" From my perspective, epistemic inquiries of this kind are key to pursuit of reliable *grounds* for moral knowledge. Similarly, I am keenly interested in such ethical questions as: "What is right action?" "What is more or less important?" "What are the most reliable grounds for our judgments about right, wrong, good, bad, in any given context?" Ethical inquiries of this kind are key to ethical action.

As Seyla Benhabib and so many others have shown, however, such inquiries depend upon our willingness and capacity to confront the following core issue: "How do we negotiate our differences ethically, effectively, and justly?" Addressing this issue requires exploration and application of the principles and methods afforded by communication ethics (more specifically, "communicative ethics"). Conversely, resolution of this issue provides invaluable (critical) resources for philosophical ethics.

From my perspective, we can most meaningfully engage such inquiries when rhetorical theory, studies of narrative and story telling, literary theory, aesthetics, cultural studies, meta-ethical inquiry, political theory, psychology, women's studies, ethnic studies, and philosophical inquiry come together. I'm gratified to see more and more of this kind of interdisciplinary, cross-disciplinary, and trans-disciplinary dialogue and scholarship today.

How would you characterize the integration of communication ethics, philosophy, and law in your work?

My early studies in philosophy of law and legal reasoning introduced me to the importance of communication ethics. Conversely, studying communication ethics has deepened my insight into sound deliberations in legal and related practical contexts.

During the past decade, much of my work has focused on exploring how people who hold fundamentally different perspectives and come from very different backgrounds and interests can come together and contribute meaningfully to their own and each other's reasoning about critical issues of the day. Few would deny that we face deeply complex and significant issues today. In the United States and across the globe, the human family faces compelling problems. Among these, are urgent challenges associated with growing socio-economic divides and poverty, injustice and inequality, environmental issues, terrorism, auto-immune deficiency syndrome (AIDS) and other pandemics, corporate control of information, corruption of public servants, abuses of technology, nuclear proliferation, and the terrible tragedy of war.

The need to connect two different facets of communication ethics—(i) developing guidelines for reasoned deliberations and (ii) fostering conditions for living well together—is more urgent today than ever before. I must confess, however, that the interdependent nature of these two diverse areas of study has only recently become apparent to me. The best way I can explain is to share a story.

One day after working for many months on our book, *Cooperative Argumentation*, Debian Marty and I confronted a difficult moment. Speaking candidly, Debian shared that she had concerns regarding the drafts I'd sent her. I replied with similar candor regarding her contributions. It soon became apparent that neither of us could understand the direction the other proposed to take. You can imagine the intensity of this moment! We had come to the realization that our collaborative effort was not working; we would need to abandon the project.

Several soul-searching hours later we experienced an epiphany. We realized that we had been writing two different books. I had assumed we were writing a volume designed to foster reasoned decision making, my obsession. She had assumed we were writing a book designed to foster conditions for living well together, her obsession. Ordinarily, these would be quite different projects. In all of our training—hers predominately in communication and women's studies and mine predominately in rhetoric and philosophy—we'd never been exposed to a marriage between these pursuits. People either studied practical reasoning or they studied how to live well together; they didn't study both simultaneously. Suddenly, however, it occurred to us that one depends upon the other. Living well together is a prerequisite for reasoning well together and vice versa. From the moment we made this discovery on, our book project flowed.

That experience has helped shaped our most recent work. Today, with our colleagues at California State University-Monterey Bay, we are moved by the commitment to explore how we as members of the human family, who cherish one another's differences, who treasure them, who see difference as a resource, can come together and make meaning together, and hear one another, and learn together; how we can come together to foster peace and prosperity and justice together. That's been our great commitment. We're fortunate because we work on a campus with rich diversity. That makes our work so exciting and rewarding, and it affords us invaluable opportunities to learn in ways we never might have imagined, which of course then re-enforces our appreciation for difference as an invaluable resource for the human family.

For me personally, the work had always been about using communication ethically and effectively in order to come together to make reasoned just, fair, equitable decisions. Today, I understand that using communication ethically and effectively to live well together is central to this pursuit.

What are your thoughts about a universal communication ethic?

I find this a deeply engaging and complex question. On the one hand, the human family today has greater access to cross-cultural values and guidelines for ethical communication than ever before. Consider, for example, the Universal Declaration of Human Rights. This remarkable document acknowledges basic rights to dignity and to freedom of thought and expression for people across cultural boundaries. The fact that this document has been reaffirmed by more than 140 sovereign nations fifty years after its first publication reflects the promise of shared commitments to common values. Similarly, truthfulness, honesty, caring and compassionate communication, and commitments to fairness and justice are among many qualities of communication granted presumption across cultural boundaries. Common ground in these and related areas offers promise for those pursuing a universal communication ethic. I find this a deeply hopeful condition.

At the same time, however, efforts to "universalize" are laden with risk. History is replete with the grave consequences of efforts to generalize the values, beliefs, and behaviors of the "ruling class" upon all other groups. In this age of surveillance, corporate control of information, and increased economic and political control by a small and overwhelmingly powerful elite, such efforts have greater potential for harm than ever. Thus, while I embrace the promises associated with pursuit of a "universal communication ethic," I join others who admonish caution in these endeavors.

How do the challenges that postmodernity presents affect argumentation and living together?

Postmodern studies have unmasked long-standing privileges, structured relations of inequality, and related relations of power. These invaluable insights have raised critical questions for all students of communication ethics. Simultaneously, technological proliferation, along with unparalleled demographic shifts, dramatically affects the communication landscape. Together, these factors profoundly affect argumentation and living well together.

Consider, for example, that someone reading the Sunday *New York Times* this week has access to more information than an educated person in the Middle Ages encountered in his or her entire lifetime. And then consider that the information accessible today is likely to seem miniscule within a decade, because it's growing exponentially. This factor alone has significant consequences for communication ethics theory, practice, and pedagogy. At the same time, consider the implications of unparalleled opportunities for cross-cultural interaction. People from radically diverse backgrounds find themselves sharing geographic space for the first time in human history. Demographic shifts across the globe are reshaping communities in ways previously unimagined. Linguistic, religious, ethnic, and other cultural boundaries are being shattered further in cyberspace as people access the Internet and share perspectives with one another.

On the one hand, such a richly diverse communication context offers the hope of democratization of information and knowledge as never before. At the same time, however, the corporatization of media controlled by a smaller and smaller group of transnationals, and the accompanying corporatization of the Academy pose significant challenges. In such a context, we face unparalleled risks of hegemony and tyranny across the globe. As George Gerbner once noted, "those who control the stories of the culture, control the culture." When such a large share of the globe's population receives its "news" of the world from a single, corporate source, we cannot ignore the power of the source's narrative to shape our destiny.

Meanwhile, technological "advances" in communications and related technologies provide powerful resources for potential manipulation of the public. At the Massachusetts Institute of Technology, for example, technologists have developed machines enabling bureaucrats to prepare a "video" recording in which a person is shown making statements he or she never made. The "image" and "sound" mixtures are so "real" that sophisticated audiences are unable to discern the misrepresentation. In the arts and humanities, new genres "mixing" documentary and creative expressive arts are becoming widely embraced. Docu-dramas, historical novels, and related artifacts are commonplace in popular culture.

Coupled with research exposing relationships of power to knowledge acquisition and dissemination, these circumstances call upon students of communication ethics to re-engage basic questions. In such a context questions such as, "What is truth?" "What is the relationship of narrative to truth?" "What is the relationship of truth to power?" "What distinguishes perception from reality, belief from knowledge?" and "How do we know?" pose especially salient challenges.

Guidelines for interaction become at once more compelling and more complex (and difficult) in such an environment. Such a time calls for deep reflection, and for concern. But it's also a fantastic time. We're hearing stories from people whose voices we have never been heard. That is so beautiful! That is so exciting! Imagine the insights, wisdom, and knowledge available to us in ways our grandparents never dreamed. In comparison, our ancestors had a very limited store of stories, if you will. And our children's children are going to have access to even more.

Demographic shifts are especially rich with opportunity. How wonderful that people who have never before had a chance to encounter one another's ideas, thoughts, ways of being, knowing, and valuing now can communicate with one another. The combination of demographic shift and technological proliferation holds so much potential.

At the same time, however, unless moral progress keeps up with technological progress, the human family will face serious dangers. We're already seeing ethnic strife and related tragedies. Sissela Bok points out that more people died as a result of military violence in the 20th century than in all the preceding centuries since the Roman Empire. More than 70% of those deaths were civilian. When you think about that, it's overwhelming. As she points out, and I agree with her, this is a time when we have to think deeply and at a fundamental level. We have to ask the most basic questions over again: "Who are we as a species?" "What are our obligations to one another?" "How can we live well together?" Communication ethics is absolutely at the core of such critical reflection. How we communicate across our differences will make a profound difference in how we ask and answer those questions in my view.

How does a person communicate ethically if he or she is deliberating with someone who holds a different perspective?

This question addresses the heart of my current research and teaching. I am deeply moved by and interested in this inquiry. One relevant contribution that has surfaced in the last several decades, that I have so deeply appreciated, is recognition of the critical role that emotion plays in reasoning. Martha Nussbaum's wonderful book *Upheavals of Thought* is especially illuminating. Although Aristotle, a number of Eastern, Meso-American, African, and other figures in the history of ideas recognized the importance of emotion to deliberation, the fields of philosophy and rhetoric have not made effective use of these potential resources for several generations. Fortunately, during the last decade exploration of this topic has resurfaced in the field.

Exploration into the role of emotion in reasoned deliberation and community building reveals that the heart is extraordinarily important in addressing the question you've raised. If you and I are going to engage in meaningful dialogue, we are going to have to open our hearts. Closed hearts imperil the process, creating impenetrable barriers to meaningful dialogue.

You and Ron Arnett have made valuable contributions in your book on *Dialogic Civility* as well. The notion that we must come together with a basic sense of mutual respect and regard if we are to reach across our differences meaningfully is a critical starting point. Of course, as we can all concede, this is often very difficult.

My colleagues often confront me with a related concern. When I speak of ethical engagement across differences, they often challenge the practicality and wisdom of my perspective. They say such things as, "Josina be real. Do you live in the real world?" The irony is they see me in so many situations that are, let's just say, very "challenging." They have to know I live in the real world—I was a dean! Others who have served as deans will attest that you cannot be a successful dean in any sense of the word and live in a fantasy world.

From my perspective, I don't lose or risk anything *that matters*, and that's the key here, *that matters* by opening my heart to you. Don't get me wrong. I risk a great deal. It's terrifying. It's scary. I risk a great deal, but not what matters—which is that the two of us have a capacity to connect, to reason well together, to serve the public good to the best of our ability, to figure out what that means, to work together, to cross our differences. Opening my heart is the only way I can contribute. Now you may not choose to. I can't control that, but I can control what I do. I understand, of course, that there are limits to that. I don't want you to misunderstand me. There are walls and barriers that are decidedly impenetrable, but it strikes me that we have to at least start by *trying*. That to me is central to addressing the concern you've raised—opening one's heart. A genuine coming to our encounter with love in our hearts and with the true desire, the true will to serve the public good, whatever that might be.

As a young person I was in competitive debate—and I'll confess I loved it—but I was disturbed early on by the realization of what was being fostered by that format. My fellow participants and I were taught to listen to others' presentations for loopholes, weaknesses, to win. I didn't listen primarily to gain insight. And in talking with fellow participants, I realized they didn't either. We were never consciously brutal; we didn't think that it would be worth any trophy to be mean. But I'll be honest with you, we were very happy to win. And if we could find a "weakness" in our "opponents'" presentations, we would seize it, not in pursuit of knowledge, truth, justice, or understanding, but in pursuit of the trophy.

In sum, our communication was not motivated primarily with the goal of learning. It was not driven primarily with the goal of understanding. We listened to others only insofar as we needed in order to get "one-up" on the other person. That was a primary lesson of our participation.

I did a lot of reading after that and paid close attention to the strategies that forensics students across the nation were taught. I want to be very clear. I absolutely understand that students in competitive debate programs learn many important skills. I want to stress that I know that; I was there. I participated. It's absolutely true, but it's at a very high cost in my view.

There is another way to teach advocacy and related critical thinking skills, within a different framework, within a different paradigm. That's where studying the Supreme Court helped. Here's what I mean.

Being a jurist requires, in the ideal sense, pursuing the *truth* and pursuing *justice*. I use those terms loosely, understanding the complexities. It seems clear, however, that a jurist's job, to the best of his or her ability, is to make the best possible decision given all the available information.

Fulfilling this responsibility requires jurists to listen well. Advocates play an absolutely critical role in this process. Speaking passionately on behalf of views you honestly embrace is vital to the pursuit of truth and justice. I subscribe to this view fully, and I teach it in my argumentation classes. However, epistemological humility is also key. Imagining at least the possibility that we are wrong enables us to contribute most fully to the pursuit of truth and justice. That's where cooperative argumentation becomes so vital. What if, in the course of our dialogue, you say something I had never considered? Without listening attentively, this invaluable insight would have slipped by me completely. I would never have had the advantage of learning from you, and would have limited my capacity to serve the community well as a result.

John Stuart Mill offered these insights long ago in his book *On Liberty*. For all of its challenges, and it has many, this work nevertheless has much of value to say to us. Mill reminds us of the reasons freedom of speech and expression are so important. As he suggests, everyone has the potential to contribute something meaningful to everyone else. If we shut the communication process down, if we don't hear one another, we risk losing access to some measure of truth, some measure of insight, some measure of wisdom.

Do you view cooperative argumentation as a more ethical way of communicating than competitive argumentation?

I'm not sure I'd say one is inherently more ethical. I would say, however, that one is more likely than the other to foster conditions for communicating ethically and effectively across differences, for collaborating in pursuit of reasoned and just solutions to complex problems, for pursuing knowledge, truth, and mutual understanding, and for building community. Additionally, in the classroom, one is also more likely than the other to facilitate development of the skills and dispositional traits associated with ethical reflection and practice. Let me explain.

Cooperative argumentation pedagogy is designed, among other things, to foster empathic and critical listening skills, mutual respect, a sense of reciprocity, critical self-reflection, balanced partiality, moral imagination, epistemological humility, accountability, and a shared commitment to working together in pursuit of reasoned and just resolutions for critical issues. Dialogue is understood as a commitment to hear and be heard, to communicate *with*, rather than "at," "for," or "to" others on this model. Cooperative argumentation fosters the "I-Thou" relationship explored by Martin Buber, Dick Johanessen, Ron Arnett, and so many others in our field. Through cooperative argumentation pedagogy, students learn to distinguish critical judgment from cynicism. They become intimately acquainted with standpoint epistemology and experience first-hand the value of reciprocal commitments to fairness in communicative action. They develop community building and cross-cultural communication competencies. And they develop knowledge, skills, and abilities critical to ethical and effective resolution of conflict across cultural boundaries.

In sum, through this pedagogical paradigm, students are empowered with knowledge, skills, and abilities for ethical reflection and practice in everyday life. My personal experiences and research lead me to believe that models privileging manipulation of others in pursuit of a prize, trophy, or other "success" fail to offer similar promise in fostering such basic dialogic virtues and skills.

For these and related reasons, I believe that cooperative argumentation pedagogy holds greater promise in equipping students with the resources they will need to live virtuous, meaningful, successful, and fulfilling lives in the multicultural, interdependent world they will encounter in the 21st century.

In addressing themes in your scholarship, you've mentioned several writers. Are there other works that you would recommend to scholars of communication ethics?

What a wonderful, but difficult question; there are so many valuable resources available! Apart from books alluded to in my responses to earlier questions, let me name a few interdisciplinary, multicultural resources outside of the "mainstream" that I've found especially helpful.

For a resource rich with insight into "communicative ethics," I recommend Seyla Benhabib's *Situating the Self*. Benhabib's insights into dialogic virtues and skills and related explorations of the "concrete vs. the generalizable other" are especially illuminating.

Renato Rosaldo's *Culture and Truth* thoughtfully addresses related issues in social analysis. His explorations into the nature of truth, objectivity, narrative, and culture are especially valuable for contemporary studies of communication ethics.

Lani Guinier and Gerald Torres's *The Miner's Canary* explores relationships between race, power, culture, and communication. The authors' insights are potentially invaluable to students of communicative ethics.

Focusing specifically on pedagogical issues, *Teaching to Transgress* by bell hooks considers education as "the practice of freedom." In this book, hooks contributes invaluably to explorations of ethical issues related to instructional communication.

Earlier I mentioned Martha Nussbaum's *Upheavals of Thought*, a book I strongly recommend for communication ethics scholars. Another of her contributions is *Cultivating Humanity*. This book explores issues related to

Socratic dialogue, the role of reason in ethics, dialogic virtues, narrative imagination, and the relationship of communication to liberal education.

Cliff Christians and Michael Traber's edited volume, *Communication Ethics and Universal Values*, contributes valuably as well. Chapters by diverse authors explore critical issues in evolving relationships among principles, norms, values and culture related specifically to communicative action.

Another valuable contribution to the field is Sharon Bracci and Cliff Christians's *Moral Engagement in Public Life*. Authors in this volume share reflections regarding the applicability of diverse theoretical frameworks in the face of postmodern challenges.

For communication ethics scholars and educators seeking a highly practical work, I recommend Sissela Bok's *Lying*. Written several decades ago, the examples may seem "outdated" to many readers. At the same time, however, Bok's exploration of the Principle of Veracity contributes valuably to our understanding of the nature, role, and limits of veracity in diverse communication contexts that are as applicable (and urgently needed) today as ever before.

Mary Field Belenky et al.'s *Women's Ways of Knowing* offers insights into diverse epistemological and pedagogical paradigms. Communication ethics scholars and educators will find a wealth of knowledge (pardon the pun!) directly relevant to the field in this volume.

There are so many, many other resources available. In the interest of time and space, however, I will close by mentioning a book I've found especially valuable for teaching. In *Ethics for the New Millennium*, the Dalai Lama thoughtfully explores the implications of interdependence to ethical reflection and practice. His explorations into the nature of wise discernment, the role of emotions in ethical and effective deliberations, cross-cultural communication and understanding, virtue ethics, and the development of cross-cultural secular guidelines for ethical reflection and practice are especially useful for today's classroom. Communication ethics scholars and educators will find a wealth of insight here.

What challenges do we face regarding communication ethics in a time of postmodernity?

In many ways, today's challenges mirror those confronting the ancients. Problems of demagoguery, issues related to deception and truthfulness, the purposes of communication, guidelines for ethical communication, grounds for moral knowledge, and related epistemological and ethical issues have changed little throughout the ages.

Similarly, today as during most previous eras, philosophers, dialecticians, and rhetoricians continue to grapple with how to find an ethical balance between pursuit of personal values and interests on the one hand, and pursuit of shared goals and service to the community on the other.

"Are there timeless, a-contextual, universal guidelines for ethical communication, or is all moral knowledge socially constructed?" "What is the most reliable means for discerning or discovering guidelines for ethical communication?" "Where can we turn for reliable *grounds* for ethical justification?" "How do we most reliably negotiate differences between diverse ethical frameworks?" "Is ethics moribund?" "Is ethics simply a tool of those in power designed to hold sway and control over the masses?" "What distinguishes cynicism from critical judgment?" "How can we best discern differences between appearance and reality?" "Does the latter exist independently of human experience?" "When 'facts' and 'Truth' appear incompatible, which should prevail in ethical reflection and practice?"

Although these questions have changed little over the ages, the human condition has changed dramatically. In this age of ubiquitous media, technological surveillance and potential abuses of technology, global information access, weapons of mass destruction, corporate control of the media and, increasingly in the Academy as well, corruption of public servants, and global interdependence, these questions carry greater complexity and significance. Reframed for the contemporary context, we face especially compelling and complex challenges.

For example, "Given the human condition as we experience it today, how can we best acknowledge, honor, respect, and embrace the rich diversity of cultures co-existing in today's interdependent world without sacrificing commitment to such cross-cultural ideals as justice, fairness, compassion, love, truthfulness, and moral courage?" "What are the strengths and limits of personal experience in 'grounding' guidelines for ethical communication?" "What about cross-cultural dialogue?" "What are its strengths and limits in 'grounding' guidelines for ethical communication?" "What are the strengths and limits of modern scientific inquiry in pursuing knowledge, truth and understanding about ethical and effective communication across cultural boundaries?" "How do we distinguish between more or less reliable narratives?" "Whose voices can and must be heard in pursuit of knowledge, truth, and understanding, justice, and peace, and how can we insure their inclusion in public dialogue and deliberation?" "What are the strengths and limits of free expression in this age of technology?" "To what and to whom are advocates for just causes morally responsible?" "Under what circumstances, if any, do the ends justify the means in public advocacy?" "Whose interests and rights should be privileged in the enforcement of guidelines for responsible public communication?" "What values should drive our uses of technology?" "Whose interests and rights should be privileged in policies related to technological development, access, and use?" "Whose interests, rights, and values should be privileged in communication pedagogy?"

More than ever, humanity's place in the future will rest upon how we confront these challenges and the opportunities associated with them. It is difficult to imagine a more fertile ground for exploration, a more dynamic and exciting time for communication ethicists, or a more compelling responsibility.

Works Cited

Aristotle. *Rhetoric*. Trans. W. Rhys Roberts. New York: Modern Library, 1954.

Arnett, Ronald C. *Dialogic Education: Conversation About Ideas and Between Persons*. Carbondale: Southern Illinois UP, 1992.

Arnett, Ronald C., and Pat Arneson. *Dialogic Civility in a Cynical Age: Community, Hope, and Interpersonal Relationships*. Albany: State U of New York P, 1999.

Belenky, Mary Field, Blythe Clinchy, Nancy Goldberger, and Jill Tarule. *Women's Ways of Knowing: The Development of Self, Voice, and Mind*. New York: Basic Books, 1986.

Benhabib, Seyla. *Situating the Self: Gender, Communication and Postmodernism in Contemporary Ethics*. New York: Routledge, 1992.

Bok, Sissela. *Common Values*. Columbia: U of Missouri P, 1995.

———. *Lying: Moral Choice in Public and Private Life*. New York: Vintage, 1979.

———. *Mayhem: Violence as Public Entertainment*. Reading, MA: Perseus, 1998.

Booth, Wayne C. *Critical Understanding: The Powers and Limits of Pluralism*. Chicago: U of Chicago P, 1979.

———. *Modern Dogma and the Rhetoric of Assent*. Notre Dame, IN: U of Notre Dame P, 1974.

Bracci, Sharon, and Clifford Christians. *Moral Engagement in Public Life: Theorists for Contemporary Ethics*. New York: Peter Lang, 2002.

Buber, Martin. *I and Thou*. Trans. Ronald Gregor Smith. New York: Scribner, 1957.

Burke, Kenneth. *A Grammar of Motives*. Berkeley: U of California P, 1969.

———. *A Rhetoric of Motives*. Berkeley: U of California P, 1969.

Christians, Clifford and Michael Traber, eds. *Communication Ethics and Universal Values*. Thousand Oaks, CA: Sage, 1997.

Cortese, Anthony. *Ethnic Ethics: The Restructuring of Moral Theory*. New York: State U of New York P, 1990.

Dalai Lama. *Ethics for a New Millennium*. New York: Riverhead Books, 1999.

Descartes, René. *The "Meditations" and Selections from the "Principles" of René Descartes (1596-1650)*. Trans. John Veitch. LaSalle, IL: Open Court, 1955.

"Ferment in the Field." *Journal of Communication* 33.3 (1983).

Friere, Paulo. *Education for Critical Consciousness*. New York: Continuum, 1990.

Gerbner, George, Larry P. Gross, and William H. Melody, eds. *Communications Technology and Social Policy: Understanding the New "Cultural Revolution"*. New York: Wiley, 1973.

Guinier, Lani, and Torres, Gerald. *The Miner's Canary: Enlisting Race, Resisting Power, Transforming Democracy*. Cambridge, MA: Harvard UP, 2002.

hooks, bell. *Teaching to Transgress: Education as the Practice of Freedom*. New York: Routledge, 1994.

Johannesen, Richard. *Ethics in Human Communication*. 5th ed. Prospect Heights, IL: Waveland, 2004.

Jonas, Hans. *The Imperative of Responsibility: In Search of an Ethics for the Technological Age*. Chicago, IL: U of Chicago P, 1984.

Makau, Josina M. and Ronald Arnett. *Communication Ethics in an Age of Diversity*. Urbana: U of Illinois P, 1997.

Makau, Josina M., and Debian L. Marty. *Cooperative Argumentation: A Model for Deliberative Community*. Prospect Heights, IL: Waveland, 2001.

Mill, John Stuart. *On Liberty*. London, UK: Watt's, 1929.

Nussbaum, Martha. *Cultivating Humanity: A Classical Defense of Reform in Liberal Education*. Cambridge, MA: Harvard UP, 1997.

———. *Upheavals of Thought: The Intelligence of Emotions*. Cambridge, MA: Cambridge UP, 2001.

Perleman, Chaïm. *The New Rhetoric: A Treatise on Argumentation.* Notre Dame, IN: U of Notre Dame P, 1969.

———. *An Historical Introduction to Philosophical Thinking.* New York: Random House, 1965.

———. *Justice.* New York: Random House, 1967.

Rosaldo, Renato. *Culture and Truth: Renewing the Anthropologist's Search for Meaning.* Boston, MA: Beacon P, 1989.

Toulmin, Stephen E. *Human Understanding.* Princeton, NJ: Princeton UP, 1977.

———. *Knowing and Acting: An Invitation to Philosophy.* New York: Macmillan, 1976.

A Conversation about Communication Ethics with Clifford G. Christians

Christians: "Could we begin with the academic's prayer?"
Arneson: "Please do."
Christians: "Dear God, lead us to the truth, but save us from those that have found it!"

How did you become interested in studying communication ethics?

It goes back to my college days. I majored in the classics. In our program we had to read the classical philosophers in the original language. Therefore, Aristotle and Plato took on special meaning to me, including their ethics. Then during my master's degree in Theology and my master's in Sociolinguistics, the questions of ethics always came to the fore as well. I was interested in theological ethics in a formal sense, but in Sociolinguistics my particular concern was the illiterate, those learning to read—those who were dispossessed of their own language. I aspired at that time to write materials for neoliterates who had just been given a language in writing, through the Wycliff translators, for example. During those graduate years in Sociolinguistics, I read Paulo Freire. He was an authority on the oppressed and issues of social justice. My Ph.D. at the University of Illinois focused on communications theory and the philosophy of communications. There we had to choose a concentration outside of communications. In my case it was philosophy, and one of the professors from the philosophy department served on my doctoral committee. So it goes back to my educational experience. All my degrees, more or less, centered on the question of social ethics.

For better or worse, most of my interests have been driven by the philosophical and, in a secondary sense, the theological world—rather than by personal experience *per se*. That's how I think of communication ethics. I'm interested in social ethics, both in theory and application. Society is an embodiment of communication. Its linkages are lingual, and those lingual connections are always value saturated. Language, communication, is society's *sine qua non* in John Dewey. He said famously, "of all things, communication is the most wonderful." No social institution is possible except as a communication system.

Rather than thinking of society as an aggregate of individuals, or seeing the social order in political or economic terms, combining communication and social ethics is a different approach. Social ethics commits us to understand those values that make society possible. Values are never held as part of one's innermost life, but they are dialogic. They are interactive, values are shared. Therefore, if one wishes to study social ethics, it seems to me, concentrating on communications is the best venue to do that. If you think of society as a communication network, then media institutions become a potent laboratory for understanding the way societies are interlinked and social values operate. We do not live in atomistic isolation, but in the social order. The over-riding question here is, "How can one understand social ethics and approach it academically?" Rather than assuming a functional or aggregate form of society, my approach is radically dialogic. The communal relations we call society are concentrated in its particular institutions or nation states or cultural groups. Coming to grips with the values embedded in their structures and organizations is one fruitful venue for understanding the moral order in general and communication ethics in particular.

Do you use the terms social ethics and communication ethics interchangeably?

"Interchangeably" mixes conceptual categories, but in my way of thinking about it, there is no pure social ethics outside of the institutions which form a society. Scholars in social ethics study political institutions, or certain regimes in society such as the military, business or religious organizations. To my mind, the media are institutions of acculturation—they produce and maintain culture. Thus in my social ethics I concentrate on communication as a phenomenon and its specific embodiments in popular culture. Through social ethics in its various forms we make judgments about the way society operates and ought to. In other words, I'm concerned about blurring the distinction between communication ethics or media ethics and social ethics, though social ethics is always shaped and directed by context. I'm interested not in meta-ethics *per se*, but normative ethics—ethics within the social order. Abstract concepts in themselves are not the emphasis, such as the nature of loyalty, power, identity, the good: "How are these issues experienced?" "What is empowerment?" "In what situations should we keep our promise?" The question for my kind of social ethics is not values-clarification, but community formation. The compelling questions for me are the extent to which the symbolic world of meaning is available to people: "How is human dignity manifested?" "For whom and under what conditions are speakers establishing the vernacular?" "How are worldviews articulated?"

How do you define communication ethics?

I use the term "communitarian ethics," and I've developed that as a concept within the larger world of social ethics. I'm thinking primarily of the Canadian philosopher Charles Taylor, of Michael Waltzer, Carole Pateman, and Michael Sandel. These scholars locate their view of ethics within the notion of society. They take the community as ontologically and axiologically situated, that is, the community in its being and in what we value is prior to the person. It's a way of working between collectivism on the one hand and libertarian individualism on the other. Collectivism out of Georg Hegel and Karl Marx has been the most powerful alternative to mainstream liberalism since John Locke. So, yes, I would characterize my work as communitarian ethics. It's a third way, a community of persons-in-relation, not merely a superficial tribute to both society and persons. Within communitarian ethics, I see it as an ethics of duty in contrast to virtue ethics. I also develop it in contrast to consequentialist ethics, such as utilitarianism.

When we wrote the book *Good News: Social Ethics and the Press*, we called chapter three "Communitarian Ethics." This is the foundational chapter of the book. The ethical theory of chapter three is examined in the rest of the book within the context of the media as a social institution. There is no media ethics outside social structures and culture, only an ethics rooted in community. Communitarian ethics is a claim about normative ethics. It is not a description of morality, and not meta-theory, but a normative ethics of community where "is" and "ought" are integrated.

There are several ways of thinking about communitarian ethics. Philosophy is a discipline. Communications is not, in my understanding of it. Communications is a problematic, a field of interest that people may have. It is an academic area but is interdisciplinary and focused on crucial issues that aren't neatly contained within a discipline's boundaries. Therefore the subject matter of ethics is driven, from my perspective, by philosophy and not by the field of communications *per se*. One works out moral problems in the context of communications, but the formulation of them is philosophical in character.

An example might be the issue of "truth." As I see it, truth is the central ethical problem within the field of communication ethics. Even as the standard of justice belongs in a particular sense to politics and the norm of stewardship to business, so truth or truth-telling is the fundamental issue in communications. To understand truth in a way that's philosophically credible, it's important for me to put it in a context of correspondence views of truth versus coherence models. That is, correspondence theories of truth are driven by the philosophical world and do not start with objectivity. Coherence approaches to truth, in the media for example, are established philosophically. We can get to questions about accuracy and precision in journalism after our bearing and way of thinking are settled into philosophical categories.

The notion of truth related to communications that I've been developing personally is what I call "interpretive sufficiency." Interpretive sufficiency works alongside or away from the realm of correspondence, since correspondence truth is obviously unsustainable in a post-Newtonian universe. But I'm not much enamored with coherence views of truth either. In narrative ethics, for example, you attempt to tell your story with overall integration and attention to the integrity of its dramatic character and to the authenticity of its plot. There are no ethical requirements for discourse beyond meeting the test of coherence. That way of understanding truth is too limited and relativistic in my perspective.

What I do is take a concept like "truth," knowing that it's crucial in the world of communications and recognize that the relationship between this problematic called communication and the discipline of philosophy is always an interactive one. I don't want to fall into the ancient Greek idea that if B follows A, B is inferior to A. Communications as a non-discipline is not inferior to the disciplines, but it's apples and oranges. Certainly the battles in the field of communications are important to take seriously. Stephen Toulmin and others have made it clear that the best philosophy is worked off the street, out of the struggles going on in real life. Debates in our homes, pain and death at the hospital bedside, controversies in parliament produce the most profound philosophical inquiry. A long tradition in philosophy sees itself as developing normative perspectives on our everyday experience. In this sense, when an issue arises such as truth in communications, one turns to a philosophical frame of reference and is theoretically serious about the problem. Therefore, to speak about objectivity and narrative devoid of coherence and correspondence views of truth is unacceptable to me. My point is, take philosophy seriously and have one's thinking driven by it while all the time integrated with the field, with that problematic, called communications.

Another example might be the issue of justice. That is, given the new technologies at hand, like digital media, cyberspace, and virtual reality, the question is "Do we have a new set of ethics on our hands?" We have new technologies. They are not merely televisual like television is, or audio technologies *per se* as radio is. They are convergent. "Are we entering a new arena different from the visual world that we've been given through cinema and television?" "Are we turning to digital technology and seeing a brand new agenda; everything else no longer matters because this technology converges all the various forms into a digital composition?" "Has technology, or will it, make today's dominant media archaic—print, television, film, computers—by reconfiguring them so dramatically that our previous work in media ethics is uninteresting or inapplicable?"

My instincts are to say that with social institutions, one typically understands them around the notion of justice. And that's how I think of the media—the social institution that is driven by the economic and ideological character of the market system. Therefore, I would be interested in coming to the question of cyberspace from those issues that philosophy has faced inescapably when working on social institutions. "How does the question about justice make an impact on internet resources?" "What about the enormous differences in equitable delivery of this technology?" Parts of the world have an abundance of it, and it serves as a recreational cabin in the woods for somebody who already has a home. Or technology provides another alternative for people who have abundant media versus those who are living with no telephone in some sections of the globe. So one comes to the issue of cyberspace from an agenda that is shaped by philosophy, not just in an abstract sense, but with philosophy and communication interacting. That is at least my way of defining the difference between meta-ethics and normative ethics. The latter works into the issues of the day but shapes them within the context of, and in terms of, the issues of philosophy.

To carry that further, the question about cyberspace from a philosophical point of view comes to a focus through the question of justice. And it's profoundly stimulating also around the issue of truth, that is, "What is being represented here?" In what sense, as we understand truth in either a correspondence or a coherence view or in terms of interpretive sufficiency, is a system of communication that transmits isolated bits of data in sequence giving us new questions about truth? "Is cyberspace opening up worlds of communication that make it necessary to elaborate what justice means philosophically?" Justice conceptually has moved from its roots in the retributive justice of law, to distributive justice, and more recently to restorative justice. As the Truth and Reconciliation Commission in South Africa has documented, no restoration is possible unless evil deeds and confession are explicitly spoken or written. The reality of communication intrudes upon and shapes the character of philosophical reflection, in this case on the nature of justice.

In addition to truth and justice, a third question from philosophy concerns the nature of the human, or philosophical anthropology. "What is going on when anonymity, in terms of sending and receiving messages in cyberspace, is a characteristic form of human interaction?" Some in the legal community argue that pornography in cyberspace cannot be considered pornography because there is no actual person who's being raped or treated violently in this technology. Pornography in cyberspace is just an exchange of artifices, of contrivances that are electronically driven. What happens with our humanity within a cyber world is important to me, but that's because the nature of the human is the longstanding philosophical issue. I'm suggesting here that philosophy as a discipline, and the history of ideas or intellectual history, shape the frame of reference; and communications, the arena in which we live and this venue in which so much of the social order is concentrated, helps me understand it better. Communications feeds back inescapably into the philosophical system.

You asked about my commitment to communitarian ethics, and from this perspective I've suggested three important issues so far that we need to work on in communications, each of them philosophical in character—truth, justice, and the nature of the human. I could speak of communitarian ethics in more generic terms as well. Communitarianism is a social philosophy that contradicts mainstream individualism. When it is developed in terms of public communication, the operating term is social responsibility.

And social responsibility has emerged within the communications literature as an important concept. I've worked on it on the international level. My colleague Kaarle Nordenstreng of Finland and I, for example, published an article in the *Journal of Mass Media Ethics* about social responsibility worldwide, trying to take note of this nomenclature as it appears in different protocols around the world. Social responsibility was first formulated in the United States by the Hutchins Commission in its 1947 *Report on the Free and Responsible Press*. The MacBride Commission in 1980, under the direction of UNESCO (United Nations Educational, Scientific, and Cultural Organization), emphasized social responsibility globally. Today, the European Union is organizing most of its understanding of cultural vitality within the Union under that label. There is more public journalism—and application of social responsibility thinking—in Latin America than in any other part of the world. Notions like social responsibility I have pursued with some interest but also a host of other generic issues that are philosophically interesting.

What kind of new questions emerge for communication ethics with the introduction of global media technologies?

The character of our society overall is technological. Rather than thinking of technologies *per se*, the fundamental issue is what Jacques Ellul calls *la technique*. *La technique* is the concept of "machineness" that underlies the technological world in which we live. The only two specific technologies that are global in scope are information and military technology, and their contradiction indicates that it is important to understand technologies individually from the inside out. If we know the different character of various technologies—as a chemist knows the differences among chemicals—we can make important distinctions between print technologies and electronic ones and distinguish the qualities of audio media from visual ones. The Canadian School of Communication, Harold Innis and Marshall McLuhan pre-eminently, have been successful at this kind of technology-focused communication scholarship.

However, the important issue, for those of us in ethics, it seems to me, is a deeper understanding of technology as an ideological system in which efficiency or instrumentalism is the dominant feature. My Ph.D. dissertation centered on the work of Jacques Ellul, since I was interested in social philosophy. Ellul's understanding of the technological society attracted me as the most helpful way of thinking about technology today, his own work rooted in Max Weber and Karl Marx. Ellul argues that in the history of the human race we were synchronized with nature—etching our livelihood out of it, the rise and fall of the seasons, day and night. The character of nature gave humans their orientation and value system. For 5,000 years it's been a different kind of ambience, away from nature and inscribed into the human and social order. Our identity and moral commitments have been human-to-human, within the social groups that are native to us.

Jacques Ellul's argument is that for the first time in human history the world essentially has become technological. Of course, we still have a human-to-nature relationship and a human-to-human one as well, but those are residual in his mind. I agree with his argument, based on Engel's law, that as quantity increases quality changes. Ellul recognizes that we have always had technologies—hoes, a stylus as a pen, the wheel, needles to sew clothes. The Roman Empire, in terms of its administration, was close to a machine. Certainly the huge armies that were built by Babylon in antiquity were technological instruments. But as quantity expands something radically different happens. A town in Pennsylvania that has 1,000 people and the Pittsburgh area with two million people are on a continuum of quantity from 1,000 to two million. But at some point on the scale, it is a village in one case and an urban center in the other. Ellul introduces the term "the technological society" for the second. There are technologies over history, but currently a technological order is present. Around the 1890s technologies like the underwater cable began to connect the world. Industry started producing technologies that created markets across the globe, and the profusion of the industrial order generated an abundance of technological forms. Industrial societies have been undergoing a shift for a century, so that today it's a technological order, one that's driven by technique, by efficiency.

Has this technological order, in a sense, become a moral order?

That's exactly right. One of the questions that you're interested in is this: What is the biggest challenge for communication ethics for future generations? I would answer that along the line of what you're implying: the huge challenge is amorality. For Jacques Ellul, the basic issue is not that the world has turned immoral, but that the instrumentalism of efficiency which characterizes technological societies makes the moral order foreign, or inaccessible, or unintelligible. It's not immorality that we contend with first of all now and in the future, but amorality. Amorality, from his point of view, means that the technological order characterizes what we are—an order that has taken on the qualitative shifts to efficiency, technique, machineness, and the mystique of the instrument. In these terms, the moral life or the moral order is instrumentalized and has no direct bearing on our humanness.

Obviously, immorality persists. Murder, fraud, physical abuse, and lying are as immoral today as always. But it's increasingly difficult to come to grips with them in our mind and conscience. In a technological society, we know the moral life exists somewhere around the edges, but it's ephemeral. The world that we live in is a world of necessity, of instrumentalism. If you use the old means-ends distinction as we typically do in ethics, means is the preoccupation of the technological order, its overwhelming commitment. Ends, therefore, have no bearing psychologically or intellectually or in the way our institutions are organized. The world of amorality means that those of us who are interested in the moral order and questions of value are speaking about a universe that the public generally does not understand. I'm over-generalizing here: specific righteous acts and institutional integrity as we witness it keep technologically sophisticated societies from darkness.

Jacques Ellul would ask, "Can a rose bush grow at the North Pole? Can ethics prosper in a technological order?" Ellul is not a nihilist or a fatalist, nor am I. He's pessimistic, but that's different. A nihilist would say that moral acts are absolutely impossible. A fatalist has so over-defined the world that amorality, in *toto*, is all that characterizes it. For Ellul, we have experienced a qualitative shift to a world of means, where ends are secondary. But one cannot conclude, therefore, that our interest in ethics and appeals to the general morality have no significance. They're an act of faith, however. Ethics is a duty whether one can calibrate substantial results or not. I believe with Ellul that we should make amorality overwhelming and inescapable without, in a fatalistic sense, saying no alternatives are possible. Amorality is definitive without being totalizing.

This is what I mean by our most formidable challenge. The increasing amorality of our technological order, by virtue of it being an instrumentalist system, concerns me the most. Thus, I'm grateful for my colleagues who include systemic failure in their study of organizational ethics. The collapse of Enron, for example, is a demonstration of wholesale failure or "wall-to-wall amorality" as Ellul would call it. The destruction of Enron is not the result of some conniving, immoral, evil leader. Amorality sometimes concentrates in leaders, but the moral failure here is the result of a corporate system consumed by means and devoid of moral ends. Enron illustrates a commitment to efficiency and instrumentalism, so that moral questions within the technological order have no resonance.

Given your interest in communitarian ethics and recognition that a global technological order is amoral, what are your thoughts about a universal communication ethic?

As with the subject matter of communication ethics, the question about universals is driven for me by philosophy. One could argue that the character of the human, philosophical anthropology, leads me to the conclusion that inscribed in our humanness is a moral dimension or proclivity that is irrepressible as far as our humanness is concerned. If one takes the field of ethics out of its epistemological and metaphysical character and makes it an ontological domain, understanding the character of being and the notion of human being, then one is compelled, from my point of view, to see the possibility of morals as a presupposition. "Protonorm" is my term here. Moral values are an underlying belief, a starting point, a faith commitment. They are primordial, deep in our being like a primal scream.

What if one were to ask, "How does that square with a technological order of instrumentalism where the moral life has no resonance?" Remember that Jacques Ellul is a dialectician. He is fundamentally influenced by Søren Kierkegaard and believes in a simultaneous "yes and no." We must face the "no" squarely, coming face-to-face with the abyss, the darkness of the technological order. At that point a leap of faith is possible. Ellul always thinks in counterpoint, "yes and no" dialectically. And this is how we should understand ethics. Resistance is not some streamlined codes of ethics that enables us to get on in the world. Ethics is speaking in the prophetic voice and calling for empowerment over against the system. Ethicists speak as prophets wanting the wayward to come home, not in condemnation as much as invitation. Underneath the declarations against evil is a wooing toward another way of life that is possible.

Ellul's dialectic "yes and no" is ultimately apocalyptic. He's a Christian and believes that when the end of the age finally comes there will be freedom from the dominance of *la technique*. Meanwhile, each of us is called to live out as much of one's own revolution as possible. Ethical acts are the first fruits of the final transformation at the end of time. In his *Autopsy of Revolution*, Ellul wants genuine revolution on the level of *la technique*, not just in terms of some problems on the surface. Revolution is swimming against the stream underneath, that is, always confronting instrumentalism, knowing that it will not basically change until the new order is introduced supernaturally. One must say "yes" while recognizing the negative.

The Kierkegaardian dialectic in Ellul is the answer to your question as I see it. Ethics can be a prophetic voice, a call to resistance, a leap of faith in which one attempts alternative possibilities. The dialectic is a long-standing intellectual tradition that we have available about the nature of the human from many different traditions, both Eastern and Western. The challenge for us is not to let dialectic disappear from the technological order.

Jean Baudrillard is of interest to me along these lines, too. The simulacrum creates through the technological world a hyper-reality, in which the real is reversed so that the hyper-real becomes the definition of reality as we know it. If we see Frontier World in Disney Land, with its assimilated and reproduced artifice of what history was like when Daniel Boone lived, then Baudrillard's argument would be that this hyper-reality becomes the frame of reference out of which we read history. The simulations within which we live, driven by the media, become reality for us, period. There is no meaningful verity that exists outside of technologically mediated frames of reference. Inversion has occurred in industrial societies. Baudrilland uses the term "implosion"—the reality that we know has imploded into hyper-reality.

There is considerable overlap between *la technique* and hyper-reality. We need more time than we have here to distinguish between the details of Ellul's world and Baudrillard's. However, on one fundamental point, I prefer the longer historical perspective in Ellul's way of thinking. Ellul is looking, either through history or through his metaphysics, for a place to stand. He seeks a location of perfect freedom and the ultimate good which are not tainted by *la technique*. At the least, he wants a prophetic voice vis-à-vis the world of necessity in which we live. Baudrillard doesn't grant us that request. I have written about Ellul and Baudrillard and argue that Ellul has the same radical understanding of technology as Baudrillard, but a far more sophisticated approach that makes prophetic resistance credible. That's how I think our stand on ethics ought to be. Ellul gives us a framework for doing ethics without skepticism.

We can also think about the world of technology in terms of what Ellul calls "self-augmentation" and machine-like growth according to the principle of efficiency. Therefore, any claims that we make about ethics are set against this evolving world constantly on the move. It is continually developing out of itself toward greater productivity. In the process of augmenting itself, it replaces anchor points for ethics—such as God, the metaphysical, and the virtuous human being—with its own instrumentalism. Therefore, the banality of evil emerges—the concerns of those who ran the Nazi concentration camps were about the sufficiency of their fuel supplies, and whether their crematoria were handling enough bodies, or whether in a 24-hour period, as a matter of fact, they have been as efficient as they were two years before, or whether Belzec's gas chambers were as effective as those in Auschwitz. The banality-of-evil phenomenon is one way to describe an Ellulian world. The social dynamics and moral qualities get reduced by technology's self-augmentation and are reformulated around the calculation of means that instrumentalism represents.

I haven't studied the military from this point of view, but those who have notice what happens when the military continues to celebrate its superior technology and makes technological refinements its primary mission. These spokesmen are integrated into military technology. SMART bombs, the ability to fly aircraft in tandem, virtually all defense combines human beings, information sophistication, and weapons. The military is a marriage of communication and weapons technology that was really evident during the Iraq War in 2003. The military celebrates the super-sophistication of military technology for giving us a cleaner approach—that the SMART bomb will not destroy entire populations as in World War II when cities like Dresden were bombed indiscriminately to near oblivion because the technology could not select from among different targets. Ellul's argument would be that as this technology becomes more and more refined, more dominant, more robotic, more of a technical artifice, the ability to use it in morally appropriate ways, or to make ethical discriminations, becomes foolhardy. For sophisticated military instruments, counter-productivity emerges, so that efficiency replaces the social ends with whatever increased technological productivity can achieve. Technologies of surveillance follow the same pattern. The technological imperative determines the goals and strategy. As the electronic ability for tracking electronic data multiplies, the instruments set the pace and standard and bury human issues of privacy and freedom in the process.

The artifice that military and surveillance technology combined with information technology has created is an amoral world. From an Ellulian point of view, to expect morally appropriate decisions by people who are trained and schooled and implicated in this technical system is absurd. It would be enjoyable to pursue this illustration some more. But it's not an area that I've investigated with the thoroughness it deserves.

Are you seeking a domain outside of technique to enable us to shape society through communication?

The argument would be that within the dialectic community, within local communities of resistance, one can develop a domain of thinking that as a matter of fact stands in counterpoint against the technological world in which we live. Many people have argued resistance and Jacques Ellul works out of this legacy. What Ellul delivers to us is a counter-culture. People during the so-called "hippie days" of the 1960s carried his book *The Technological Society* around as their bible. Ellul does insist that the first step one must take is withdrawal from it. The only forms of resistance that are really available to us from his point of view are communities of nonviolence in which the proto-norm, the sacredness of life, is honored. His critics have complained that all he makes available to us is a non-technological island within a raging technological environment. But actually Ellul is not content with that. Max Weber's bureaucratization is a direct parallel to Ellul's *la technique*. Ellul's machineness is not just in our tools, but in bureaucracies. The government and education are machine-like in character. In his case, the Reformed church in France of which he was a part was a stifling, choking bureaucracy. So he starts a church in his own home. He develops a men's club and a film study group, and refuses to drive a car. In various ways, he is living alongside of the materialist world of which he is a part. The argument would be to enable and empower local resistance, developing groups dialogically, interactively, those that nurture human values, the proto-norms that I'm talking about. Certainly truth and justice and nonviolence are entailed by the sacredness of human life, and resistance then also takes the form of a non-instrumental nurturing of values. That nurturance is not an individual escape but takes place interactively among the like-minded.

Jacques Ellul has written about the Middle East, and it is too complicated to cover adequately here. He would want to see groups of Palestinians and Israelis working together on water projects, on health, on education, on creating a world of nonviolence in the face of the overwhelming violence driven by military technology. Part of my interest in ethics is to spend more time telling the stories of these resistance groups, of people who are trying to articulate, vis-à-vis the instrumentalism of our society, the way of peace and human values. Our research tends to emphasize the major entities and large-scale issues. We examine the *New York Times*, CNN, Hollywood, the global conglomerates, and neglect the small, authentically counter-cultural. To claim that the only alternative is to wait until the world ends and we live in heaven with divine peace would be contrary to Ellul's thinking. In the dialectic of saying "yes" in the face of the "no," we thereby resist and empower one another. To the extent we can make public these acts of critical consciousness, as Freire would call them, we inspire others to authentic humanity in their own time and space.

In addressing themes in your scholarship, you've mentioned several writers. Are there others who have influenced your work in communication ethics?

Thanks for the question. This gives me an opportunity to take note of several intellectual colleagues I haven't already introduced: Reinhold Niebuhr, W. D. Ross, and Edith Wyschogrod. Niebuhr was one of the most influential thinkers of mid-twentieth century America. His Christian realism showed us how to take divine command theory out of metaethics and root it in justice and social reform instead. His *Moral Man and Immoral Society* and two-volume *Nature and Destiny of Man* are heavyweight books that continue to invigorate my thinking on the problem of structural evil and the distinctive character of the human. W. David Ross in his *The Right and the Good* developed the most influential critique of utilitarianism ever written. In the process, he established an ethics of duty as the most credible alternative and has encouraged my own predilections for a communitarian duty ethics.

And with the relational center to social ethics, feminist moral theory has been indispensable to me, also. Feminist ethics demonstrates how we can start over conceptually rather than be trapped in the individual autonomy of mainstream Western ethics. Edith Wyschogrod represents the dialogic tradition of Emmanuel Levinas, and in doing so demonstrates how the actual moral existence of the saintly few is the best venue for understanding Otherness. She makes inescapable the need in our ethics to account for the surgeon from the Royal College of London serving in a leper colony in Cairo. Ethical reflection on the Holocaust cannot concentrate exclusively on the atrocities of the Third Reich but must include the heroics of Anne Frank.

Even as I mention these inspirations of mine, I need to underscore my indebtedness to classical philosophical tradition. I don't treat Aristotle, John Stuart Mill, and Immanuel Kant in scholastic terms; in fact, my communitarian social ethics isn't a contemporary version of any of them. Our theorizing is never *ex nihilo*. We do not create new models *de novo*. Theories engage the *status quo*; they rectify weaknesses in existing paradigms. Theories are oppositional claims. The classic thinkers in the academic enterprise we call "ethics" give us a legacy to work from, without which we merely re-invent the wheel. The intellectual masters are not canonical but provocateurs, essential to our thinking even while we contradict them and create models that are foreign to their age and expertise.

Works Cited

Aristotle. *Nichomachean Ethics*. Trans. H. Rackham. Cambridge, MA: Harvard UP, 1934.

Baudrillard, Jean. *Simulations*. Trans. Paul Foss, Paul Patton, and Philip Breitchman. New York: Semiotext(e), 1983.

Christians, Clifford G., and Jay M. Van Hook, eds. *Jacques Ellul: Interpretive Essays*. Urbana: U of Chicago P, 1980.

Christians, Clifford, John P. Ferré, and Mark Fackler. *Good News: Social Ethics and the Press*. New York: Oxford UP, 1993.

Christians, Clifford, and Kaarle Nordenstreng. "Social Responsibility Worldwide." *Journal of Mass Media Ethics* 19 (2004): 3-28.

Christians, Clifford G., and Michael Traber, eds. *Communication Ethics and Universal Values*. Thousand Oaks, CA: Sage, 1997.

Dewey, John. *Human Nature and Conduct: An Introduction to Social Psychology*. 1922. New York: Modern Library, 1930.

Ellul, Jacques. *Autopsy of Revolution*. Trans. Patricia Wolf. New York: Knopf, 1971.

———. *The Technological Society*. Trans., John Wilkinson. 1954. New York: Knopf, 1964.

Freire, Paulo. *Pedagogy of the Oppressed*. Trans. Myra Bergman Ramos. 1970. New York: Continuum, 2000.

Hegel, Georg. *Hegel's Philosophy of Right*. Trans. Thomas Malcolm Knox. Oxford: Clarendon P, 1952.

Innis, Harold A. *The Bias of Communication*. Toronto: U of Toronto Press, 1951.

Kant, Immanuel. *Lectures on Ethics*. Eds. Peter Heath and J. B. Schneewind. Trans. Peter Heath. Cambridge, UK: Cambridge UP, 2001.

Kierkegaard, Søren. *Either/Or: A Fragment of Life*. Trans. David F. Swenson and Lillian Marvin Swenson. Princeton, NJ: Princeton UP, 1944.

Levinas, Emmanuel. *Ethics and Infinity: Conversations with Philippe Nemo*. Trans. Richard A. Cohen. Pittsburgh, PA: Duquesne UP, 1985.

Locke, John. *The Works of John Locke, in Nine Volumes*. London, UK: C and J Rivington, 1824.

Marx, Karl. *The Economic and Philosophic Manuscripts of 1844*. 1932. Trans. Martin Mulligan. Moscow: Progress, 1959.

McLuhan, Marshall. *Culture Is Our Business*. New York: McGraw-Hill, 1970.

Mill, John Stuart. *The Ethics of John Stuart Mill*. Ed. Charles Douglas. London, UK: Blackwood, 1897.

Niebuhr, Reinhold. *Moral Man and Immoral Society*. New York: Charles Scribner's Sons, 1960.

———. *The Nature and Destiny of Man*. 2 vols. 1941, 1943. New York: Charles Scribner's Sons, 1964.

Pateman, Carole. *The Problem of Political Obligation: A Critique of Liberal Theory*. Cambridge, UK: Polity 1985.

Plato. *Plato in Twelve Volumes*. Cambridge, MA: Harvard UP, 1980.

Ross, W. David. *The Right and the Good*. Oxford, UK: Clarendon P, 1930.

Sandel, Michael. *Liberalism and the Limits of Justice*. 2nd ed. Cambridge, UK: Cambridge UP, 1998.

Taylor, Charles. *Philosophical Arguments*. Cambridge, MA: Harvard UP, 1995.

Toulmin, Stephen. *Human Understanding*. Princeton, NJ: Princeton UP, 1977.

Walzer, Michael. *Politics and Passion: Toward a More Egalitarian Liberalism*. New Haven, CT: Yale UP, 2004.

Weber, Max. *The Theory of Social and Economic Organization*. Trans. A. M. Henderson and Talcott Parsons. Glencoe, IL: Free P, 1947.

Wyschogrod, Edith. *Saints and Postmodernism: Revisioning Moral Philosophy*. Chicago: U of Chicago P, 1990.

A Conversation about Communication Ethics with Michael J. Hyde

How did you become interested in studying communication ethics?

I did my graduate work in the Department of Communication at Purdue University. Both my M.A. and Ph.D. programs, however, included intensive study in philosophy under the guidance of Calvin Schrag. I was especially interested in continental philosophy: existentialism, phenomenology, hermeneutics, critical theory, and deconstruction. It was a wonderful education that influenced me to think about how these two disciplines could be brought together for the benefit of both. Clearly one of the linchpins was ethics and its relationship to the theory and practice of rhetoric.

A major catalyst for my work in communication ethics was my father suffering renal (kidney) failure. He had that disease for four years. It proved to be a horrible adventure in the hell of high tech medicine. The experience incited me to narrow my focus in communication ethics. A central question for me became how advancements in medical technology were affecting the health-care expectations of patients. I was awarded a fellowship from the W. K. Kellogg Foundation that allowed me to concentrate on this topic. One result of my research was my book *The Call of Conscience: Heidegger and Levinas, Rhetoric and the Euthanasia Debate*. Communication ethics was a central concern of this 10-year longitudinal study of the moral justifiability and social acceptability of physician-assisted suicide.

How do you define communication ethics?

The study of communication ethics entails an appreciation of "rhetorical competence"—how people go about making cogent and persuasive arguments, how they tell stories that can move others to think and act in morally just ways. From a philosophical standpoint, what fascinated me about the topic was its ontological status, as clarified by such phenomenologists as Martin Heidegger. Although he does not see himself as an "ethicist," Heidegger is certainly interested in uncovering those conditions that make possible the human capacity for rhetorical competence and its ethical ("authentic") use.

My approach to communication ethics also receives much guidance from the work of Hans-Georg Gadamer, Paul Ricoeur, Jürgen Habermas, Jacques Derrida, and Emmanuel Levinas. These philosophers certainly do not walk hand-in-hand when it comes to an appreciation of communication ethics.

Nevertheless, I find their respective projects to be essential in generating a robust appreciation of the scope and function of the topic. I attempt to illustrate this point in my most recent book, *The Life-Giving Gift of Acknowledgment (A Philosophical and Rhetorical Inquiry)*. The book draws heavily from continental philosophy in making a case for how we need acknowledgment as much as we need such other easily taken-for-granted things as air, blood, and a beating heart. Without the life-giving gift of acknowledgment, we are destined to exist in ways that are marked by the loneliness of social death. One senses the presence of this state of being, for example, in the lives of college students who "don't fit in with the crowd" or who are suffering from a disturbance brought on by breaking up with their girlfriend or boyfriend. "Where art thou?" Not hearing a familiar "Here I am!" can sometimes even lead a young person to admit that he or she "feels like dying." Like their teachers who publish so as not to *perish* and who then worry incessantly over who, if anyone, is even reading their work, students are an especially vulnerable population when it comes to dealing with the hurt of being unacknowledged by their peers—*and*, to be sure, their teachers. Acknowledgment has much to do with communication ethics and rhetorical competence.

Do you prefer the term "rhetorical ethics" rather than "communication ethics" because of the issue of rhetorical competence?

Not necessarily. Although when one is thinking as a rhetorical critic, he or she is interested not just in "what" a text means, but primarily in "how" it means. The effectiveness of a discourse has much to do with how it is structured, arranged, designed for the audience at hand. For example, it's one thing for a doctor to say to a patient, "We just got back your tests, and I'm sorry to report to you that you have cancer," and then he or she walks out of the room. The communication is very clear, but it doesn't take into consideration all the other things that are going on in and affecting that patient's life and health. When you start to consider carefully, "How should I say this to this individual?" you are emphasizing a rhetorical turn in your behavior. For me, communication ethics necessarily includes rhetorical ethics. It is the rhetorical dimension of communication that plays an essential role in transforming space and time into "dwelling places" (*ethos*; pl. *ethea*), where people can deliberate about and "know together" (con-scientia) some matter of interest. Such dwelling places define the grounds, the abodes or habitats, where a person's ethics and moral character take form.

Would you talk about the themes in your scholarship related to communication ethics?

Shortly after I received my Ph.D., I published the edited volume *Communication Philosophy in the Technological Age*, which contained original essays by philosophers of communication and rhetoric. The book reflected my interest in how ethical issues arise as communication becomes more and more technologically oriented. My specific work in communication ethics and medicine grew out of this early interest, which, in turn, led to my "infatuation" with the phenomenon of "the call of conscience." As both Martin Heidegger and Emmanuel Levinas make clear, an ontological appreciation of this phenomenon reveals how human existence is structured spatially and temporally at any given moment and how this structure calls on us to assume the ethical responsibility of affirming our freedom through resolute choice as we attempt to give meaning to the world. Assuming this responsibility is especially crucial when a personal crisis happens in our everyday interactions with things and with others. Today's ongoing euthanasia debate is a result of such a crisis, whereby people must decide what constitutes the "good life" and the "good death." In *The Call of Conscience* I examined how rhetoric functions to sound such a call. With this book, I came to realize that whether people are on the side of the "right to die" or the "right to life," the issue of acknowledgment is right in one's face. Being all alone when you are sick and dying is a terrible way to live and a terrible way to go. Such is the case whether the patient's call of "Where art thou?" is intended as a plea for life or for death.

The Life-Giving Gift of Acknowledgment was thus the necessary next step in my research program in communication ethics. The book contains 11 case studies that address the question "What would your life be like if nobody acknowledged your existence?" Taken together, the case studies unfold as an ontological theory of acknowledgment. With all of these cases I kept confronting the issue of how, as beings in need of acknowledgment, we embody a "metaphysical desire" for perfection: achieving a state of completeness in our lives. This issue warranted more careful consideration than I had so far given it; hence, my current book project on "coming to terms with perfection." For me, conscience, acknowledgment, and perfection walk hand-in-hand.

Like both conscience and acknowledgment, perfection admits a certain ontological significance: it is something that is essential to our well-being. "What would life be like if it were never informed by moral consciousness?" "What would life be like if no one cared enough to give you the time of day?" "What would life be like if we lacked any desire to improve the human condition, to perfect the goodness it is capable of producing?"

I thus hope to stimulate an awareness of a relationship, a process, that is too easily taken for granted and forgotten by people who are satisfied with their particular take on what they understand perfection to be and who therefore are too easily blinded to the negative consequences that may follow from their respective worldviews. I submit that it is important to keep these specific matters in mind, especially in an age like ours when, for example, science and technology are being employed more than ever before to create what has been termed our ever-growing instant-makeover, self-improvement culture, where anything less than perfection is pathology. Kenneth Burke provides important direction for grasping the problem with his discussion of how human beings are "rotten with perfection." Coming to terms with the nature of perfection defines a requirement for maintaining the well-being of our personal and public existence. Human survival and dignity call for some degree of perfection operating in our lives, although how we define, express, and live whatever this perfection is can be quite problematic. The euthanasia debate, for example, certainly raises the issue of perfection with all of its rhetoric on "the good life" and "the good death."

In thinking about the applications you are now drawing for Martin Heidegger's work in a postmodern era, are there aspects of his writing that remain consistent across time?

People like Jacques Derrida, Emmanuel Levinas, and others who were influenced by Martin Heidegger's work admit that its richness and ambiguity encourage a constant reconsideration of his philosophy. Indeed, Heidegger's theory of hermeneutics emphasizes this very point.

I think it's fair to say that the way I go about doing work in communication ethics involves turning to certain philosophical schools of thought for directives that provide ways for deepening an appreciation of the role of rhetoric in our everyday lives. At the same time, however, I am interested in showing how a fundamental understanding of rhetoric may provide directives for dealing with the shortcomings of the philosophy that I am using. I always try to have my work exhibit this double movement.

My recent essay "A Matter of the Heart: Epideictic Rhetoric and Heidegger's Call of Conscience" is a case in point. The essay appears in *Heidegger and Rhetoric*, edited by Daniel Gross and Ansgar Kemmann. The contributors are both philosophers and rhetoricians. We were asked to read Heidegger's as-yet untranslated 1924 lecture course on Aristotle's *Rhetoric* and to discuss how Heidegger's interpretation of Aristotle contributes to the rhetorical tradition. How important was rhetoric to Heidegger? I think people are going to be amazed when his lecture course is translated because they are going to see, as Nancy Struever put it in her contribution, that what you have with Heidegger's lecture course is one of the most original and important readings of Aristotle in the 20th century.

With my contribution, I tried to use Heidegger to take us beyond Aristotle's notion of epideictic rhetoric, while at the same time using Aristotle's notion of epideictic to critique Heidegger, especially as he moves away from the importance of everyday discourse in his later philosophy. The critique reflects my commitment to the teachings of Cicero. I see myself as an advocate of civic republicanism, or what is sometimes called civic humanism. Here you have the argument that training in philosophy is essential for the education of the orator, but it is the art of eloquence (*oratio*), practiced by this advocate of the *vita activa*, that instructs one on how to equip (*ornare*) knowledge of a subject in such a way that it can assume a publicly accessible form and function effectively in the social and political arena. In Cicero's words, the "severance between the tongue and the brain" is an impediment to this civic-minded, persuasive, and moral endeavor. For the good of the community, philosophy and rhetoric must work together. Cicero would have it no other way. To be drawn by philosophical study away from active life is contrary to moral duty. As Heidegger developed his philosophy, a sincere concern for the authenticity of rhetoric disappeared from view.

Throughout the history of Western philosophy, such a disappearance has never been a healthy sign for rhetoric. In *Being and Time*, Heidegger still mentions how the practice of rhetoric has an important role to play in the building of authentic community. But after that, his ontological investigations of the "essence" of language and its relationship to the "event of Being" are more attuned to the "poetic" ways of discourse, to how "language speaks" the "truth" of things through discursive acts of disclosure. This nonrhetorical orientation, however, is not without its problems. For example, when caught up in the midst of life's contingencies, of sociopolitical happenings that can bring us to our knees and perhaps send us to our graves, can we afford to merely sit back and wait and see what the event of Being has in store for us? When the sufferings of others provoke us to hear the call of conscience, is it enough to release ourselves from the practical and ethical matters at hand so that we may properly stay attuned to "the call of Being"? The later Heidegger seems oblivious to Cicero's warning about the danger of allowing a severance to occur between the tongue and the brain. This danger must always be a central concern of communication ethics.

My interest in communication ethics has me look at everyday existence to see what is actually going on *now* in the social and political arenas in order to determine how research in communication ethics might help us improve the process. If that requires that I seek direction from the classical period or the postmodern period, so be it. Sometimes Aristotle and Cicero fit the bill; other times Heidegger, Levinas, and other postmodern thinkers can prove quite helpful in directing and advancing one's theoretical gaze.

People can get so caught up in analytic frames that we lose sight of the social world in which people live and make ethical choices.

Yes, theories can get in the way of one's seeing what is actually going on before one's eyes. Being blinded by a commitment to Aristotle's or Heidegger's or Levinas's philosophical worldview is always a problem. Still, the appropriation, revision, and construction of theory is an invaluable endeavor. One must learn the notes before one attempts to write the symphony. At any given moment, one must turn from emphasizing theory to leaping head-first into the muck and mire of everyday existence in order to ensure the empirical integrity of the research at hand. If you're doing work in communication and rhetoric, it seems to me that sooner or later you have to come back to earth, take your theory and apply it to see if it has any real purchase. I am an advocate of the case study approach to scholarship. Phenomenology and hermeneutical philosophy are my favorite theoretical ways of getting to the ontological heart of the matter at hand. Unlike Levinas, I do not believe that ontology comes *after* ethics.

Can you clarify that last point?

Emmanuel Levinas maintains that Heideggerian ontology subordinates our relationship with others to the relationship with Being in general. Hence, according to Levinas, Heidegger's thinking on the call of conscience leads us down the wrong path. For this call originates, Levinas claims, not in "the temporality of Being," but rather in the "the temporality of the interhuman," in the face-to-face encounter between the self and the other. This encounter, according to Levinas, defines the primordial domain of ethics—a domain where the self, existing as it does in constant proximity to the other, is always in the situation of trying to come to terms with the otherness or alterity of the other, with what the self can never totally be in mind and body, with a fundamental difference embedded in life that forms the existential basis of all forms of social critique because its mere presence calls into question the self's egoist tendencies and know-it-all attitudes. Although Heidegger's philosophy does not focus on the moral character of human being, he certainly makes clear that this being (ontology) must be existing before there can be any talk about any form of otherness. Jacques Derrida, for example, makes much of this very point in his critical assessment of both philosophers. Still, as Heidegger admits, otherness is necessarily a part of the self's existence. Borrowing one of his phenomenological terms, I think it would be fair to say that ontology and ethics are "equiprimordial."

What are your thoughts about a universal communication ethic?

That's a good follow-up question. And a difficult one, too. I am presently struggling with the question in my work on perfection, which I referred to earlier.

A universal communication ethic necessarily raises the issue of perfection. Perfection is at work in our everyday lives—in our thoughts and actions—as we attempt to sustain and advance the progress we have achieved in the struggle to survive, understand the world, be better persons, and live the good life. Our passion for perfection is admirable; it defines who we are as metaphysical animals, creatures who have a longing, a nostalgia, for security, comfort, and completeness in our lives. This same passion is humbling, too. The 18th century Enlightenment philosopher David Hume reminds us of this fact when he notes how we can form ideas of perfection (e.g, God) that go beyond the empirical limits of everyday experience and, in so doing, call attention to our own contemptible limitations. Indeed, despite our many excellences, human beings are still animals, fallible creatures. At our best, we live lives that, at one and the same time, advance and forever fall short of our ever having it all together before we pass away. There is a *significant insignificance* to our being. Hume goes as far as to say that "the life of man is of no greater importance to the universe than that of an oyster." Perhaps he is right.

Unlike David Hume, however, I am not ready to admit that in the great cosmological scheme of things, human beings are of no greater importance than some marine bivalve mollusk. Such a skeptical assessment of humankind is called into question by the openness, the objective uncertainty, of our spatial and temporal being. We are always underway toward what is not yet. The future lies before us. The openness here allows for hope. Despite our shortcomings, we are creatures capable of good things. Coming to some agreement about what exactly constitutes such goodness calls on our capacity for collaborative deliberation and thus the communicative and rhetorical competence that allows us to speak our minds about contestable matters. Is not this entire process a dynamic in communication ethics?

I turn to philosophers like Martin Heidegger and Emmanuel Levinas to answer this question in a positive and, I hope, robust and instructive manner. Jürgen Habermas provides the most famous affirmative answer to the question with his "theory of communicative action." Here we are told of the "validity conditions" of "the ideal community of communication," wherein "competence" of "communicative rationality" can thrive. These conditions include: choosing a comprehensible expression, intending to communicate a true proposition, expressing intentions truthfully, and choosing an appropriate expression with respect to the dialogical situation at hand.

I find Habermas's work instructive; he provides us with at least a scaffolding for a universal theory of communication ethics. His theory can serve the interests of rhetoricians who would expose the ideological element of authority that inhibits collaborative deliberation in a given rhetorical situation. What he omits, however, is a major concern of the rhetorical critic: *how* discourse is invented and arranged in order to be expressed in an appropriate, truthful, and effective manner. To repeat, the rhetorical critic is concerned not only with what a text means, but also with *how* it means—for example, how a certain story is arranged such that it enhances a given argument being developed by a speaker or writer. Habermas fails to appreciate certain "positive" functions of rhetoric that make possible collaborative deliberation and that, as I argue in my work, conscience, *ethos*, and acknowledgment are fundamentally related to the ontological, hermeneutical, and moral structure of human being.

This is not to suggest, however, that the kind of work that I do provides the way to discover last remaining elements that are needed to discover a universal communication ethics. If anything, the philosophical and rhetorical nature of my work suggests that this discovery is always dependent on the particular situation at hand. As Aristotle long ago noted, the business of rhetoric is to deal with what is in the main contingent. The openness of human existence is the ultimate source of contingency. Who can say for sure what will happen tomorrow? The material of communication ethics is always *situated* in an ever-changing world. Knowing how to stir the soul rhetorically is essential because existential questions concerning the livelihood of society are not usually decided with the equations of demonstration or the syllogisms of dialectic. Existence is a gamble based on probabilities, and the emotional outlook of an audience influences its judgment at the time the bet is placed. Questioning is an ongoing activity for rhetorical critics who would do what must be done in order to ensure the livelihood of their tradition.

And in the questioning we are able to discern what theoretical applications of rhetorical ethics are appropriate for what particular rhetorical context.

That's correct. As Albert Jonsen and Stephen Toulmin make clear in their study of casuistry, a case study approach can abide by what is thought to be "universals" when examining a particular piece of discourse, but these universals must always remain flexible. The specific circumstances at hand might call for an amending of some thought or principle that heretofore was considered to be a "permanent" truth. Research in communication ethics fails to adhere to an essential feature of its practice when it neglects to remain *open* to such a call. With its temporal and spatial structure, human existence commends openness as being a truthful and ethical way to live. This easily taken-for-granted event lies at the heart of the teachings of existentialism, phenomenology, hermeneutics, and deconstruction, at least as these philosophical outlooks come to us from such thinkers as Søren Kierkegaard, Friedrich Nietzsche, Karl Jaspers, Martin Heidegger, Hans-Georg Gadamer, Emmanuel Levinas, and Jacques Derrida. These thinkers, to be sure, have their differences, but their respect for openness defines a common thread in the fabric of their respective works.

What is the biggest challenge for communication ethics in a time of postmodernity?

I am interested in the origins and the practices of communication ethics. Western religion is well known for equating these origins with God. Directed by the Darwinian theory of evolution, Western science, on the other hand, feels compelled to associate this source of perfection more simply and soundly with our species' biological and evolutionary drive for survival. Cognitive scientists, in fact, have identified structures in the human brain that can account for our metaphysical tendency to associate this drive with "God's call"—which is not necessarily to say that God exists, but only that the evolved "wiring" of our brains allows us to invent this linguistic construction and feel comfortable and secure with its mysterious referent and supposedly ultimate form of perfection. As Steven Pinker argues, language is first and foremost the product of a well-engineered biological instinct, an evolutionary adaptation that consists of "a form of mental software" ("grammar") made possible by specific genetic structures in the brain.

Western religion teaches that the significance of human being lies in our unique ability to answer God's call, no matter how insignificant we think ourselves to be in the ever-expanding vastness of the cosmos that began with a Big Bang approximately fifteen billion years ago. Indeed, coming to terms with God's truth takes place on a small planet in a galaxy that shares space and time with approximately 10^{11} (1,000,000,000,000) other galaxies in the observable universe. Each galaxy contains about as many stars and each is typically 100,000 light years across. Still, the Old and New Testaments tell stories about how our evolving power of consciousness has an essential role to play in God's plan for the universe to become aware of itself, better itself, and, in so doing, achieve as much perfection as possible as we make our way from our home on earth to our home in an even better world to come. The ever-developing field of cognitive science demands empirical evidence of this plan, which it continues to provide in disclosing the mechanisms of brain function. Research in communication ethics is well advised to keep in touch with the findings of their scientific colleagues. That certainly is one way of building theory from the ground up. But another essential piece of ground is the temporal and spatial structure of human existence. Here is where language, communication, and rhetoric do their everyday social and political work. The data that can be found here and used in instructive ways to educate us about all that is "good" and "bad" in life are no less important for "postmodernity" than the data collected by cognitive scientists. The future of communication ethics lies in attending carefully to the world's present-day scientific, social, political, and spiritual development and to the discourses that inform and are informed by such progress. Our goal as researchers should be to discover things about our being and its language that might truly improve the moral quality of everyday existence.

Works Cited

Burke, Kenneth. *Language as Symbolic Action: Essays on Life, Literature, and Method*. Berkeley: U of California P, 1966.

Cicero, Marcus Tullius. *Cicero: De Oratore*. Trans. E. W. Sutton. Cambridge. MA: Harvard UP, 1942.

Derrida, Jaçques. "Violence and Metaphysics: An Essay on the Thought of Emmanuel Levinas." *Writing and Difference*. Trans. Alan Bass. Chicago, IL: U of Chicago P, 1978. 79-153.

Gadamer, Hans-Georg. *Truth and Method*. 1960. New York: Crossroad, 1986.

Habermas, Jürgen. *Moral Consciousness and Communicative Action*. Trans. Christian Lenhardt and Shierry Weber Nicholsen. Cambridge: MIT P, 1990.

Heidegger, Martin. "*Grundbegriffe der Aristotelischen Philosophie*." Unpublished transcript of Heidegger's 1924 Summer Semester lecture course at Marburg. Marcuse Archive, Stadtsbibliotek, Frankfurt.

―――. *Being and Time*. Trans. John Macquarrie and Edward Robinson. New York: Harper and Row, 1962.

Hume, David. *Essays Moral, Political, and Literary*. Ed. Eugene F. Miller. Indianapolis, IN: Liberty Classics, 1985.

Hyde, Michael J., ed. *Communication Philosophy in a Technological Age*. University: U of Alabama P, 1982.

―――. *The Call of Conscience: Heidegger and Levinas, Rhetoric and the Euthanasia Debate*. Columbia: U of South Carolina P, 2001.

―――, ed. *The Ethos of Rhetoric*. Columbia: U of South Carolina P, 2004.

―――. *The Life-giving Gift of Acknowledgment (A Philosophical and Rhetorical Inquiry)*. West Lafayette, IN: Purdue UP, 2005.

―――. "A Matter of the Heart: Epideictic Rhetoric and Heidegger's Call of Conscience." *Heidegger and Rhetoric*. Eds. Daniel M. Gross and Ansgar Kemmann. Albany: State U of New York P, 2005. 81-104.

―――. *Coming to Terms with Perfection*. Book ms. in progress.

Jaspers, Karl. *Way to Wisdom: An Introduction to Philosophy.* Trans. Ralph Manheim. London, UK: Gollancz, 1951.

Jonsen, Albert R., and Stephen Toulmin. *The Abuse of Casuistry: A History of Moral Reasoning.* Berkeley: U of California P, 1990.

Kierkegaard, Søren. *Philosophical Fragments, Or, A Fragment of Philosophy by Johannes Climacus* [pseud.]. Trans. David F. Swenson. Princeton, NJ: Princeton UP, 1936.

Levinas, Emmanuel. *Totality and Infinity.* Trans. Alphonso Lingis. Pittsburgh, PA: Duquesne UP, 1969.

———. *Difficult Freedom: Essays on Judaism.* Trans. Sean Hand. Baltimore, MD: John sHopkins UP, 1990.

Nietzsche, Friedrich. *Complete Words: The First Complete and Authorized English Translation.* 10 vols. Ed. Oscar Levy. New York: Russell and Russell, 1964.

Pinker, Steven. *The Language Instinct: How the Mind Creates Language.* New York: HarperCollins, 1994.

Ricoeur, Paul. *Time and Narrative.* Trans. Kathleen McLaughlin and David Pellauer. Chicago, IL: U of Chicago P, 1984.

Struever, Nancy S. "*Alltäglichkeit*, Timefulness, in the Heideggerian Program." *Heidegger and Rhetoric.* Eds. Daniel M. Gross and Ansgar Kemmann. Albany: State U of New York P, 2005. 105-130.

A Conversation about Communication Ethics with Julia T. Wood

How did you become interested in studying communication ethics?

I think my interest in ethics really came about before I labeled it as that. Early in my career, in the 1980s, some issues of gender in communication, specifically power differences between women and men, were quite extraordinary. I think they have waned a bit in the years since but they were quite extraordinary in the early 1980s. I became interested in how communication really establishes power, and then more generally, got interested in how power is used to create categories for people in groups within a society and used to decide whose voices are heard and whose are not. My general interest in power has, in many ways, gone in some specific directions that people probably associate with my work. Power was perhaps the dominant issue that got my initial attention. The way that power leads to positions and understandings about how the world works that are indeed quite partial and sometimes quite perverse, because they aren't informed about the range of voices and the perspectives of those voices.

My work is probably more in the interpersonal domain. That's simply my background and training so I gravitated toward that initially. At the same time I would say that it's not absolutely restricted to that. For instance, I'm very interested in what happens with groups that are economically poor, often communities of color that are faced with toxic landfills and dumps and so forth in their communities. The sets of regulations about public hearings often exclude them because their voices are non-expert or scientific, and the hearings are often held at times when they can't attend. That kind of issue interests me, as do some of the things happening within social movements. I think interpersonal communication is a clear focus of mine, but it can't stay just there.

Do you prefer the term "communication ethic" or "communication ethics"?

I have a lot of reservation about the term "communication ethic" or, even worse, *the* communication ethic. To me that implies a single ethic for communication. If we recognize only one ethic, there is a very strong inclination toward some universal applications and judgments that are not really informed by a range of people in their practices. One way I can qualify that is to say I think I could be comfortable with perhaps a short list of quite abstract ethics of communication as long as each of those allowed for some variations as to how it is applied in a given case. Ethics can be situated in particular people and groups and situations and cultures and historic locations. Now for instance, maybe we could agree to an ethic that called on us to communicate respectfully with others, but what constitutes "respectful" communication would be quite different in low context and high context cultures. So a communication ethic would be very abstract, perhaps on a level of form, but the content of what respectful communication would be would vary.

I was just thinking of something Josina Makau and Ron Arnett said in the preface of their book *Communication Ethics in an Age of Diversity*. They noted that communication can't ever be understood in a vacuum because it's shaped by so many forces that are social, political, economic, and historic. That's really, in many ways, the basis of my reservation about a universalist ethic. I tend to think more about ethics of communication and ones that are rather flexible and applied as opposed to being formulaically thought through.

One of the other sorts of issues involved in this question of how we define and approach communication ethics is how we differentiate communication ethics from, say, philosophical views of ethics and philosophical scholarship. It seems to me that one of the real gifts of the communication field is a continuous and insistent emphasis on praxis as differentiated from abstract ethical rules. Perhaps because we are richly informed by rhetorical traditions, our questions circulate around, "How does this work in a given case? How do we apply it?" Philosophical ethics, at least as I studied them, are in many ways easier to deal with than applied ethics. Who would not agree with the idea of a "veil of ignorance"? Who would not agree with an ethic based on what's better for the majority of people? It's when you get down to the given case that the ease of philosophic abstraction sort of dissipates in front of you. It's not that simple and not that clear-cut. A given situation is fraught with all kinds of constraints that are particular to the situation that are not part of the abstract consideration of an appropriate ethic.

My approach to communication ethics is practical and I think there are some criteria that guide me. "Ethical" to me seems to be inclusive of a range of voices and experiences and perspectives. So that to me is always a key issue. Am I behaving ethically or do I judge this to be an unethical kind of a pronouncement or policy? Ethics is informed by multiple voices. So that's clearly part of it. I guess the key is to have equity and respect.

One of my former doctoral students is a man named Tim Muehlhoff. He and I have worked a great deal, not so much in writing as in conversation with each other, on this notion of trying to understand—not just meet the other, but to really understand—where the other is coming from. If you can find out what are the assumptions that inform, say, President Bush's policies, or the viewpoints of someone who sets up and manages a hate site on the web; if you can understand those, then you ask, "If I believed what that person did, then would I believe what else follows from this person?" I think that it's, to me, a very uncomfortable thing to say, "Ok, now. Let's see if I endorse this assumption that someone who engages in hate speech and hate acts does." To even temporarily put myself in that position is exquisitely uncomfortable. Yet, if I'm to really try to meet that other person, it means meeting them in that fullness, which is not, of course, the same as agreeing with them. I think we have to have some understanding that people's actions and communication practices do not emerge out of nowhere. They are always very rooted.

In a recent study, "Monsters and Victims" in the *Journal of Social and Personal Relationships*, I did follow-up on some work on my earlier research on intimate partner violence. In the earlier study, I interviewed women who had been victims of intimate partner violence to learn about their perspectives. That's pretty much the way the research has gone. You interview women victims and you castigate the terrible men that would do these things. I didn't see anything in the research that really looked at intimate partner violence from the perspective of perpetrators who are predominately men. I asked, "What is it that they believe? How do they do this? How do they see what they are doing?" The joke around my house is that I spent the summer in prison, and indeed that is what I did. I went to a prison to interview men who had harmed or sometimes killed wives or girlfriends. It was the most difficult research I've ever done, because I was really trying to understand how it could make sense to them and be right in their minds in some way. It was difficult, not only as a human being but as a steadfast feminist, to listen to these men. I think what really troubled me most was when I came to a point in the research where I did understand them. Where I could see that their violence toward women in their lives made sense from their perspective. I was enough in their perspective to understand it. That is just a shocking moment for a person whose most violent act is to kick a door when I'm really angry, but I could understand it.

One of the men I talked to had viciously beaten a woman and later murdered her. As we talked, I found out that when he was five years old on the playground with his older brother who was his hero, one of his other brothers had come by and shot the brother that was his hero. Now what would I think of violence if at five years old I'd seen one of my brothers against another brother? That perspective begins to make sense—it's the way that he dealt with things and, for him, it was natural as breathing air.

I behave in the ways that I was brought up to behave, in many respects. I was always taught violence isn't how we solve problems. We don't hit people; we don't do these things. But the man I interviewed was also behaving according to what he was taught. Now I don't think we stay in this "everything is relative" morass. I think intimate partner violence is absolutely unacceptable, and I can't say that his actions were right. But I can say that they are understandable given the experiences and narratives that framed his life. They make sense. That gives us some real ideas for interventions. Of course, the really effective interventions in a situation like that may not be for that man. We are talking about very early childhood, very massive kinds of work. It means that society has to sign on to it.

What are your thoughts about communication ethics and the historical shift to postmodernity?

I think the postmodernist viewpoint that has emerged rejects decisively the idea of coherent autonomous identities and the idea of grand narratives for societies. In place of those modern forms, postmodernism offers us a view of multiple fluid sorts of selves and societies and spheres that are contingent, always arguable, as are actions within them. Now I think that is really helpful in breaking us away from some of the modernist universals, which of course were false universals because they were definitely from a quite particular standpoint. I think postmodernism has been helpful in breaking us away from that.

Yet at its extremes, particularly in its earlier parts, maybe a decade or 15 years ago, as postmodernism was emerging, it invited an epistemology of really radical and unstable subjectivity, which allows no basis for making judgments that some practices are better than others. Now I think that's been tempered a good deal and I think that's very good news indeed. I appreciate the de-centering inclinations of postmodernism very much. I think they were important. I think they are benefiting from some tempering these days. I'm not convinced that individuals in cultures are so completely fragmented.

I'm dubious of the idea that we cannot create some sort of grand narratives that can be more inclusive than those of the past. In other words, the critique of grand narratives may be to a large extent the particular grand narratives that gained sway and not necessarily of the idea that we could have some quite broad narratives. Then, with that, I share the viewpoints of people such as you and Josina Makau and Ron Arnett that ethical communication these days has got to heed the postmodernist challenges to purely abstract universalism which ignores or devalues the local. There's got to be some kind of coming together. The temptation to reject any and all collective identities in favor of specific group identifications fosters even more social fragmentation than we have today. I don't think that we can go there. That's one reason for the cultural wars today that are breaking out all over. While many folks tend to see what separates them from others, more than noticing what connects them to others; it's always both. Yes, we are different. Yes, we are similar. I think that there are some things from modernity that we need not throw out in terms of some broad collective notions and narratives and beliefs. We need to somehow reconcile those with the idea that there are also very localized beliefs and variations on whatever our broad narratives are, but it's not either-or.

Universals were never 'universal'—they were simply a particular perspective or vision.

Or visions of members of a privileged group, let's say—mistaking the viewpoint that is cultivated by membership in that group and that serves the interests of that group as everybody's viewpoint. It's what I think Donna Haraway refers to as "the god trick," little "g" god. The god trick is saying, "I'm the voice and the perspective from everywhere and nowhere in particular," but of course, it is from a particular place. When you think about how the laws were made in this nation, they were from the perspective of white, able-bodied, more or less Christian—at least in theory if not always in practice—property-owning males. That's not the viewpoint of everyone. One of the great exposés of that, if you will in a particular form, is Howard Zinn's *People's History of the United States.* You read that book and you say, "Oh!" The history someone of my generation learned in grade school and college was from a particular viewpoint, and guess what—there were some other viewpoints there that wouldn't have called it the same way. That's what I mean. Whenever you have dominant groups that can make their views seem to be the normal, the right, the natural ones.

I think I knew that in some way, but I couldn't quite label it. Therefore, of course, I couldn't conceive it and think about it in any serious way until I began reading and working with standpoint theory, which is really what I credit with giving me that insight and helping me extend it. Standpoint theory addresses how our perspectives are shaped by the social, symbolic, and material conditions of our life and not our lives as individuals. For instance in our case, being white women, or white heterosexual women, or white heterosexual middle class women, shapes how we understand the world. Now I see that is not truth in the sense that it's not the only way to understand the world. Then, of course, standpoint has led me to see more and more particular views have been privileged as right.

One of the more interesting angles within this is Shirley and Edwin Ardener's muted group theory of speech. Anthropologists were initially trying to understand cultures and they were talking to only the men in the cultures, because they basically thought the men were more interesting. When they finally began talking to women, they discovered a whole other realm of what the cultural life is about, through the practices and everyday activities of the women. Women understood and participated in the culture in ways that were not only not understood by men but also not in any way encoded in the language that the men created.

Given that a "universal" is politically based, would a universalist communication ethic be impossible?

Not "impossible;" that's not the right word. Going back to the beginning of our conversation, I'm not sure you could have a universalist ethic like, what counts as "respect."

Given existing power relations, it's almost inevitable that some cultures and groups will dominate while shaping the discourse, while others are going to be marginalized. Back in the early 1990s when I was inquiring into "care" and how care is defined in a culture, it became very clear that men, and, more accurately, masculine perspectives, defined care and caregivers in Western culture. This has extraordinary implications, both benefits and burdens, for women who were defined as caregivers. It still does, for that matter.

So, communication ethics depends on how one defines the parameters of ethics within the relationship as it's negotiated between people who are situated in and understand the world differently?

That's right. In a relationship—for example a romantic relationship, a professional relationship, collegial relationship, or people who write together—there's supposed to be some significant understanding of each other's perspectives and an honoring of that. The minute one says "It's my book and I'll tell you what to do with it," or "It's my marriage and I'll tell you the rules of it," the minute it's that way, you have something less than an ethical relationship. To violate ethical principles of inclusion and equity is to do violence to the relationship, and to both parties. It's obvious that you do violence to the party who's being silenced or in other ways oppressed. I think we also do it to ourselves when we oppress.

In your research with men in prison, did any of them recognize that they had done violence to themselves by oppressing their partners?

Some of them did. I wound up titling the piece "Monsters and Victims: Male Felons' Accounts of Intimate Partner Violence"—which is not an aside; it's really directly relevant to your question. I entered the study knowing these men were absolute monsters. They weren't worthy of human attention or consideration. Part of the learning experience of the research for me was that I could understand that they were also equally victims of their own violence and what it did to them. Some of them lost women who were deeply important to them. Another thing I didn't believe before the study was that men actually deeply loved some of the women they hurt and killed. Before the study I would have said you can't deliberately hurt somebody you love. I was persuaded differently, because many of the men had also been victims of being on the lowest rung of a society with no way out. They were being told "here are the ideals of manhood" and yet they had no way to meet those ideals. It was not so nice and clear-cut. You can't say they're either monsters or victims. They are both.

Some of them did know they had hurt themselves. Mainly, they didn't know of options. What's another way to be in the world? A lot of the men came from a standpoint that didn't necessarily assume one did or should respect others. The idea was that you beat them up before they beat you up. So, we're back to one of my frames for looking at the world. The values you and I would talk about for "respect" aren't necessarily present in some people's viewpoints.

What is the role of an educator for instilling communicative ethics?

I think one of the fundamental responsibilities all educators have, particularly people in communication, is teaching our students to participate effectively and ethically in a world that is characterized by diversity. One of the key terms in our field is "perspective," but so far it's been applied largely to inappropriate situations. "Perspective" is broader than that and includes perspective-taking, teaching people to deeply take perspectives. I'm not just talking about role-taking, but I mean to really ask questions like "What would it be like to see one of my brothers shoot my other brother when I was five years old?" Really try to move into that. Read the whole narrative from the man who gave me the story, and read his entire interview, and sit in his place, his mind, his world for a while.

I think that a lot of efforts to teach about diversity and different viewpoints and all have been in many ways somewhat shallow and have tended to be satisfied with group generalizations. We'll say this about "black speech," and this about "women's speech." I think we need those generalizations, but you also need to understand that within any group perspective, there are also variations, and then we can begin to understand. Some men have seen one brother shoot another and not become violent. Now what's the difference? It becomes very complex. I don't think we can necessarily get there in all cases. I think it is worthwhile to try to hold ourselves to that as an ideal ethic and ask our students to do the same.

One of the most influential essays I've ever read was Linda Alcoff's "The Problem of Speaking for Others." In that essay she asks, "When do we have a right to speak for others? When don't we?" It's such a smart essay because she didn't lay it out as "here's the five rules," or the guidelines or one principle. What she ended up developing was a set of interrogatories that a person should ask himself/herself before choosing to speak for others. Asking them, working through them, may help you decide that you shouldn't or you should, or you could, or you must. In different cases, you might come to different decisions. It's like rhetoric. There are no absolutes, but there are interrogatories. There are ways of deliberating about appropriate courses of action. Educators can recommend a process that may be productive, but you can't always guarantee a result from a student. There are some processes that are likely to lead to ethical communication. A process somehow requires us to look at perspectives other than our own. It's more likely to lead to decisions that yield good practices, rather than a process that doesn't require us to do that. The process helps us understand more who we are, who others are, what the situation is. It is much, much messier than having the abstract, "the greatest good for the greatest number." I think, from my viewpoint, it's better. I think it is richer.

Clearly, I'll be able to understand some perspectives more than others. I'll never be able to understand the black or gay perspective as fully as I do a white or heterosexual perspective, but I can do more than say, "I'm not black, I'm not gay. So I don't understand it at all." That's a cop-out, too. If I can understand to some degree those different perspectives, then not only are people likely to think in ways that are more informed by multiple perspectives, and I think this is so fundamentally important, I'm also consistently disproving that the way I see the world as the way the world is. I'm always asking, "How could this person be seeing the world? How exactly do I deal with that assumption?" Where would I be if I could no longer hold onto the illusion that my viewpoint is *the* viewpoint?

Technology is training us to be so much more passive. When we talk about the interactive games and activities, and so forth. They're within a structure that's set for us. We don't have to go outside. We're within a set structure, which is in itself passivity. Then we can't get out of the structure because we've given up the right to question or to imagine an alternative.

For his thesis project, Tim Muehlhoff conducted a study with a group of born-again Christians and gays and lesbians who are in a cultural war with each other, inviting them to imagine an alternative. He led them to create their own narrative and explain the things that they considered as basic in that narrative. In really trying to understand that, and keep walking in those words, they had a couple of breakthroughs that go beyond empathy and paraphrasing. They talked about understanding what it means to live in a world. He's actually teaching his students ways to walk in the words of another, and in a way, enter a perspective in a way that you can't really enter without knowing another's language. Knowing the perspective of the other is necessary to interacting with them ethically. All the skills in the world won't help us if we don't have that richer understanding within perspectives.

In addressing themes in your scholarship, you've mentioned several writers. Are there others who have influenced your work in communication ethics?

My thinking has been shaped by a number of writers who use critical lenses to examine families—who counts as a family, who takes responsibility for family life and well-being. An early influence was Susan Moller Okin's book, *Justice, Gender, and the Family*, which critiqued normative beliefs and practices that assume women have primary or exclusive responsibility for home and family. One of Okin's arguments with which I particularly resonate is that the family not only operates in more or less ethical ways, but also that it teaches ethical frameworks to its youngest members, children. In other words—ethical principles are *learned* and one of the key sites for learning them is the family. Okin makes the point that if children see parents operating in inequitable ways—for example, mothers doing most or all of the work required to keep home and family functioning—then children are likely to regard gender inequity as acceptable, as ethical. Nel Noddings makes a similar argument about the importance of teaching all children to care and to take responsibility for the caregiving that is required for families and society to work.

A more recent book, *Left Legalism/Left Critique*, edited by Wendy Brown and Janet Halley, includes a number of very powerful analyses of laws and social policies that confer various privileges and rights on socially approved familial forms—marriage, to be precise—and withhold those privileges and rights from other familial units such as gay and lesbian families. In my judgment, there are keen ethical questions to be asked about cultural structures and practices that restrict to only certain people those things that are required for any of us to live a good life—basic health care, the right to insure loved ones, equity among family members in responsibilities for family well-being, and so forth.

Because I am very interested in how people's lives are regulated, I'm naturally drawn to Michel Foucault's work. He offers incisive analyses of a multitude of ways in which families and the lives they can live are regulated. What particularly intrigues me about Foucault's analyses of power is that he attends to two types, or levels, of power that regulate human rights, actions, and so forth. He gives good consideration to centralized forms of power such as laws that institutionalize rights and prerogatives. Yet Foucault doesn't stop there. He also attends to decentralized forms of power such as social norms and expectations. He brings a keen eye to the ways in which these decentralized forms of power shape—discipline, to use one of Foucault's favored terms—everyday life, including our understandings of who counts as a family and what rights and privileges should be conferred on various associations such as gay partnerships, single parents, and so forth. In highlighting the importance of disbursed, decentralized forms of power, Foucault provides an opening for thinking about some of the non-dramatic ethical choices—routine, everyday ones—that we make in our roles as agents in the social world.

I might tell students—it might sound like I'm saying this because you co-authored this book but I'm quite serious—to start with *Dialogic Civility*. It's eloquent and extended. Be with others in a common sense world and respect them—even, and perhaps particularly, when their perspective differs from our own. That book starts with the idea of perspective taking and engages in it across contexts—everything from policy and social movements to interpersonal relations to organizational communication. Framing something—a situation, event, choice, or other phenomenon—in one particular way and rigidly viewing it only in that way inhibits students from taking the perspective of another. That's the bottom line whether we're teaching public speaking, group communication, or interpersonal relationships. Whatever we're teaching, perspective taking has got to be a part of it.

What is the biggest challenge for communication ethics in a time of postmodernity?

Postmodernity recognizes the multiplicity of both selves and the social world. It proclaims that there is no unwavering center and certainly no unassailable "True Perspective." Given this, it is more important than ever that we all learn to take multiple perspectives—to see from a range of viewpoints. It's what María Lugones, in a delightful word choice, calls "world traveling"—learning to cross from one way of seeing the world to a different one, and then another different one, and another. Doing this enlarges our own understandings by making them multiple, complex, and usefully unsettled.

Another danger of postmodern conceptions of self and the social world is nihilism, the denial of any absolute basis of meaning. If identities, values, ethical principles are all radically subjective, there can be no clear or stable basis for judgment that some beliefs, codes of ethics, practices, and so forth are better than others. One hope for resisting such radical relativism is to turn to rhetorical theory, which offers rich advisories about making practical judgments in an inherently contingent world. Rhetorical theories don't rely—at least not primarily—on absolute and *a priori* principles or criteria for making judgments. Instead, they encourage us to consider the specific circumstances, people, and options available in the given case and to work to make sound judgments about attitudes and actions—not absolute judgments, not judgments that are beyond question or argument, and not the only possible judgments, but sound ones that are cognizant of the particularities of the given case. This way of acting in the world doesn't give us the comfort of believing we've found the unalterably, undeniably "correct" judgment. Yet, if there is no capital-T truth, then such comfort would be false because it would be based on a misunderstanding of ourselves and the world in which we live. It is no small challenge to learn how to live and act in a world and with selves that are more shifting than those we previously believed in.

Works Cited

Alcoff, Linda. "The Problem of Speaking for Others." *Cultural Critique* (Winter 1991-92): 5-32.

Ardener, Edwin. "Belief and the Problem of Women: The Problem Revisited." *Perceiving Women*. Ed. Shirley Ardener. London: Malby P, 1975. 1-27.

Ardener, Shirley. *Defining Females: The Nature of Women in Society*. New York: Wiley, 1978.

Arnett, Ronald C., and Pat Arneson. *Dialogic Civility in a Cynical Age: Communication, Hope, and Interpersonal Relationships*. Albany: State U of New York P, 1999.

Brown, Wendy, and Janet E. Halley, eds. *Left Legalism/Left Critique*. Durham, NC: Duke UP, 2002.

Foucault, Michel. *Power/Knowledge: Selected Interviews and Other Writings: 1972-1977*. Ed. Colin Gordon. Brighton, UK: Harvester, 1980.

———. "The Subject and Power." *Michel Foucault: Beyond Structuralism and Hermeneutics*. Eds. Hubert Drefus and Paul Rabinow. Chicago: U of Chicago P, 1993.

Haraway, Donna. *Simians, Cyborgs, and Women: The Reinvention of Nature*. New York: Routledge, 1991.

Lugones, María. "Playfulness, 'World'-Travelling, and Loving Perception." *Making Face, Making Soul/Haciendo Caras: Creative and Critical Perspectives by Feminists of Color*. Ed. Gloria Anzaldúa. San Francisco: Aunt Lute, 1990. 390-402.

Makau, Josina M., and Ronald C. Arnett, eds. *Communication Ethics in an Age of Diversity.* Urbana: U of Illinois P, 1997.

Muehlhoff, Tim. "Walking in the Words of Another." MA thesis. The University of North Carolina at Chapel Hill, 1997.

Noddings, Nel. *Caring: A Feminine Approach to Ethics and Moral Education.* Berkeley: U of California P, 1984.

———. *Starting at Home: Caring and Social Policy.* Berkeley: U of California P, 2002.

Okin, Susan M. *Justice, Gender and the Family.* New York: Basic, 1989.

Wood, Julia. "Monsters and Victims: Male Felons' Accounts of Intimate Partner Violence." *Journal of Social and Personal Relationships* 21 (2004): 555-576.

———. "That Wasn't the Real Him": Women's Dissociation of Violence from the Men Who Enact It. *Communication Quarterly* 47 (1999): 1-7.

———. *Who Cares?: Women, Care, and Culture.* Carbondale: Southern Illinois UP, 1994.

Zinn, Howard. *A People's History of the United States: 1492-Present.* New York: Harper Perennial Modern Classics, 2005.

A Conversation about Communication Ethics with Kenneth E. Andersen

How did you become interested in studying communication ethics?

It really grew out of my doctoral dissertation. I had done a historical study for my master's thesis. When I went to University of Wisconsin for doctoral work, Fred Haberman looked at me and asked, "What are you going to do for a dissertation?" I said, "Well, I've done a historical study. I guess I'd like to do something empirical, experimental." He said, "Fine. On what subject?" I said, "Well, I've always been kind of intrigued by the area of *ethos*." This was in my first interview, mind you. He said, "Good. That's something you ought to pursue," and that sort of set the train in motion.

I was classically oriented, so I began going back to Aristotle and all the original sources. Aristotle talks about ethical proof as something you create on the occasion. One of the difficulties of being an empiricist is you have to be able to operationally define terms. So I was casting about for definitions of *ethos*. I talked to a lot of the scholars and one of them particularly struck me. Wilbur Samuel Howell said, almost in Supreme Court language, "I don't know what it is, but I know it when I see it."

I said, "That doesn't quite cut it." When I was looking at a lot of the research that had been done on *ethos*, I found that people would sometimes talk about prior reputation of a communicator. Sometimes they would talk about the content of the speech. They would say if you had these things, these things, and these things—that creates ethical proof. The problem, of course, is ethical proof for whom? I became very focused in my research on the notion that *ethos* had to be defined in terms of the perceptions of the receiver. If we're going to talk about ethical proof or what is seen as good moral character—if we're going to use the Aristotelian approach—we have to talk about moral character in terms of the perceptions of the audience, if you will. I became very listener centered or receiver centered. That was kind of a genesis of a lot of my thinking about communication ethics.

The real breakthrough for me came when I was asked to write *Persuasion: Theory and Practice* for Allyn & Bacon Publishers. At that point, I had to say, "Well, I need to have a chapter on ethics, that's an obvious perspective." That forced me to think through a lot of things, including the effort to ground persuasion in what I call an ethical context: namely, that ethics exists to serve the community, to serve the polis. Ethics does not exist just to serve the source or the immediate receiver, but in a larger sense serves the whole polity. Then one begins to say rhetoric has an ethical function, because rhetoric has to be ethical if it's going to serve the interest of the collective. So that is sort of how it all began to fit together for me.

How do you define communication ethics?

In my view, we've got to start out with an assumption, I guess, that ethics is a dimension in all the communication process. It is a dimension that is relevant to all the actors in the communication process—the source or the originator, the person that initiates communication; the person who receives, interprets, hears, reads communication; and people, who in effect are further agents of transmission—the Tom Brokaws of the world, or the friend that you say, "Don't tell that guy, but I really am interested in him," with exactly the intent of saying, "You go tell him as fast as you can!"

So, one begins to say that in all the activity of communication, in whatever role we may happen to be in at the moment, there is an ethical dimension. This doesn't mean we're conscious of it. In fact, I'm very much of the view that so much of our communication is habitual that we often don't call to mind the ethical dimension. I'm a believer in habit. I'm a believer in Aristotle's notion that virtues are matters of practice that become habitual and recurring. You begin to talk about an ethical dimension where people are behaving in a particular pattern, which is more or less ethical in that situation. I think of communication ethics as being a study of the various dimensions of the good. I use "the good" not in a practical utilitarian sense but in a value oriented sense—much as Aristotle would—of the good in communication activity.

To tease out the ethical ramifications has been one of my projects. For example, when I was doing the lecture circuit as the NCA President Elect, I talked about the responsibility of third parties in the ethical pattern. I'll back up. When I did my first persuasion book I articulated what I called the 200% Theory of Responsibility. I said that the source has an obligation to assume the fullest measure of responsibility that one is capable of fulfilling. That responsibility falls upon the source at a 100% level. Simultaneously for the receiver, you don't want to give over to someone else the responsibility or the right to make your decisions. So you have a 100% responsibility to listen, to be critical, to evaluate, to reject, to demand more information, to reject, whatever the case may be.

I started out saying responsibility involved the active parties, the whole audience. Then it occurred to me there is really another dimension to that.

There is a larger society, a larger arena in which we can talk about third persons. I mentioned Tom Brokaw who narrated the news. I am reminded of David Brinkley's eyebrows and the concern by some of the President's people that Brinkley was making sarcastic remarks about them and he would flick his eyebrow at certain statements when he was reading them. There are all kinds of third party roles. You overhear somebody on the subway. You see your neighbors abusing a child. You have intermediary roles that you're serving. There are a lot of third party roles that we assume in the society. There is a responsibility that includes those individuals too. Now those responsibilities in every case will be unique to the situation, unique to one's ability to fulfill the role of intermediary.

There are all kinds of things one can talk about here as to the limits of how you determine one's responsibility. À la Aristotle, the amount of responsibility that falls on each individual is an individual thing. It's determined by the capacities of the individual, the specific situation, a whole set of exigencies and circumstances. To really assess the amount of responsibility any communicator, listener, receiver, and third party has, one has to take into account the wholeness of the situation in trying to make a judgment of what that responsibility may be.

Each person makes his or her own communicative choice to be ethical.

Yes. You have to take account of the capacities of the individual in the particular case. I'm a great believer in Aristotle's doctrine of choices. You don't ask a five-year-old to accept the same level of responsibility you expect a 15-year-old to accept. You don't expect someone of diminished mental capacity, or you don't expect someone who has not the access to certain pieces of information, to behave in the same way as somebody that has fuller access. On the other hand you can hold people responsible for refusing to get access to the information that would have made a difference. So it's a very complicated equation to work out. The goal, I think, is to sensitize people to the ethical dimension and to develop habit patterns that will move you along in the direction of consistently making more optimal ethical choices.

Do you understand communication ethics as distinct from rhetorical ethics?

You're talking about continua here. It's like the fallacy of the beard, how many hairs does it take to be a beard? One hair doesn't constitute a beard—

1,000 hairs don't do it. Well, you're going to end up saying that a million hairs won't do it because at some point you're going to have to identify a specific number and the fallacy trips over. I think that obviously we deal in different communicative situations. When you think about something as a rhetorical situation, speaker to audience, then you conceive of the situation differently than when you're talking to your spouse or to your children, or in a small group of people.

It doesn't seem to me that the issue of the communication activity and judgment of what is ethical and unethical in communication necessarily change depending on the size of the situation, of the audience. There are factors that come into play. It's a different situation if the same speech that someone is making to a large audience is transmitted by radio. It's a different situation if it's printed in the newspaper, such as *The New York Times*, even if they do include *ad hoc* interjections. There are differences, but the notion that one does not therefore have to talk about the ethical continua here is important. I'm looking for an ethic that is, in effect, grounded in the nature of the communication process. The ethical values should be those that serve the ultimate goal of that communication process for all involved—including the existing society and the one yet to be. Now, I'll tell you frankly that gets you into real difficulty if you were to say, "Well, my goal is to steal people's gold eyeteeth!"

One of the things I included in my persuasion book that I've always been very proud of, and nobody else has really paid any attention to, was a chapter on a totalitarian ethic. "What would a persuasion theory look like if I were writing it from a totalitarian society perspective, where I could control the ability to reward or punish at will?" One could talk about Saddam Hussein, where one has the ability to manipulate all the rewards because he holds all the power. This gives you a very different persuasion theory and "ethical" theory than one presumes in a democratic society.

Implicitly, I think one has to say, "The ethics I'm talking about are necessarily grounded in a particular concept of democratic interaction, of freedom of choice, of respect for the individual as someone of moral worth, of several other constituents of the rhetorical dynamic. I'm not talking about those other settings unless I specifically identify differences." Now, that may give us a problem when we begin talking about such things as universal ethical constraints et cetera, but we'll talk about that later.

What is the relationship between an individual's ethical choice and institutional enactments of ethical choice?

I think responsibility ultimately devolves on individuals. Although I've made the argument elsewhere, and it's one I hold to, society is also responsible for the kind of ethical norms it creates. It seems to me that whenever we begin to communicate one with another and when we communicate within society, we're tacitly negotiating the ethical constraints. We're agreeing how far we can go with x, y, and z. It still comes down to the individual who has to assume that degree of responsibility which is proper for him or her. At the same time one has the right to presume that other people are going to assume the responsibility they have and ask/insist that they do so.

One of the things that I would sometimes get on my students about, when I had students, was about their refusal to critique one another: "I'm not going to 'dis' somebody else." To which my comment was, "You don't respect them enough to challenge their idea? You don't respect them enough to say you're worthy of my disagreeing or my saying, 'Have you thought about this, that, and the other?'"

One of the views I have is that whenever one sticks one's head up to become a rhetorician, to raise your hand, you make yourself vulnerable. Not just in the sense that people may reject your ideas, but that the exchange in communication may cause you to reject your own ideas. You may passionately advocate today what you tomorrow may say is wrong. You're caught in a kind of conundrum: "I've got to advocate and tell you what I believe, but I do that in a provisional sense and maybe I'll discover that this isn't right."

Please talk more about "my perception of your unethical behavior." How do we negotiate differences without just saying, "You think differently, I think differently; c'est la vie"?

Well, it depends. I think there are times when it's all right to say, "*C'est la vie.*" My wife will sometimes say, "Do you like this pin or do you like this scarf?" It doesn't really matter to me one way or the other. It's fine with me. But on serious matters it's clear that we do need to be able to talk to one another and try to work out some kind of basis on which we can operate. If we're going to try to build a peace treaty, if we're going to try to build a relationship, if we're going to work out how we're going to relate to one another in future, we have to establish a communication process that enables us to define how we will approach those kinds of things.

Often people can start with very different premises, different foundations, different groundwork. Ultimately it'll come down to some kind of *modus operandi* where there is agreement between parties about a preferred process. Some people may develop an ethic that is heavily grounded in religious tradition; other people may come from a humanist background. It might well be that they find certain things on which they will agree as a pattern of behavior. This is a basis on which we can work and relate. I think so often we assume that our values are shared when upon exploration we discover they are not. Sometimes we don't understand the implications of the differences in grounding that we have.

I don't think democracy ever said, "Everything goes!" You and I might well disagree about whether pornography is this or that. I will have to tell you candidly that I was thrilled that *Avenue Q* won the Tony Award, because I think it is one of the most stimulating and provocative and useful musicals that we've seen in a long time. On the other hand it opens with the song "My Life Sucks." It goes on from there using an awful lot of four letter words that I'm not always comfortable saying, and it's not at all a vulgar show. It's a wonderfully revealing show of what it is like to be a brand new English major trying to make your way in the cruel, cruel world among other things.

I think that certain of the concepts that we have that are requirements of a democracy are in long term the protection against the excesses of democracy. You can make arguments. You have a right to express your free will. You have a right to take up competing positions. Those are important correctives it seems to me. On the other hand, I think there are issues where the state, if you will, treads at its peril. John Cribbet, a law professor and former Chancellor at Illinois said, "Societies are sometimes better known by the laws they do not need to pass, than the laws they do pass." I think we often make a mistake of trying to legislate morality with rules that do not take account of all the situational realities. While I'm a kind of rule-person, I like to think about what's the utilitarian value, if you will, of having this rule? Maybe a better expression would be, let's have a robust generalization that will help guide my behavior. I certainly believe in that concept. I also know that in any particular case I may have five or six values I'm trying to achieve. I've got to decide which is more important in this situation, which is most harmful, most violent. There are a whole lot of things that go into working out a response.

I think that you are going to see a return in our society to the question of whether or not we can do some of the stem cell research stuff. I think that

Reagan's death, Nancy Reagan's plea, et cetera, is going to open up that arena. I think you're going to see important public policy debate on that. I think you're going to see some attitude change in the American public. There will be people who will be convinced that's not the right move. There will be other people who will be convinced that it's a long overdue move. So we'll work that one out. It is also to say that you can disagree without being disagreeable. You can disagree for your own personal value. On one hand you are entitled to your own personal value structure, but you are not entitled to impose that on another person, in particular kinds of cases.

What are your thoughts about a universal communication ethic?

That's a very troubling question for me. I doubt that it is possible. If you look at family units, or if you look in certain structures, you can see communality. The problem is that the ethical bases don't extend beyond that unit. One can think about a tribe or a clan having certain principles in which they are committed to each other, and they respect each other as beings of moral worth, people who are worthy of protection and support. On the other hand they may define an awful lot of people as outside of that, not worthy of respect, not human. At some level you can find commonalities; but the difficulty comes up when you begin saying, "How far will you extend these views? How far will you go out beyond family, or clan, or tribe, or race, or religious entity, or whatever?"

I think there are universals to which we would aspire. If you think about The Declaration of Independence, I think there are some universals there. If you think about The Declaration of Human Rights, it seems to me that those aspirations are valuable and we could, in a sense, see them as models. Now, granted there are some people who would reject those as being inappropriate and not reasonable.

I'm an optimist about the notion that on the whole we as people are making progress toward a better global situation. One can think about Aristotle and the whole notion of slavery, and the irrelevance of women to anything that matters. Then consider the fact that in even in Africa, female circumcision is slowing down. People are beginning to speak against it. You're seeing in Iran and Iraq some groups are talking for a more democratic, a more flexible kind of regime. One could look at the tensions within the Catholic Church. My wife was a member of a denomination that did not ordain women. She changed denominations and became ordained. I think there are things that are habits and customs that we can see and evolve beyond.

The whole idea of aspiration is exceedingly crucial. We need to set a goal that is not so far above where we are that it's just ridiculous to even conceive of it. On the other hand we need to set a goal that's better than where we are at the moment. You and I can disagree about what those goals are, but if we talk about the notion of spiraling upward, as we begin to move up toward achievement, then we'll see a higher level. You begin to spiral upward, or you could do the reverse and spiral downward into a bad situation. I think again that's the modification of Aristotle's doctrine of choices. You make a good choice that makes possible a new range of good choices, which makes possible another new range of good choices, et cetera.

We're in an information age. The amount of information that we have available to us doubles every six months or less. Some individuals may have more or less information that is actually accessible to them. But if you think about the spread of communication across the world through the media—radio, television, movies—and granted a lot of people don't have access, it seems to me that we're creating an environment in which it's more and more possible for these general universals to begin to develop. If you show a vision of a better life to people, they want the better life. Some people may want something that is a vision of a better life that I personally don't think is a better life. I do think there is a possibility of progress in this sense. It seems to me that the notion of respect for other human beings, of the conception that human life is valued, that you're going to accord people certain rights and responsibilities, is a vision that is going to increasingly spread across the world.

What would be some of the elements that would either inhibit or enhance the possibility of respect for other human beings?

Well, I think the ability to communicate across boundaries is absolutely amazing. You think about the development of a world economy that's going to bind us together. It used to be what happened in China didn't matter to people outside that country. That's certainly not true any longer. People who are losing jobs in this country are beginning to worry about what's happening in India. They're beginning to worry about poverty and pay scales, about diseases spread with modern air transportation. There's no protection anymore, there's no insulation; Formosan termites are loose in New Orleans. We're in a different world than we were before.

Our world is one in which we have to deal with the world *qua* world. I think it's going to take us a while in public policy to make that shift. We really have to adopt a very different view about how the world is going to function. If you look at the history of the state, you go from the cities and states to nations, to confederations, to the European Common Market. I'm not saying we're necessarily going to have a world government, but we're moving in a direction that to some degree means we have to have worked out relationships with a whole lot of people. While trade and contact and other things perhaps precede this in some sense, they are also dependent on ethical relationships.

I'm very worried about the degree to which knowledge has become so specialized and so compartmentalized. I worry that we're not preparing our students with, what I would call, a really core liberal arts education: to communicate, to reason, to think. In one sense higher education was always about getting a job, about preparing you for a career of some sort—but it was preparing you for a lifetime in which you would "flourish" in your existence. It seems to me we've tipped the scales too much to getting a job and away from the notion of laying the groundwork for a constantly enriching life. It's the life of the mind, the aesthetic dimensions, and the arts—the richness of an integrated human being. I think we've fallen short in a lot of our higher education. That's something we really need to go back to or more forward to for all of society—not just some of it. We need to stress the core liberal arts that are basic to everything we do. Then you lay a job, a business orientation, a major, and other things on top of that and they feed back and forth to each other. I think that's something we've got work on. From my point of view, the exposure and the development of extensive discussion of communication ethics is an essential component of higher education. You can go through an awful lot of classes and programs and there will never once be a reference to an ethical dimension. That's scary.

I think we have lost sight of some very crucial values. Anytime you say there is this single goal, this object, that determinant, I get very worried. We need to live in a much more multi-dimensional world in which we see an array of different goals, different intensities, different priorities. We have to think about the degree to which any action doesn't subvert one set of values or one particular value at the same time it enables you to move forward toward what you want.

You said that ethical values serve the ends of communication. Would you talk more about that?

I think I would see those as reciprocal processes. If you think about the ongoing pattern of things, the one becomes the other in my view. You are trying to get some short-term goal that you have at a particular moment. But simultaneously you're also trying to serve other long-term goals, perhaps not fully consciously. In persuasion class, I used to talk about the salesman that succeeds in selling some poor product, but then has to go back and try to sell it the second time around. You got the first sale and you blew all the other sales. When you think about your reputation, you develop that reputation over a long period of time. We are always engaged in the multiplicity of goals we're trying to serve. We're defining ourselves, and at the same time we're being ourselves we're defining our self. Our communication on one hand is designed to influence other, but at the same it necessarily influences ourselves.

Rhetoric serves many purposes from the individual's point of view, but it also serves many purposes from the receiver's point of view. You want information, you want advice; you want exchange of material. I like to know if there's a new car out; I like to know what the price of gasoline is this week at the local gas station; there are zillions of things I want from the communication process. "What does the society want? Does society want some standard, if you will, on the basis for how we conduct discourse with one another?" It wants to provide a mechanism by which people can make coordinated decisions.

I think back to the Carroll C. Arnold speech I did last fall to reinvigorate the whole notion of the civic culture. We want a dynamic civic culture in which people are involved in making cooperative decisions in which they'll live with the results even when their view does not prevail. When you hear a lot of the attacks on those terrible justices that are making all these decisions; that really is a signal, I think, to say that the democratic process didn't have the chance to play out in full. Take the gay marriage issue. I would hope, as an example, that we don't have any kind of preemptive decision one way or the other coming down from above; either the national Supreme Court or from the Federal Constitutional Amendment. Let's see how that dynamic plays out. You know it was not many years ago that if I had married a black woman, we were not married in a lot of states in this union—even though I had been legitimately been married in my own state. We have made some progress. Other people will say it is not enough. And it isn't. But, I remember the shock when I went to Dallas, Texas and saw the blue sign for colored water fountains in 1956. I was just stunned. I grew up in Iowa. I didn't know.

We need to talk about the functions that communication processes serve for all the individuals engaged in the communication activity and for the larger polis as a whole. Then one can begin to say there are certain ethical imperatives that one can discern, discuss, and agree need to be the norm.

In addressing themes in your scholarship, you've mentioned several writers. Are there others who have influenced your work in communication ethics?

I need to qualify my answer by saying that my "teachers"—including students and colleagues—were for me more important than books. In part that is because they introduced me to the books; they commissioned papers; they asked me to comment on dissertation chapters; they disputed my interpretations.

Lil Wagner, my undergraduate debate coach, was my professor in at least five courses. She taught the seminar on classical rhetoric, argumentation, advanced public speaking. And we talked about ethical issues a lot for several years.

How can I leave out the impact of Ted Clevenger, of my wife Mary with her coauthoring of the *ethos* chapters in the persuasion book, her dissertation on basic textbooks' treatment of ethics, of Charles Follette's dissertation on Richard Weaver, et cetera, et cetera?

Perhaps the most important book for me is one that never saw print. B. J. Diggs, Philosophy professor at Illinois, directed work I did in two separate semesters of a program of "Study in a Second Discipline" at Illinois. I participated in many courses through that program and several seminars with Diggs. In one we reviewed a manuscript on ordinary morality he was writing, rewriting, and rewriting. It was never published. But it opened a whole world to me. And Diggs was very much one to bind ethics to the larger society in government and in law.

Key authors obviously include Aristotle—*On Rhetoric*—first in the Lane Cooper version and then in much more valid and extensive translations. *The Politics. The Poetics.* But most of all, *Nichomachean Ethics* coming well after its grounding the *On Rhetoric*. Second, John Rawls—a source that has largely been ignored by our field. I find that incomprehensible. He was one of the giants of philosophy of the 20th century. We know him not. *A Theory of Justice* has profound ethical implications for communication although they need to be derived from his work—they are not bullet-pointed for us. Third, Sissela Bok's *Lying: Moral Choice in Public and Private Life*. I used this in my ethics class and loved it. A rich resource, as is *Secrets*. Fourth, Frank Haiman's *Speech and Law in a Free Society*. Haiman understood there is an ethical dimension relevant to communication activity and links this to free speech concerns. I could add lots of sources from our own field: Dick Johannesen, Ron Arnett, Tom Nilsen, Jim Jaksa and Mike Pritchard, and on and on. We have so many colleagues to value.

Works Cited

Andersen, Kenneth E. *The Carroll C. Arnold Distinguished Lecture 2003: Recovering the Civic Culture: The Imperative of Ethical Communication*. Boston: Pearson Education, 2005.

———. *Persuasion: Theory and Practice*. Boston: Allyn and Bacon, 1971.

Aristotle. *Nichomachean Ethics*. Trans. H. Rackham. Cambridge, MA: Harvard UP, 1934.

———. *Politics and Poetics*. Trans. Benjamin Jowett and S. H. Butcher. New York: Heritage, 1964.

———. *On Rhetoric: A Theory of Civic Discourse*. Trans. George A. Kennedy. New York: Oxford UP, 1991.

Arnett, Ronald C. "Dialogic Civility as Pragmatic Ethical Praxis: An Interpersonal Metaphor for the Public Domain." *Communication Theory* 11 (2001): 315-338.

Arnett, Ronald C. and Pat Arneson. *Dialogic Civility in a Cynical Age: Community, Hope, and Interpersonal Relationships*. Albany: State U of New York P, 1999.

Bok, Sissela. *Lying: Moral Choice in Public and Private Life*. New York: Vintage, 1989.

———. *Secrets: On the Ethics of Concealment and Revelation*. New York: Pantheon, 1983.

Haiman, F. S. *Speech and Law in a Free Society*. Chicago: U of Chicago P, 1981.

Jaksa, James A., and Michael S. Pritchard, eds. *Responsible Communication: Ethical Issues in Business, Industry, and the Professions*. Cresskill, NJ: Hampton, 1996.

Johannesen, Richard L. *Ethics in Human Communication*. 5th ed. Prospect Heights, IL: Waveland, 2002.

Nilsen, Thomas R. *Ethics in Speech Communication*. 2nd ed. Indianapolis, IN: Bobbs-Merrill, 1974.

Rawls, John. *A Theory of Justice*. Cambridge: Belknap P of Harvard UP, 1971.

Communication Ethics: The Dialogic Turn[1]
Ronald C. Arnett, Pat Arneson, and Leeanne M. Bell

This essay engages a "community of memory" (Bellah, Madsen, Sullivan, Swidler, and Tipton 152-155), revisiting the conversation of previous scholarship in communication ethics. Robert Bellah (1985) and Alexis de Tocqueville (1835/1969) in different historical moments outlined the importance of a community of memory. Within this commitment, we begin by revisiting Marie Hochmuth Nichols's 1977 *Central States Speech Journal* article, "When You Set Out for Ithaka ..." in which she contended that there was no community of memory in the area of communication ethics inquiry.

> I do not believe that speech communication people are in a position to answer Derek Bok's question, 'Can Ethics Be Taught?' We have not seriously tried either directly or indirectly. We have not seriously studied the various systems of ethics; nor have we seriously studied social norms to which ethics is related. Idealism is not enough either in life or in communication books, nor are idealistic prescriptions. (150)

Nichols's chastisement called for attentive response to communication ethics scholarship. The discipline responded with original scholarship, summary articles, books, conferences, and organizations devoted to the study of communication ethics. This essay outlines how communication scholars answered and continue to answer Nichols's charge, "Where is the body of communication ethics scholarship?"

Introduction

This essay reviews a community of memory about communication ethics scholarship, updating Ronald C. Arnett's "The Status of Communication Ethics Scholarship in Speech Communication Journals from 1915-1985" and outlining the evolution of communication ethics scholarship: (1) identifying metatheoretical surveys of the literature, (2) engaging Kant's metaphor of "ought" (55) to understand communication ethics as a "good," and (3) reviewing scholarly journal articles addressing communication ethics categorized into six separate themes with a significant scholarly article serving as standard-bearer for each theme. This final contribution frames the theoretical and practical movement from a communication ethic to the postmodern reality of a multiplicity of communication ethics. The "dialogic turn" embraces this multiplicity of "goods," seeking to meet, learn from, and negotiate with difference. Communication ethics are central to the dialogic process of negotiating contending social goods in a postmodern society, an era of narrative and virtue contention.

In an era defined by difference, it is not surprising that both prescriptive and descriptive understandings of communication ethics shape the discourse. Prescriptive imposition of communication ethics works from the assumption that a universal correction communicates a social good that redirects the other person, altering the "wrong" or unethical behavior. An ethical prescription imposed on the other omits the reality of differing standpoints. Prescriptive facilitation of communication ethics represents the move from a universal understanding of truth with the human as the temporal carrier of truth. A descriptive understanding of ethics responds to the communicative practices in place rather than imposed standards. This movement from a prescriptive to a descriptive understanding of ethics provides the theoretical substance of Alasdair MacIntyre's changing character types in *After Virtue*—from the priest who announces truth given *a priori* to his pronouncement to the therapist who assists an individual to describe his or her own values and practices. This essay recognizes the ongoing hegemony of prescriptive and descriptive studies of communication ethics, while outlining dialogic ethics as a third alternative—a turn responsive to a historical moment in which negotiating contending social goods in an era of narrative and virtue contention is normative communicative competence.

Once the Enlightenment presuppositions of paradigmatic stability, progress, and universal certainty collapsed as coordinates of normative agreement, the study of communication ethics became an effort of learning through dialogic engagement of the other. With the ground of universal certainty shattered, petite narratives provide mobility of ground that situates embedded agents, offering temporal footing for meeting and addressing the world, offering a temporal place for interpretive understanding in search of negotiated communication "habits of the heart" (Tocqueville 267).

The Communication discipline's concern for communication ethics reflects the pragmatic currency of ethical questions that emerge in an era of competing narrative and virtue structures. It would be difficult to find anyone unaware of the importance of ethics, from the collapse of Enron to ongoing war to repeated tragedies of violence in our public classrooms. Alasdair MacIntyre in *After Virtue* refers to the "moral calamity" (ix) of our time. This essay sees not a moral crisis but a dialogic opportunity for learning, which is the natural by-product of meeting difference.

Communication Ethics Scholarship

Public evidence documenting an ongoing record of accomplishment in communication ethics scholarship offers a community of memory that constitutes a story of varied approaches to communication ethics. This evidence includes the National Communication Association (NCA) Communication Ethics Division, publications in *Communication Yearbook* and special issues of scholarly journals, presentations by leaders of professional communication organizations, historical surveys, books, and journal articles.

The NCA Communication Ethics Division, created in 1984, currently has 279 registered members. The Division sponsors conference papers at the annual meeting of the NCA and sponsors a bi-annual summer conference devoted entirely to research on communication ethics. Several book publications have emerged from the summer conference (Bracci and Christians; Jaksa and Prichard *Responsible*; Makau and Arnett), in addition to research from the conference appearing in other scholarly outlets.

Communication Yearbook has published scholarship examining ethical issues across a wide range of communication contexts (Allen, Gotcher, and Seibert; Boynton; Cameron, Sallot, and Curtin; Johannesen; Rimal, Fogg, and Flora). Lea Stewart has edited three journal issues dedicated to communication ethics. These include the 1997 issue of *Electronic Journal of Communication* (Jaffe; D. A. Kernisky; I. F. Kernisky; Pym; Tompkins), the 1996 issue of *Electronic Journal of Communication* (Arnett and Arneson; Ford; Lepper), and the 1990 issue of *Communication Quarterly* (Arnett; Bloom; Brown and Singhal; Deetz; Ferré; McEuen, Gordon, and Todd-Mancillas; Tompkins Pribble).

Kenneth Andersen's 2003 NCA Carroll C. Arnold Distinguished Lecture, "Recovering the Civic Culture: The Imperative of Ethical Communication," addressed the topic of communication ethics, continuing his contribution begun in 1983 as the Vice-President and then President of NCA. Andersen gave communication ethics scholarly currency, identifying this area of inquiry as the theme of the 1983 NCA conference. In this era, scholarship about communication ethics works with one "given": there are multiple communication ethics, making the notion of "difference" (Derrida, *Of Grammatology* 36) a trope akin to a first principle of philosophical communication ethics in the postmodern age.

Historical Surveys of Communication Ethics Literature

Five primary surveys of communication ethics situate our understanding of the diversity of approaches to communication ethics (Arnett "The Status"; Chesebro; Jensen "An Analysis," "Teaching Ethics"; Johannesen "Communication Ethics"). Each of these scholarly pieces provides insight into how communication ethics "works" in daily interactions.

J. Vernon Jensen addressed the instruction of ethics in speech communication education. In 1959, he evoked deliberation by one simple question, "Should a teacher of speech teach the ethical considerations in speaking in addition to the techniques of speaking?" ("An Analysis" 219). By 1985, Jensen ("Teaching Ethics") answered this question, framing communication ethics as central to the communication discipline.

James Chesebro provided a summary of the primary ethical standards proposed in communication. First, "ethical standards in communication should be patterned after the political structure of the society" (106), therefore consistent with a democratic government. Second, "ethical standards in communication should reflect a more universal, humanistic perspective of humans...consistent with the principles which ensure the development and expanded opportunities for the individuals" (106). Third, "ethical communication should concentrate upon the means used to attain an end. As a result, fairly specific and prescriptive sets of standards that are designed for means evaluation" (106) would emerge. Fourth, "the best framework for ethical communication focuses upon standards which enhance communication itself" (106). Fifth, some writers state they would "avoid the establishment of any universal set of standards for all cases, but argue that the situation or the context in which communication behavior occurred should determine when and if ethical standards of any kind should be employed" (106).

James Chesebro's ethical standards continue to shape communication ethics deliberation. Ronald C. Arnett ("The Status") examined the literature on communication ethics from 1915 to 1985, adopting Chesebro's four categories of communication ethics (democratic ethics, procedural standards and codes, universal humanitarian ethics, and contextual ethics) and adding a fifth category, "narrative ethics" (52-54).

Richard L. Johannesen ("Communication Ethics") examined seven trends in communication ethics scholarship: the proliferation of books on media and journalism ethics, an emphasis both on individual ethics and on social or institutional ethics, the recognition of the interrelationship of freedom and responsibility, scholarship taking place in ethics in organizational communication contexts, diverse feminist contributions to communication ethics, scholarship from the viewpoint of an ethic of care, and an application of the ancient Greek tradition of virtue ethics to contemporary communication contexts. He also explored six controversies or challenges in the development of communication ethics: "Can we develop a viable concept of the 'self' as an ethical agent in communication?" "Can we develop postmodern ethic or ethics of communication?" "Can we legitimately search for some minimum transcultural ethical standards for communication?" "Can we recognize the roles that diversity and marginalization play in developing communication ethics?" "Can we develop a viable communication ethic for the internet and cyberspace?" and "Can some conception of 'shame' be legitimate for communication ethics?" (216-226). Johannesen's work set forth important trends and controversies that creatively inspire contemporary communication ethics scholarship.

These works by J. Vernon Jensen, James Chesebro, Ronald C. Arnett, and Richard L. Johannesen reveal historical and contemporary considerations in the study of communication ethics. Additional books and edited anthologies augment their theoretical understanding of communication ethics and this area of inquiry. The summaries work at a descriptive level. They are akin to paths upon which people walk that naturally invite an architect to construct a stone sidewalk, offering even more guidance. Johannesen's work moves us to emerging paths: from communication ethics categories of engagement to communication ethics questions. The next section considers book-length treatments of protection: What is the "good" that one "ought" to protect? The communicative action of "protection" shapes a given communication ethic.

Books Addressing Communication Ethics

In this section, we identify how various works revolve explicitly or implicitly around Immanuel Kant's notion of "ought" (55). The changing engagement of "ought" moves the discussion of communication ethics in different and, at times, contrasting directions. "Ought" is the marker that directs communicative attention to a "good," functioning as an engine for a given communicative ethic. The following discussion traces communication ethics with hermeneutic attentiveness to the "ought" and the "good" that a given work seeks to protect. This brief analysis follows a chronological history by publication dates of selected books and chapters in scholarly anthologies.

George Gerbner, in the foreword to Thomas W. Cooper et al.'s book *Communication Ethics and Global Change*, states "American social authority is divided between public and private spheres. Private owners...are constrained only by their own private interests and those of investors, advertisers, and sponsors. But their own governance, insulated though it may be from public government, sets the terms for a community's pursuit of the common good" (xi). A communicative ethic "ought" to protect both the public and private spheres of communicative life.

Fred Dallmayr in *The Communicative Ethics Controversy* states the essays collected in their volume "do not offer a 'final word' or a resolution of the issues under discussion. Since the essays were written, the controversy surrounding communicative or discourse ethics has gathered momentum, with contending positions being steadily intensified or sharpened in the process" (18). Dallmayr reveals that in postmodernity there is no "final word" on what is ethical. There "ought" to be no "final word" in discourse ethics.

Robert E. Denton, Jr. follows this path in *Ethical Dimensions of Political Communication* when he writes, "The central theme that emerges from the essays is that we cannot depend upon the politicians, their handlers, or even the media or the press to correct real or perceived problems of ethics in American politics. The task is ours. Only as citizens can we alter or affect the quality of the polity" (xiv). Denton seeks a communicative ethic recognizing that we "ought" to protect the speech of the citizen.

J. Vernon Jensen, in his foreword to Karen Joy Greenberg's edited work *Conversations on Communication Ethics*, states "[t]his volume converses with us on a host of ethical concerns in communication. We grapple with the tension between relativistic and absolute ethics, between ends and means, between the 'is' and the 'ought' and between private and public goods" (xi). Jensen recognizes that communication in the public sphere "ought" to advance the public good.

James A. Jaksa and Michael S. Pritchard in *Communication Ethics: Methods of Analysis* note:

> As a normative study, ethics is concerned with determining what values are worthy of our acceptance. Our intent in this book is to assist readers in undertaking a normative study of morality, specifically in regard to human communication. To some

extent it will be important to discuss what moral values people actually accept, but this will always be with an eye on normative questions about what moral values ought to be accepted. (4)

Jaksa and Pritchard understand that the communication ethics scholar attends to the tension between the "is" and the "ought" in communicative life.

James A. Jaksa and Michael S. Pritchard in *Responsible Communication: Ethical Issues in Business, Industry, and the Professions* raise "critical questions about the role of communication in dealing with ethical problems that range from the local to the global.... These chapters serve as an invitation to join the authors in trying to understand and explain the communication challenges facing technologically advanced societies and those whose lives they touch" (13). Jaksa and Pritchard suggest a communication ethic "ought" to be attentive to the simultaneous concern for the particular and the comprehensive, the local and the global.

Fred L. Casmir states in *Ethics in Intercultural and International Communication*,

> the concept of dialogue will be repeatedly used in the discussions and in some of the models included in this book. Such a dialogue is made more difficult when it has to take place across cultural or political lines of demarcation or division. Differences become more readily apparent, or are more readily supposed to exist, when we deal with those who can be easily identified as being *different* from us. Thus important dimensions for misunderstandings, confrontations, and serious conflicts are added to what, in many cases, are already common difficult processes of interpersonal or group interactions within any one culture. (x)

Casmir recognizes that in a postmodern era, communicators "ought" to protect difference.

Clifford G. Christians and Michael M. Traber in *Communication Ethics and Universal Values* noted:

> The multicultural comparative ethics developed here does not aim at geographic representation. The approach is topical and issue oriented. The study process for this book has demonstrated that cultures in all their differences also reflect common humaneness and humanity. This book thus shows the many different entranceways that can lead to a common ethical discourse on a global scale, centered on truth-telling, human dignity, and no harm to the innocent. (xv)

Christians and Traber point to an "ought" beyond the postmodern disruption of narrative consensus, suggesting that part of our conversation "ought" to include minimal, temporal universals for the global community.

J. Vernon Jensen in *Ethical Issues in the Communication Process* defines ethics as:

> the *moral responsibility to choose, intentionally and voluntarily,* oughtness *in values like rightness, goodness, truthfulness, justice, and virtue, which may in a communicative transaction significantly affect ourselves and others. Ethics* refers to theory, to abstract universal principles and their sources, whereas *moral* implies practicing those principles of applied ethics, or culture-bound modes of conduct. (4, italics in original)

This definition combines theory and practice in determining how one "ought" to communicate.

Josina M. Makau and Ronald C. Arnett write in the preface to *Communication Ethics in an Age of Diversity*:

> Particularly noteworthy in this regard is the evidence of postmodern influences on the majority of the essays. Many of the authors challenge enlightenment approaches to ethical issues, calling for the abandonment of abstract ideological frameworks. Emotions receive acknowledgment and serious attention in many of the chapters. The chapters also share a recognition that fruitful scholarship on communication ethics integrates theory and *praxis*. The authors reject modernist tendencies to denigrate applied research. Significantly, however, most of the authors in this volume affirm the enlightenment's critique of privatized truth. Most of the authors also reject the postmodern tendency to abandon the quest to find meaningful ways to deliberate across differences about ethical issues. The chapters in this volume are written with the hope of contributing to this critical but difficult search. (x-xi)

Makau and Arnett implicitly suggest that one "ought" to understand and learn the diverse views of the "good" that guides differing communication ethics. They recognize a postmodern "ought" to move from a universal assumption of the "good" to understanding and learning from cultural and human difference.

Matthew W. Seeger in the introduction to his book *Ethics and Organizational Communication* states, "ethical questions, issues, and dilemmas are inherent to our humanness....Any comprehensive model of organization must incorporate an understanding of the role of values and ethics. Although it is easy to adopt an ethically neutral approach when discussing organizations and communication, this is simply not an option" (xii). Seeger follows this path, asserting one "ought" to place ethics as a first principle of communication.

Julia T. Wood, in her foreword to Ronald C. Arnett and Pat Arneson's book *Dialogic Civility in a Cynical Age: Community, Hope, and Interpersonal Relationships*, states:

> To replace the therapeutic model, the authors propose a model grounded in historicality, which is best understood as a willingness to meet the demands of a particular moment. Reflecting the authors' long-standing commitment to a dialogic approach to communication, the model they advance respects the preferred stories of all communicators. The model assumes that each individual's previous or established story moves into dialogue with the stories of others, as well as the constraints and commonsense questions of the present moment. Respectful dialogue that opens self and other to the possibility of change is fostered when all communicators embrace the authors' proposed narrative of dialogic civility—with narrative understood as a story held in the public domain by a group of people. (xiii)

Ethical communicators "ought" to attend to the historical moment, answering its call to "keep the conversation going" (Rorty 378).

Elaine E. Englehardt in *Ethical Issues in Interpersonal Communication: Friends, Intimates, Sexuality, Marriage, and Family* noted that communication ethics are important in interpersonal relationships because communication ethics "help the individual with self-understanding; they help the individual think critically about the multifaceted environment; and they demonstrate how self-understanding encourages an approach to ethics that begins with avoiding harm and focuses on doing good for and with others" (vi). The first section in Englehardt's edited book, "What Is Ethics?," introduces the importance of studying interpersonal communication ethics as "a system of guidance that assists each of us in living within a society" (vi-vii). The contributors embrace a Socratic "ought" to "know thyself" (Cornford 28) in order to better assist others in changing interpersonal environments.

Robert E. Denton, Jr. states in *Political Communication Ethics: An Oxymoron?*, "[b]y better understanding our political process and its ethical implication, we hope to empower readers with a sense of purpose and to resolve to protect our civic culture" (xvii). Denton's work suggests communication ethics "ought" to protect civic culture.

Michael J. Hyde in *The Call of Conscience: Heidegger and Levinas, Rhetoric and the Euthanasia Debate* recognized, "With this evocation, this acknowledging call to others, rhetoric demonstrates its 'physicianship' as it helps to promote reasoned judgment and civic virtue and thereby lends itself to the task of enriching the moral character of a people's communal existence" (13). The aspect of "physicianship," inherent in rhetoric, is an "ought" that requires attentiveness and care for others.

Richard L. Johannesen, in *Ethics in Human Communication*, states:

> My primary intentions ... are: (1) to provide information and insights concerning a variety of potential perspectives for making ethical judgments about human communication; (2) to sensitize participants in communication to the inherency of potential ethical issues in human communication process; (3) to highlight the complexities and difficulties involved in making evaluations of communication ethics; (4) to encourage individuals to develop thoughtfully their own workable approach to assessing communication ethics; and (5) to aid individuals in becoming more discerning evaluators of communication through enhancing their ability to make specifically focused and carefully considered ethical judgments. (xi)

Johannesen's descriptive analysis asserts that one "ought" to have choice in how one communicates one's thoughts in words and deed.

Josina M. Makau in the preface to Sharon L. Bracci and Clifford G. Christians's edited book *Moral Engagement in Public Life: Theorists for Contemporary Ethics* wrote:

> So called universal principles have proven inadequate (and often counterproductive) to resolution of many, if not most, 'real world' moral challenges. Similarly, pursuit of value neutrality has proven to be both fruitless and undesirable, particularly given the demonstrable role of power in human relations and social structures. Disregarding the key role of the heart in ethical deliberation and action, traditional paradigms have undermined the very foundations of spirituality and other critical resources for ethical interaction. Rich ontological, epistemological, and ethical traditions have been undermined gravely by adherence to such narrow and misguided perspectives. (ix)

She suggests that one "ought" to attend to the "heart" and communication ethics as the first human principle.

Jeffrey W. Murray in *Face to Face in Dialogue: Emmanuel Levinas and (the) Communication (of) Ethics* wrote "ethics is 'announced' prior to communication, this work suggests that that primordial 'announcement' or 'call' often requires communication in order to be effectively and enduringly heard over the subsequent clamor of cultural assumptions, stereotypes, prejudices, and prejudgments" (vii). The rhetorical "ought" of Murray's work concurs with Levinas—ethics is a philosophical first principle, the first principle of humanness. Ronald C. Arnett in *Dialogic Confession: Bonhoeffer's Rhetoric of Responsibility* and Michael J. Hyde's *The Life-Giving Gift of Acknowledgement* suggest the communication ethics that we "ought" to protect is a pragmatic humility of confession in meeting diversity and the fundamental importance of acknowledging the face of another in human meeting.

Summary

Insights from these scholarly books guide our understanding of the study of communication ethics as seeking to protect the following "oughts" or understandings of the "good" appropriate for a postmodern era: 1) the public and private spheres of communicative life; 2) admission that there is no "final word" in discourse ethics; 3) the free speech of the citizen; 4) the expectation to advance the public good; 5) simultaneous concern for the particular and the comprehensive, the local and the global; 6) engaging difference as the foundation for learning; 7) minimal temporal universals for the global community; 8) theory and practice in determining how one "ought" to communicate; 9) understanding and learning from differing communication ethics; 10) ethics as a first principle of communication; 11) attentiveness to the voice of the historical moment; 12) the importance of Socrates's Delphic injunction to "know thyself" (Cornford 28) in changing interpersonal environments; 13) understanding the assumptions of a given civic culture; 14) "physicianship" (Hyde, *The Call* 13) as attentiveness and care for others; 14) choice in how one communicates one's thoughts in words and deed; 15) attention to the "heart" (Makau, "Preface" ix) in ethics as a first human principle of communication; 16) ethics as the first principle of humanness; 17) pragmatic humility/confession in meeting diversity; and 18) the fundamental importance of human meeting in which one acknowledges the face of another person.

The dominant connection in these works remains Immanuel Kant's notion of "ought" (55), which is a communicative call to attend to a given good. To understand a communication ethic, one must ask "What is the 'ought' that implies a 'good' that underscores the communication?" Stated differently, within the spirit of Jürgen Habermas, we ask "What 'interest' is being protected and promoted?" Once a sidewalk, a publicly paved path, exists for given categories of communication ethics or questions about communication ethics, the protection of a given communication ethic returns us once again to connecting ethics to "ought"—not as a universal but as a form of ethics lived out in *Communicative Praxis* (Schrag). Calvin O. Schrag outlines communicative praxis as the interplay of theory, action, and contextual discernment. He uses the terms "by," "about," and "for" (viii) to bring communicative praxis into ongoing engagement with ethics. While various understandings of communication ethics privilege action (by), theory (about), and contextual discernment (for whom) in differing proportions, the interplay of this conceptual trinity illuminates the following discussion.

Scholarly Journal Articles Addressing Communication Ethics

This section updates Ronald C. Arnett's article "The Status of Communication Ethics Scholarship in Speech Communication Journals from 1915-1985." That work reviewed 128 articles related to ethics of communication published in disciplinary journals from 1915-1985. This essay reviews an additional 73 articles from 1986-2004. Following Arnett, the primary guidelines for inclusion of articles in this review were the use of the term "communication ethics" in the title and/or that the article was closely connected to human communication ethics. To identify journal articles, the term "communication ethics" was typed into multiple library search engines (i.e., Ebscohost, Communication Institute for Online Scholarship (CIOS) Index, ComAbstracts, and Proquest) at Duquesne University. Media and Journalism ethics were not included; summaries of that work are available elsewhere (Christians "Fifty Years," "Review Essay").

We examined the following journals from 1986-2004: *Argumentation and Advocacy*, *Communication Education*, *Communication Monographs*, *Communication Quarterly*, *Communication Reports*, *Communication Research*, *Communication Studies* (includes previously titled *Central States Speech Journal*), *Communication Theory*, *Communication Yearbook*, *Electronic Journal of Communication*, *Howard Journal of Communication*, *Human Communication Research*, *Journal of Applied Communication Research*, *Management Communication Quarterly*, *Philosophy and Rhetoric*, *Southern Communication Journal*, *Text and Performance Quarterly*, *Western Journal of Communication* and *Quarterly Journal of Speech*. A bibliography of the communication ethics articles published in these journals appears at the end of this essay. Although additional communication ethics articles appeared in other communication journals (including but not limited to *Business Communication Quarterly* and *Journal of Business Communication*), only the above list of journals were included in this review. Our goal is to provide a representative picture of the state of communication ethics scholarship through 2004.

Following the process used in Ronald C. Arnett's content analysis, the identified articles were reviewed and placed in one of the following categories of communication ethics: democratic communication ethics; universal-humanitarian communication ethics; codes, procedures, and standards in communication ethics; contextual communication ethics; and narrative communication ethics. Responding to Julia T. Wood's ("Foreword") suggestion, we also identify essays that offer a "history" of communication ethics in our discipline (Arnett "The Status"; Chesebro; Christians and Lambeth; Jensen "An Analysis," "Teaching Ethics"; Johannesen "Communication Ethics"; McEuen, Gordon, and Todd-Mancillas; Sproule). Our analysis reconfirmed the five categories and announced a sixth category, "dialogic communication ethics." This new category is central for navigating a postmodern era in which narrative and virtue agreement no longer exist.

A significant work published in the communication discipline was selected to represent each of the six categories of communication ethics scholarship. While identifying a single contribution to serve as a standard-bearer for an approach to communication ethics is an arguable task, what is clear is that each selected work outlines the horizon of that particular approach to communication ethics. We do not suggest that the selections are "the" representative of a given category; however, in these works researchers will find the central theme that frames and shapes the common center for each category. The following section organizes communication ethics scholarship within these six themes, offering a discussion and analysis of each category. We begin with a discussion of democratic communication ethics, followed by universal-humanitarian communication ethics; codes, procedures, and standards in communication ethics; contextual communication ethics; narrative communication ethics; and dialogic communication ethics.

Democratic Communication Ethics

The category "democratic communication ethics" is fundamental in our discipline, consistent with our early rhetorical roots in Greek democracy and previous examinations of communication ethics literature. We utilize the understanding that "Democratic Communication Ethics are based on a public 'process' ethic, an open airing of diverse opinions and control by majority vote" (Arnett, "The Status" 46). "The democratic ethic in communication studies is a 'public' process for forging mass collaboration on ideas, customs, and rights" (48). Additionally, we recognize that a democratic communication rests within an argumentative communicative framework dependent upon a public process, a procedural understanding of rationality.

Karl R. Wallace's article "An Ethical Basis of Communication" published in *Speech Teacher* is identified as a standard bearer in this category. In that work, Wallace outlined four basic habits that comprise a democratic communication ethic: the "habit of search" requiring knowledge-fueled continual learning; the "habit of justice" reminding us of fairness, accuracy, and respect for fact over opinion; the "habit of preferring public to private motivations" in a democracy must trump private impulses—accurate information rather than personal opinion needs to shape the public sphere; and the "habit of respect for dissent" which presupposes that a democracy never concludes but continues by reshaping itself with new ideas, new information, and new insights (6-9). Wallace states, "It is these four 'moralities'—the duty of search and inquiry; allegiance to accuracy, fairness, and justice in the selection and treatment of ideas and arguments; the willingness to submit private motivations to public scrutiny; and the toleration of dissent—which provide the ethic of communication in a free society" (9). For Wallace and for many scholars in the discipline, a democratic communication ethic either explicitly or implicitly guides public and private assessment of fair and just discourse.

Our review revealed 11 articles that address democratic communication ethics appearing in communication journals from 1986-2004 (Arnett "The Practical Philosophy"; Batt; Dowling and Marraro; Garver "Essentially Contested," "The Ethical Criticism"; Haas; Johnstone "Reagan"; Muir; Schwarze; Tompkins; Ulmer and Sellnow). Those articles privilege the following ideas: evidence, controversy, upholding principles, social responsibility, free speech, competing publics or public, controversies, debate, argument, practical rationality, democracies need free and open debate,

Athenian heritage, rhetorical practice, significant choice, critical publicity, public knowledge of events, and reasoned opinion. These ideas are the "about" (Schrag viii), or the ethical "goods," addressed by scholars who promote or support a democratic world view for persons in contexts resistive or unresponsive to a democratic appeal.

A democratic ethic fundamentally lives upon one basic pragmatic assumption: informed choice matters. Communication strategies that encourage and enhance informed choice underscore the intimate connection between free speech and communication ethics. A democratic ethic is procedural in that it privileges the communicative process of argumentation and debate, which presupposes the existence of rationality that in practice encourages good decision-making. A democratic commitment assumes informed choice. Star A. Muir wrote, "Firm moral commitment to a value system...along with a sense of moral identity, is founded upon unreflexive assessments of multiple perspectives....We must progressively learn to recognize how often the concepts of others are discredited by the concepts we use to justify ourselves to ourselves" (291). A democratic communication ethic enters a postmodern world of difference with a reminder to not discount the other or the other's ideas. Learning and informed choice must trump unreflective normative agreement. A democratic communication ethic is not alien to universal-humanitarian communication ethics.

Universal-Humanitarian Communication Ethics

Universal-humanitarian communication ethics requires "a select intelligentsia to announce 'principles' that should guide communication behavior. However, the principles are *not created* by the intelligentsia; rather they are universal, *a priori* principles announced, supported and if necessary, fought for by an 'enlightened' and 'insightful' minority" (Arnett, "The Status" 48). We draw upon this definition with one additional supporting caveat that underscores that a universal-humanitarian ethic rests in an Enlightenment ideology that presupposes an *a priori* understanding of rights and principles for human interaction. This category is the home of Platonic thought carried through the Enlightenment commitment to rational discernment of the truth—discerning and making the "already" (the *a priori*) visible.

Christopher Lyle Johnstone's article, "Ethics, Wisdom, and the Mission of Contemporary Rhetoric: The Realization of Human Being," is a standard bearer for universal-humanitarian ethics. Johnstone frames the necessity of uplifting inherent human features such as resourcefulness, lovingness, and receptiveness to beauty, emotion, insight, and imagination. Universal-humanitarian communication ethics emphasizes a passionate commitment to the growth of the human being within what could be called humanizing *topoi* that lead one to reason on behalf of the "good." As Johnstone states:

> The humanist commitment demands a dedication to nurturing and treasuring those characteristics in ourselves and each other that underlie our capacity for bringing quality into our lives. There is, I suggest, general agreement on what these characteristics are, at least on how they can be labeled. What is lacking is knowledge of and attachment to them on a personal level. This humane knowledge, moreover, is always a potentiality inherent in the relating of one human being to another. When we attempt to 'reason together' in order that we might live together productively and happily, we lead each other and ourselves to the edge of the human soul. (188)

Johnstone reminds us of universal presuppositions about a human soul committed to beauty, choice, and reason.

Our review identified 12 articles addressing universal-humanitarian communication ethics (Arnett "The Responsive 'I'"; Condit; DiTomaso, Parks-Yancy, and Post; Ferré; Fischer; Ford; Griswold; Gunson and Collins; Herrick; McCaleb and Dean; Pym; Seeger and Ulmer). Those articles privilege the following terms: an *a priori* commitment to the other's potentiality, institutionalizing procedures for discourse ethics' reason or moral understanding, public morality, goodness, creativeness, perfection, and responsiveness to a transcendent ideal. Using Calvin O. Schrag's (viii) language, the "about" casts itself in Enlightenment language "by" those assuming inalienable rights and "for" persons in contexts unresponsive to universal appeals to human dignity.

A universal presupposes value-laden terms about a "good" life that can be rationally made visible, ever connected to an *a priori* conception of the good, the beautiful, and the responsible. The "good" of universal-humanitarian communication ethic protects the *a priori* of rationality; the communicative "ought" is the ethical demand to discern and make visible truth and beauty before us. The connection of truth to the *a priori* of rationality gives way to responsiveness to codes, procedures, and standards, as public announcements that inform choice about participation in a given organizational context. Universal-humanitarian ethics and codes, procedures, and standards as different approaches to communication ethics share a basic commitment to informed choice.

Codes, Procedures, and Standards in Communication Ethics

Codes, procedures, and standards conceptually and behaviorally frame communication in varying contexts. These guidelines are established as the "guardians of appropriate ethical conduct" (Arnett, "The Status" 50). Ronald C. Arnett states, "Standards and codes are important to most organizations in crisis and in beginning identity formation, as long as they are not taken too legalistically. The value of codes lies more in their ability to promote discussion, than in the total regulation of behavior" (51). Codes, procedures, and standards in communication ethics "rely on a select number of guardians of appropriate ethical conduct. The members create the codes and procedures; they are not discovered *a priori* principles" (50). The key to such an approach to communication ethics is two-fold: discussion of direction and enforcement. This understanding is augmented with a stress on prescription and public disclosure. Codes procedures and standards both prescribe (presuppose) and publicly proclaim communicative limits and constraints (public procedure). Restated in another way, codes, procedures, and standards publicly announce contextual "oughts" (the do's and don'ts) of communication ethics.

Kenneth Andersen's 2003 NCA Carroll C. Arnold Distinguished Lecture, "Recovering the Civic Culture: The Imperative of Ethical Communication," is a standard bearer for the category of codes, procedures, and standards. He began his presentation by returning us to two credos or standards adopted by the National Communication Association: "The Credo for Ethical Communication" and "The Credo for Free and Responsible Communication in a Democratic Society." These credos frame communicative respect for persons, information, and difference. Codes and credos are not value free; they rest upon democratic and universal-humanitarian presuppositions. Andersen's lecture reminds us of communicative ethics standards that keep a democratic tradition vigilant against totalitarian action, whether that of the state, a ruler, or oneself.

Our review identified six recent articles addressing codes, procedures, and standards for communication ethics (Anderson; Bloom; Boynton; Jaques; Kirkwood and Ralston; Tompkins Pribble). Those articles privilege the following terms: objectives, ethical conduct, professional communicative standards, government structures, professionalism, ethics codes, professional duty, standards, and effective coordination of action. Drawing upon Calvin

O. Schrag's (viii) understanding of communicative praxis, the "about" suggests public standards "by" those wanting to protect particular professional interests "for" contexts in which those working within or utilizing the services of a given organization are assured of codes of conduct.

The development of communication standards and codes are often too quickly dismissed as simply a public window for how persons in a position of power would guide communication. However, when codes and standards are formed through repeated conversation, they provide public communicative guidance and assurance for the participants. In addition, they can enhance a communicative terrain of trust, a set of "best professional practices" responsive to persons and a given organization. "L'Etang (1992) presented evidence that deontological, or Kantian, ethics provide the most suitable foundation for the development of ethics codes" (qtd. in Boynton 254) which characterize conduct in various contexts. A procedure, standard, and/or code is a public admission of a given "good" that "ought" to guide communicative life in a given context.

Contextual Communication Ethics

A contextual communication ethic encompasses and "justifies different communication standards for different audiences, cultures, and relationships" (Arnett, "The Status" 52). Contextual communication ethics presuppose "difference." However, the difference originates not from the communicative agent but from the place, the situation, in which the communicative agent engages others. Contextual communication ethics suggest that a given context gives birth to temporal standards appropriate for guiding communication ethics conduct in that situation. The standard for "good" and "bad" communication lives within the context itself.

Perhaps the most famous contextual approach to ethics was Joseph Fletcher's *Situational Ethics: The New Morality*. Fletcher, a pastor, understood the confines of contextual ethics within the Judeo-Christian narrative. Although beyond the scope of this essay, one could conclude that Aristotle's work was a form of contextual ethics, defined within the confines of the polis. Phronesis, practical wisdom, is creative implementation responsive to a background that offers limited options. Today the term "contextual" most often refers to the place of decision; however, its original intent was to take a story-laden set of limits to a given context for communicative engagement.

The postmodern understanding of contextual communication ethics adds a relativistic and "emotivist" understanding of ethics. Alasdair MacIntyre in *After Virtue* states, "emotivism is the doctrine that all evaluative judgments, and more specifically all moral judgments, are nothing but expressions of preference, expressions of attitude or feeling, insofar as they are moral or evaluative in character" (11-12). When emotivism is introduced, contextual communication ethics adheres to "'private' reliance on individual discernment at the moment of decision" (Arnett, "The Status" 51). The term "contextual" is now more akin to the immediate place of discernment that knowingly or unknowingly brackets an ethical *a priori* that one takes to the context, the place of ethical discernment. A contextual communication ethic does not produce objective standards of proof. There is a celebration of the absence of standards of proof, ever-responsive to the importance of the particular—a particular group, a particular audience, and a particular occasion. The context shapes an ethical response or argument.

Malcolm O. Sillars's article "Audiences, Social Values, and the Analysis of Argument" is a standard bearer for contextual communication ethics. Sillars states:

> The development of a system of argumentative analysis for general argumentation requires that we understand argumentation as a kind of communication addressed to an audience, that we abandon objectivist notions and arbitrary designations about proof, that we recognize argumentation as an ongoing process where societal values are vital. It requires, as well, that argumentative analysis return to its grounding in the social sciences and the humanities to learn the potential value systems of the society....[T]he ways in which we arrange values are not hierarchies in different situations. It is not an easy task, but it is worth taking. (302-303)

Sillars's freedom works within a context that presupposes what is potentially valuable. The contextual approach allows flexibility within limits. Sillars's work, written over 30 years ago, suggests that ethical discernment is not shaped by the routine, but by the unique and the particular.

Our review identified 17 recent articles addressing contextual communication ethics (Arnett and Arneson; Booth-Butterfield and Cottone; Cameron, Campo, and Brossard; Granville and Hermodson; Hallstein; Jaffe; Johannesen "The Ethics"; Lepper; Marin, Sherblom, and Shipps; McGuire, Stauble, Abbott and Fisher; Medhurst; Nkomo; Reinsch; Stablein; Steiner; Winegarden and Fuss-Reineck; Wood "Ethics"). Those articles privilege the following terms: standpoint, context, socialization, responsiveness to the contingent nature of communication, communicative environment, communicative norms, organizational diversity, situational, community, embedded, situated, culturally embedded, and norms of ethical conduct. Drawing upon Calvin O. Schrag's (viii) work, the "about" of contextual ethics assumes appropriate fit, doing the "right" action at the "right" moment. The "about" requires listening to the communicative context. The "by" emphasizes a communicator who understands the responsive role of a communicative actor attentive to standpoint and context. Standpoint theory (see Harding) shifts the theoretical ground of contextual communication ethics; standpoint and contextual communication ethics, taken together, offer insight "for" ethical navigation of a world of competing narrative and virtue structures.

A contextual communication ethic is responsive to culture and standpoint. The term "contexts" presupposes difference and multiplicity. Sandra Harding discusses standpoint as a socio-cultural action construct that shapes a context from which decisions emerge: "Recall that a standpoint is not a perspective; it takes a science and politics to achieve a standpoint. Standpoints are socially mediated, perspectives are unmediated" (276). Standpoint theory takes us from the naïve assumption that the situation alone offers communicative ethics insights to drawing upon the power and limits of a given context to ethically engage the situation. This approach offers a two-sided understanding of context. The communicative "ought" is listening to the needs of a given context before offering ethical response. The "good" that is protected is attentiveness to the unique. The narrative ethics approach discusses the portability of ethical practices in the meeting of a given context.

Narrative Communication Ethics

This section "includes articles directly related to 'narrative ethics' and others that have paved a conceptual path to this approach" (Arnett, "The Status" 52). Discussion of communication ethics attentive to a speech act, a story, or narratives, all of which guide people and offer insights, reside within this category. "Narrative or story provides a community with a...context for action and rhetoric of practice" (53). We add a cultural component to narrative ethics; a culture functions as an implicit story supported by a web of communicative practices that orchestrate communicative behavior by guiding and delimiting communicative possibilities for a people.

Walter R. Fisher's work *Human Communication as Narration: Toward a Philosophy of Reason, Value, and Action* serves as a standard bearer for a narrative communication ethic. He outlines a narrative as a "good" story that situates "good reasons" (48, 57) for an argument and embraces both probability and fidelity in the implementation of communicative action. The paradigmatic innovation of the focus on narrative is that Fisher implies a form of mobile ground or temporal standpoint. Unlike the universal-humanitarian communication ethic, a narrative is a petite housing of good reasons. The universal presupposes the *a priori* totality of rationality. A narrative paradigm does not abandon rationality, but it does pragmatically situate rationality within a humble story that must compete with other stories. A narrative is not a universal truth but a coherent story of bias. Fisher's theoretical contribution is populist; he makes rationality available to all. He privileges the importance of identity, situated not around the person but around a given story that shapes good reasons that guide a person.

Our review revealed only four articles that directly address narrative communication ethics appearing in communication journals from 1986-2004 (Hyde and Sargent; Mattson and Buzzanell; Struever; Whaley, Nicotera, and Samter). Those articles privilege the following terms: story, from public to publics, interactive play, and living historical entities. Communicative praxis in narrative ethics, drawing upon Calvin O. Schrag's (viii) work, is "about" story, whether petite or long standing. The "about" is the direction of a given story—"Where does it take us?" Narrative ethics is engaged "by" a communicator aware of the muddiness of narrative life; narratives blind us, give us sight, limit us, and offer us new possibilities. Additionally, narratives change as new historical moments and communicative actors affect them. A narrative, unlike an ideology, is ontologically constituted "for" the possibility of change. Competing narratives define postmodernity; they contend against modernist ideology, the metanarrative of progress, and the autonomous self. Modernity houses ideology and postmodernity calls forth the reality of narratives in contention with one another.

In the introduction of ideas there are, at times, major theoretical contributions that resituate understanding within the intellectual community. The introduction of narrative to the field of communication was such a contribution. We agree with Jean-François Lyotard who recognized that in a postmodern era we live in a time of petite narrative structures. Confidence in the meta-narrative or a universal is absent; rather petite narratives, that both guide and assume limitations, are the temporal common ground of postmodernity. Within a multiplicity of narratives structures, the conceptual foundation for a given communication ethic becomes a temporal backdrop for understanding and engaging the foreground issues of communicative implementation and engagement.

Narrative ethics are carried by a story, even the story of science. "The scientist's duty is to place herself [or himself] in a community of inquirers and in this way orient herself [or himself] within a matrix of beliefs, dispositions, and habits of action. The practice is antisolipist" (Struever 103). The scientist who understands rationality as constrained within narrative limits experiences a postmodern moment of narrative contention. In a pragmatic minimalist sense of hope this contention invites the "between" of dialogue—learning from difference. Instead of a focus on the agent, narrative embeds the person within the mud of a story-laden life and dialogic ethics. The narrative paradigm provides theoretical and practical ground for an emerging approach to communication ethics, "dialogic ethics."

Dialogic Communication Ethics

Dialogue is understood as the communicative exchange of embedded agents standing their own ground while being open to the other's standpoint, conceptualizing meaning that emerges in discourse situated between persons while engaging a common text in their communicative event. A dialogic ethic assumes an embedded communicative agent, recognizing that a human being lives within an ongoing conversation that began well before a specific interpersonal interaction begins. This understanding of dialogue presupposes the importance of narrative; narrative gives birth to a given set of social practices, virtues, and understandings of the "good" that are carried forth in a dialogue. A dialogic ethic begins with the presupposition that we enter into an ongoing human conversation that is never concluded.

John Stewart and Karen Zediker's work "Dialogue as Tensional, Ethical Practice" serves as a standard bearer for dialogic communication ethics. They assert that all approaches to "dialogue" are not the same. Drawing upon Aristotle's *Nichomachean Ethics*, Stewart and Zediker recognize that dialogue can be understood descriptively or prescriptively. Prescriptive approaches to dialogue foreground the relational and tensional qualities of "human meaning making" and emphasize epistemological concerns. Prescriptive approaches "affirm this relational epistemology *and* foreground axiological concerns" (239, italics in original).

There are ethical implications in the choice to approach dialogue as descriptive or prescriptive interaction. A prescriptive approach to dialogue

> requires participants to make choices between and among multi-vocal, tensional perspectives and assertions. As praxis, dialogue involves the processes of making and evaluating moral judgments about and through communication. From this perspective...he or she not only becomes an active agent shaping the quality of the relationship, but also assumes responsibility for the ways in which communicative practice facilitates relating. (Stewart and Zediker 240)

Dialogic communication ethics presupposes the importance of situated difference in communicative interaction, ever vigilant and responsive to emergent insight owned by neither party, the communicative result of the dialogue, itself.

Our review revealed 18 articles that address a dialogic communication ethic (Arnett "Dialogic Civility"; Deetz; Engnell; Fenske; Fulkerson; Garvey; Johannesen "Nel Noddings's Uses"; Jovanovic; Lipari; Mattson and Stage; Murray "Bakhtinian," "The Face," "An Other Ethic," "An Other-Burkean," "The Paradox"; Pinchevski; Reich; Stewart and Zediker). Those articles privilege the following terms: invitational not prescriptive, responsive, between persons, responsive to the other, the ethical call of responsibility between self and other, propelled by learning not power, attentive to a human face, cognizant of difference and alterity, interpersonal negotiation, relational ethic, unfinished, emergent, respectful of the text/content, and relationally embedded. From the perspective of communicative praxis (Schrag viii) the "by" of dialogic ethics is emergent; it is not the product of any one communicative partner. The "about" is engagement—the interplay of historical moment, biased ground the communicators bring to the table of conversation. Communicators exhibit a willingness to listen "for" the emergent, the unexpected, what Martin Buber called the "between" (72-88).

A dialogic communication ethic is responsive to a relational space the invites content and insight to emerge between persons. Dialogic ethics lives in creative possibilities invited between communicative partners that have neither prescriptive ambitions nor descriptive roots. A dialogic ethic both invites and prescribes—prescribing an alternative to individualism that precludes attentiveness to the other.

> The primary philosophical and pragmatic goal of...'dialogue' was not just to have people recognize the inherently relational nature of all human being....[but to urge

people] to make the ethical choice of changing their dominant monologic communication patterns toward more dialogic ones. This is the sense in which Buber's writings about dialogue are fundamentally prescriptive. (Stewart and Zediker 227)

Dialogue ethics are, additionally, prescriptive as one understands them as communication implementers of a narrative sense of the "good." Dialogic ethics is both perspective and transcendent in that new ideas emerge "between" persons of difference.

Articles about communication ethics in communication journals from 1986-2004 cluster around six approaches to communication ethics: democratic communication ethics; universal-humanitarian communication ethics; codes, procedures, and standards in communication ethics; contextual communication ethics; narrative communication ethics; and dialogic communication ethics. Each of these approaches contributes to our holistic understanding of ethics in communication. The emergence of dialogic ethics in the postmodern era represents the significance of communication ethics in negotiating competing social goods.

Negotiating Social Goods: The Dialogic Turn

From James Chesebro to Ronald C. Arnett ("The Status") to Richard L. Johannesen ("Communication Ethics"), we learn that there are multiple ways of engaging the texture of communication ethics scholarship. One of the central issues is choice. Johannesen stated the importance of this view of communication ethics. The importance of choice continues with a dialogic communication ethic. Dialogue works as communicative invitation, rejecting the short-term advantage of demand. Aristotle was unwilling to list shame as a virtue; his decision rested with the recognition that ethics and demand are contrary to one another.

The dialogic turn is a form of choice that presupposes that competing positions on communication ethics contend with one another. The dialogic turn privileges choice that requires constant learning, a willingness to engage interpretive understanding of diversity over argumentative condemnation of difference. The crucial element of dialogic ethics is the choice to learn; learning requires content—one needs to learn "something." The ethical content comes from the narrative structure upon which a person in dialogue stands; dialogue requires one to know one's own position and that of the other person.

The evolution of dialogic ethics owes much to the philosophical and practical discussion of narrative. Narrative ground is the moral source of a person in dialogue. This narrative ground is "prescriptive" with dialogue turning prescription into learning. John Stewart and Karen Zediker stated accurately that Martin Buber's position is prescriptive. Emmanuel Levinas discusses the prescriptive nature of ethics as responsibility for the Other. Narrative ground situates a dialogic ethic, but when one turns toward the Other, understanding an insight from the Other's narrative ground, the insight that emerges "between" persons moves dialogue to negotiating difference and communicative learning.

The dialogic turn toward the Other begins with prescription. One learns from understanding "difference" and negotiating ethical differences that emerge from the narrative ground of communicative partners, from insight emerging "between" persons, and from the communicators' attentive responsive to changes in the historical moment. There is little that is mystical about dialogic ethics—at a minimum it presupposes learning from the narrative or ground of self and Other and, in a larger sense, it implies discovering new possibilities that emerge from the "between" of difference. Dialogic ethics does not guarantee that one will convince another; however, it does require learning if minimum requirements are to be met. An approach to dialogic communication that begins with prescription and then moves to learning from diverse sources offers a beginning for negotiating "difference."

A dialogic ethic acknowledges one's own ground, learns from the ground of the Other, enables insight to emerge "between" persons, and changes in the historical moment. Such learning reveals different social goods—and negotiating competing "social goods" (Arnett, "Paulo Freire" 157). Negotiating competing social goods is the communicative answer to an era in which there is no "one" single communication ethic—there are multiple communicative ethics. A single communication ethic, supported by universal rationality, no longer exists, if it ever did.

Communication ethics from a dialogic perspective is an ongoing negotiating of rival social goods. All approaches discussed in this essay are co-present rival traditions in this historical moment; they compete for the communicative enactment of communication ethics. Dialogically this difference fuels learning—leading us to a communication ethic that begins with narrative ground, a "community of memory" (Bellah, Madsen, Sullivan, Swidler, and Tipton 152-155), that contains a particular understanding of social goods requiring particular communicative practices in the implementation of a given set of goods to communication ethics, which then becomes the home of a particular social good and the clashing of social goods. Kant's "ought" (55) and the communicative protection of a "good" continues, only the stress on learning from difference and the negotiating of difference separates a dialogic approach from all the others. This interpretive work understands dialogic ethics as centered in learning, which offers choice while negotiating rival traditions, each of which privileges differing social goods in various contexts.

Alasdair MacIntyre suggests in his book *Three Rival Versions of Moral Enquiry: Encyclopaedia, Genealogy and Tradition* that competing understanding of "goods" shape ongoing philosophical and pragmatic argument. These rival understandings include encyclopedic, genealogical, and tradition; each works as an interpretive grid that frames understanding and learning. The encyclopedic perspective presupposes the possibility of categorizing varying approaches to communication ethics (e.g., Jensen *Ethical Issues*, Johannesen *Ethics in*). The genealogical perspective looks at the intellectual heritage of ideas and authors (e.g., Johannesen "Nel Noddings's Uses"). The tradition perspective presupposes the emergence of ideas from ground under one's feet (e.g., Wood, "Ethics"). The literature of communication ethics engages each of these modes of inquiry.

Jacques Derrida recognizes that this "philosophical tremor" (*Adieu* 11) of contention points to the postmodern turn. According to Alasdair MacIntyre, contending schools of philosophical thought gather their significance from the good of effectiveness and the good of excellence. Modernity privileges the "good" of effectiveness, which is dependent upon implementation of effective strategies. The "good" of excellence is dependent upon negotiating competing incommensurable narratives. We contend that the dialogical turn is responsive to contending with the "good" in the postmodern historical era. Competing narratives bring together a "unity of contraries" (Buber 111): (1) the prescriptive and the emergent, (2) narrative ground and temporality, and (3) competing traditions and attentiveness to the uniqueness of the historical moment. A dialogic call to communication ethics rests in oxymorons such as "restrained freedom," "biased learning," and "fuzzy clarity." Dialogic ethics rests in conviction tempered by Søren Kierkegaard's reminder of *Fear and Trembling*. Dialogic ethics is a communicative call to a postmodern common sense that accepts the necessity of ground and the potential of fallibility of one's choice.

Giambattista Vico's *sensus communus* or common sense rests not upon agreed commonality of communicative practices and narrative commitments, but within a dialogic scope of understanding, learning, negotiating, and willingness to unite fragility of insight with temporal clarity. Dialogic ethics begins in narrative bias that situates an ethic. The dialogic turn takes us to the Otherness of temporality and conviction walking side-by-side with doubt, vulnerability, and a willingness to learn. The doing of dialogic ethics is akin to Mahatma Gandhi seeking truth:

> But how is one to realize their Truth....By single-minded devotion (*abbyasa*) and indifference to every other interest in life (*vairagya*)—replies the Bhagavad Gita. In spite, however, of such devotion, what may appear as truth to one person will often appear as untruth to another person. But this need not worry the seeker...there is nothing wrong in everyone following Truth according to one's light. Indeed it is one's duty to do so. Then if there is a mistake on the part of any one so following Truth, it will automatically be set right...[if] one takes to the wrong path one stumbles, and is thus redirected to the right path. (Duncan 42)

Dialogic ethics unites ground and the temporality aptly stated by Maurice Friedman with the metaphor *Touchstones of Reality*. Dialogic ethics begins with conviction, engages differences, and engages learning that recasts the conviction—sometimes ever so slightly, sometimes dramatically, and sometimes standing firm upon one's own ground—ever aware that the ground of conviction is a "touchstone," a temporal fragile place to stand.

Summary

This essay engaged a "community of memory" (Bellah, Madson, Sullivan, Swidler, and Tipton 152-155), revisiting scholarship including publications in *Communication Yearbook* and special issues of scholarly journals, presentations by leaders of professional communication organizations, historical surveys, books, and journal articles. We followed the process used in Ronald C. Arnett's "The Status of Communication Ethics Scholarship in Speech Communication Journals from 1915-1985" for reviewing communication journal articles from 1986 to 2004.

We outlined communication ethics as the process of protection and competition among competing goods that "ought" to shape discourse. Immanuel Kant's metaphor of "ought" (55) is a marker that focuses communicative attention on a "social good" (Arnett, "Paulo Freire" 157) that drives a given communicative ethic. Differing approaches to communication ethics engage action ("by"), theory ("about"), and contextual discernment ("for") in different ways (Schrag viii). This interpretive work suggests a communicative ethics responsive to "negotiating social goods." Negotiating goods coalesces around the term "dialogue." Communication ethics is central to the dialogic process of negotiating contending social goods in a postmodern society. The dialogic turn privileges choice that requires constant learning and a willingness to engage interpretive understanding of difference over argumentative condemnation of difference. The ethical content comes from the narrative structure upon which a person in dialogue stands. Communication ethics from a dialogic perspective suggests the "ought" of learning and significance of negotiating "social goods" in a time of competing narrative and virtue structures.

Note

1. This essay was previously published in *The Review of Communication* 6 (2006): 62-92. The authors would like to thank Taylor & Francis Group for granting permission to reprint this article. All rights reserved.

Works Cited

Allen, M. W., J. M. Gotcher and J. H. Seibert. "A Decade of Organizational Communication Research: Journal Articles 1980-1991." *Communication Yearbook 16*. Ed. S. A. Deetz. Newbury Park, CA: Sage, 2003. 252-330.

Andersen, Kenneth E. *The Carroll C. Arnold Distinguished Lecture 2003: Recovering the Civic Culture: The Imperative of Ethical Communication*. Boston: Pearson Education, 2005.

Anderson, James A. "Forum Response: Ethics in Business and Teaching." *Management Communication Quarterly* 17 (2003): 155-164.

Aristotle. *Nichomachean Ethics*. Trans. M. Ostwald. Indianapolis: Bobbs-Merrill, 1962.

Arnett, Ronald C. "Dialogic Civility as Pragmatic Ethical Praxis: An Interpersonal Metaphor for the Public Domain." *Communication Theory* 11 (2001): 315-338.

———. *Dialogic Confession: Bonhoeffer's Rhetoric of Responsibility*. Carbondale: Southern Illinois UP, 2005.

———. "Paulo Freire's Revolutionary Pedagogy: From a Story-Centered to a Narrative-Centered Communication Ethic." *Moral Engagement in Public Life: Theorists for Contemporary Ethics*. Eds. Sharon L. Bracci and Clifford G. Christians. New York: Peter Lang, 2002. 150-170.

———. "The Practical Philosophy of Communication Ethics and Free Speech as the Foundation for Speech Communication." *Communication Quarterly* 38 (1990): 208-217.

———. "The Responsive "I": Levinas's Derivative Argument." *Argumentation and Advocacy* 40 (2003): 39-50.

———. "The Status of Communication Ethics Scholarship in Speech Communication Journals from 1915-1985." *Central States Journal* 38 (1987): 44-61.

Arnett, Ronald C., and Pat Arneson. "Interpersonal Communication Ethics and the Limits of Individualism." *Electronic Journal of Communication* 6.4 (1996). Retrieved March 14, 2005, from http://www.cios.org/getfile/Arnett_V6N496.

Batt, Shawn. "Keeping Company in Controversy: Education Reform, Spheres of Argument, and Ethical Criticism." *Argumentation and Advocacy* 40 (2003): 85-104.

Bellah, Robert N., Richard Madsen, William M. Sullivan, Ann Swidler, and Steven M. Tipton. *Habits of the Heart: Individualism and Commitment in American Life*. Berkeley: U of California P, 1985.

Bloom, Melanie M. "Sex Differences in Ethical Systems: A Useful Framework for Interpreting Communication Research." *Communication Quarterly* 38 (1990): 244-254.

Booth-Butterfield, Steve, and Rocco R. Cottone. "Ethical Issues in the Treatment of Communication Apprehension and Avoidance." *Communication Education* 40 (1991): 172-179.

Boynton, Lois A. "Professionalism and Social Responsibility: Foundations of Public Relations Ethics." *Communication Yearbook 26*. Ed. William B. Gudykunst. Mahwah, NJ: Lawrence Erlbaum, 2002. 230-265.

Bracci, Sharon L., and Clifford G. Christians, eds. *Moral Engagement in Public Life: Theorists for Contemporary Ethics*. New York: Peter Lang 2002.

Brown, William J., and Arvind Singhal. "Ethical Dilemmas of Prosocial Television." *Communication Quarterly* 38 (1990): 268-280.

Buber, Martin. *The Knowledge of Man: A Philosophy of the Interhuman*. New York: Harper and Row, 1966.

Cameron, Glen T., Lynne M. Sallot, and Patricia A. Curtin. "Public Relations and the Production of News: A Critical Review and Theoretical Framework." *Communication Yearbook 20*. Eds. Brant R. Burleson and Adrianne W. Kunkel. Thousand Oaks, CA: Sage, 1997. 111-156.

Cameron, Kenzie A., Shelly Campo, and Dominique Brossard. "Advocating for Controversial Issues: The Effect of Activism on Compliance-Gaining Strategy Likelihood of Use." *Communication Studies* 54 (2003): 265-281.

Casmir, Fred L., ed. *Ethics in Intercultural and International Communication*. Mahwah, NJ: Lawrence Erlbaum, 1997.

Chesebro, James. "A Construct for Assessing Ethics in Communication." *Central States Speech Journal* 20 (1969): 104-114.

Christians, Clifford. "Fifty Years of Scholarship in Media Ethics." *Journal of Communication* 27 (1977): 19-29.

———. "Review Essay: Current Trends in Media Ethics." *European Journal of Communication* 10 (1995): 545-558.

Christians, Clifford G., and Edmund B Lambeth. "The State-of-the-Art in Teaching Communication Ethics." *Communication Education* 45 (1996): 236-243.

Christians, Clifford G., and Michael M. Traber, eds. *Communication Ethics and Universal Values*. Thousand Oaks, CA: Sage 1997.

Condit, Celeste Michelle. "Crafting Virtue: The Rhetorical Construction of Public Morality." *Quarterly Journal of Speech* 73 (1987): 79-98.

Cornford, Francis Macdonald. *Before and After Socrates*. London, UK: Cambridge UP, 1966.

Dallmayr, Fred. Introduction. *The Communicative Ethics Controversy*. Ed. Seyla Benhabib and Fred Dallmayr. Cambridge, MA: MIT P, 1990. 1-20.

Deetz, Stanley. "Reclaiming the Subject Matter as a Guide to Mutual Understanding: Effectiveness and Ethics in Interpersonal Interaction." *Communication Quarterly* 38 (1990): 226-243.

Denton, Robert E., Jr., ed. *Ethical Dimensions of Political Communication*. New York: Praeger, 1991.

———. *Political Communication Ethics: An Oxymoron?* Westport, CT: Praeger, 2000.

Derrida, Jacques. *Adieu to Emmanuel Levinas*. Trans. Pascale-Anne Brault and Michael Nass. Ed. Werner Hamacher and David E. Wellbery. Stanford, CA: Stanford UP, 1999.

———. *Of Grammatology*. Trans. Gayatri Chakravorty Spivak. Baltimore, MD: Johns Hopkins UP, 1982.

DiTomaso, Nancy, Rochelle Parks-Yancy, and Corinne Post. "Structure, Relationships, and Community Responsibility." *Management Communication Quarterly* 17 (2003): 143-150.

Dowling, Ralf E., and Gabrielle Marraro. "Grenada and the Great Communicator: A Study in Democratic Ethics." *Western Journal of Speech Communication* 50 (1986): 350-367.

Duncan, Ronald, ed. *Gandhi: Selected Writings*. New York: Harper and Row, 1972.

Englehardt, Elaine E., ed. *Ethical Issues in Interpersonal Communication: Friends, Intimates, Sexuality, Marriage and Family*. Fort Worth: Harcourt College, 2000.

Engnell, Richard A. "Toward an Ethic of Evocative Language: Contemporary Uses of Holocaust-related Terminology." *The Southern Communication Journal* 66 (2001): 312-322.

Fenske, Mindyl. "The Aesthetic of the Unfinished: Ethics and Performance. *Text and Performance Quarterly* 24 (2004): 1-19.

Ferré, John P. "Communication Ethics and the Political Realism of Reinhold Niebuhr." *Communication Quarterly* 38 (1990): 218-225.

Fischer, Norman. "Frankfurt School Marxism and the Ethical Meaning of Art: Herbert Marcuse's *The Aesthetic Dimension*." *Communication Theory* 7 (1997): 362-381.

Fisher, Walter R. *Human Communication as Narration: Toward a Philosophy of Reason, Value, and Action*. Columbia: U of South Carolina P, 1987.

Fletcher, Joseph. *Situational Ethics: The New Morality*. Philadelphia: Westminster Press, 1966.

Ford, Wendy S. Zabava. "Ethics in Customer Service: Critical Review and Research Agenda." *Electronic Journal of Communication* 6.4 (1996). Retrieved March 14, 2005, from http://www.cios.org/getfile/Ford_V6N496.

Friedman, Maurice. *Touchstones of Reality: Existential Trust and the Community of Peace*. New York: E. P. Dutton, 1972.

Fulkerson, Gerald "The Ethics of Interpersonal Influence: A Critique of the Rhetorical Sensitivity Construct." *Journal of Communication and Religion* 13 (1990): 1-14.

Garver, Eugene. "Essentially Contested Concepts: The Ethics and Tactics of Argument." *Philosophy and Rhetoric* 23 (1990): 251-270.

———. "The Ethical Criticism of Reasoning." *Philosophy and Rhetoric* 31 (1998): 107-130.

Garvey, Gregory T. "The Value of Opacity: A Bakhtinian Analysis of Habermas's Discourse Ethics." *Philosophy and Rhetoric* 33 (2000): 370-390.

Gerbner, George. Foreword. *Communication Ethics and Global Change*. Eds. Thomas W. Cooper, Clifford G. Christians, Frances Forde Plude and Robert A. White. White Plains, NY: Longman, 1989. xi-xii.

Granville, King, III, and Amy Hermodson. "Peer Reporting of Coworker Wrongdoing: A Qualitative Analysis of Observer Attitudes in the Decision to Report versus Not Report Unethical Behavior." *Journal of Applied Communication Research* 28 (2000): 309-330.

Griswold, Charles L., Jr. "Rhetoric and Ethics: Adam Smith on Theorizing about the Moral Sentiments." *Philosophy and Rhetoric* 24 (1991): 213-237.

Gunson, Darryl, and Chik Collins. "From the 'I' to the 'We': Discourse, Ethics, Identity and the Pragmatics of Partnership in the West of Scotland." *Communication Theory* 7 (1997): 277-300.

Haas, Tanni. "Toward an Ethic of Futurity." *Management Communication Quarterly* 16 (2003): 612-618.

Habermas, Jürgen. *The Structural Transformation of the Public Sphere: An Inquiry into a Category of Bourgeois Society.* Trans. Thomas Burger. Boston, MA: MIT P, 1991.

Hallstein, D. Lynn O'Brien. "A Postmodern Caring: Feminist Standpoint Theories, Revisioned Caring, and Communication Ethics." *Western Journal of Communication* 63 (1999): 32-56.

Harding, Sandra G. *Whose Science? Whose Knowledge?: Thinking from Women's Lives.* Ithaca, NY: Cornell UP, 1991.

Herrick, James A. "Rhetoric, Ethics, and Virtue." *Communication Studies* 43 (1992): 133-149.

Hyde, Michael. *The Call of Conscience: Heidegger and Levinas, Rhetoric and the Euthanasia Debate.* Columbia: U of South Carolina P, 2001.

———. *The Life-Giving Gift of Acknowledgement: A Philosophical and Rhetorical Inquiry.* West Lafayette, IN: Purdue UP, 2006.

Hyde, Michael J., and Kevin D. Sargent. "The Performance of Play, the 'Great Poem,' and Ethics." *Text and Performance Quarterly* 13 (1993): 122-138.

Jaffe, Cella I. "Ethics in the Family: A Ninth Century Mother Trains her Sons." *Electronic Journal of Communication* 7.1 (1997). Retrieved March 14, 2005, from http://www.cios.org/getfile/Jaffe_V7N197.

Jaksa, James A., and Michael S. Pritchard. *Communication Ethics: Methods of Analysis.* 2nd ed. Belmont, CA: Wadsworth, 1994.

———, eds. *Responsible Communication: Ethical Issues in Business, Industry, and the Professions.* Cresskill, NJ: Hampton, 1996.

Jaques, Elliot. "Ethics for Management." *Management Communication Quarterly* 17 (2003): 36-142.

Jensen, J. Vernon. "An Analysis of Recent Literature on Teaching Ethics in Public Address." *Speech Teacher* 8 (1959): 219-228.

———. *Ethical Issues in the Communication Process.* Mahwah, NJ: Lawrence Erlbaum, 1997.

———. Foreword. *Conversations on Communication Ethics.* Ed. Karen Joy Greenberg. Norwood, NJ: Ablex, 1991. x-xii.

———. "Teaching Ethics in Speech Communication." *Communication Education* 34 (1985): 324-331.

Johannesen, Richard L. "Communication Ethics: Centrality, Trends, and Controversies." *Communication Yearbook 25.* Ed. William B. Gudykunst. Mahwah, NJ: Lawrence Erlbaum, 2001. 201-235.

———. *Ethics in Human Communication.* 5th Ed. Prospect Heights, IL: Waveland, 2002.

———. "The Ethics of Plagiarism Reconsidered: The Oratory of Martin Luther King, Jr." *Southern Communication Journal* 60 (1995): 185-194.

———. "Nel Noddings's Uses of Martin Buber's Philosophy of Dialogue. *Southern Communication Journal* 65 (2000): 151-160.

Johnstone, Christopher L. "Ethics, Wisdom, and the Mission of Contemporary Rhetoric: The Realization of Human Being" *Central States Speech Journal* 32 (1981): 177-188.

———. "Reagan, Rhetoric, and the Public Philosophy: Ethics and Politics in the 1984 Campaign." *Southern Communication Journal* 60 (1995): 93-108.

Jovanovic, Spoma. "Difficult Conversations as Moral Imperative: Negotiating Ethnic Identities During War." *Communication Quarterly* 51 (2003): 57-72.

Kant, Immanuel. *Grounding for the Metaphysics of Morals.* Trans. James W. Ellington. 3rd ed. Indianapolis, IN: Hackett, 1993.

Kernisky, Debra A. "Point: All the Information Fit to Be Reported—Negotiating American Symbolic Reality." *Electronic Journal of Communication* 7.1 (1997). Retrieved March 14, 2005, from http://www.cios.org/getfile/Dkernisk_V7N197.

Kernisky, Ivan F. "Counterpoint: All the Information Fit to Be Reported—Fabricating American Symbolic Reality" *Electronic Journal of Communication* 7.1 (1997). Retrieved March 14, 2005, from http://www.cios.org/getfile/Ikernisk_V7N197.

Kierkegaard, Søren. *Fear and Trembling.* Trans. Alastair Hannay. New York: Penguin, 1985.

Kirkwood, William G., and Steven M. Ralston. "Ethics and Teaching Employment Interviewing." *Communication Education* 45 (1996): 167-179.

Lepper, Tammy Swenson. "Ethical Sensitivity, Cognitive Mapping, and Organization Communication: A Different Approach to Studying Ethics in Organizations." *Electronic Journal of Communication* 6.4 (1996). Retrieved March 14, 2005, from http://www.cios.org/getfile/Lepper_V6N496.

Levinas, Emmanuel. *Emmanuel Levinas: Basic Philosophical Writings.* Eds., Adriaan T. Peperzak, Simon Critchley, and Robert Bernasconi. Bloomington: Indiana UP, 1996.

Lipari, Lisabeth. "Listening for the Other: Ethical Implications of the Buber-Levinas Encounter." *Communication Theory* 14 (2004): 122-141.

Lyotard, Jean-François. *The Postmodern Condition: A Report on Knowledge.* Trans. Geoff Bennington. Minneapolis: U of Minnesota P, 1984.

MacIntyre, Alasdair. *After Virtue: A Study in Moral Theory.* 2nd ed. Notre Dame, IN: U of Notre Dame P, 1984.

———. *Three Rival Versions of Moral Enquiry: Encylopaedia, Genealogy and Tradition.* Notre Dame, IN: U of Notre Dame P, 1990.

Makau, Josina M. Preface. *Moral Engagement in Public Life: Theorists for Contemporary Ethics*. Eds., Sharon Bracci and Clifford G. Christians. New York: Peter Lang, 2002. vii-x.

Makau, Josina M., and Ronald C. Arnett, eds. *Communication Ethics in an Age of Diversity*. Chicago: U of Illinois P, 1997.

Marin, Mary J., John C Sherblom, and Therese B. Shipps. "Contextual Influences on Nurses' Conflict Management Strategies." *Western Journal of Communication* 58 (1994): 201-228.

Mattson, Marifran, and Patricia M. Buzzanell. "Traditional and Feminist Organizational Communication Ethical Analyses of Messages and Issues." *Journal of Applied Communication Research* 27 (1999): 49-72.

Mattson, Marifran, and Christina W. Stage. "Toward an Understanding of Intercultural Ethical Dilemmas as Opportunities for Engagement in New Millennium Global Organizations." *Management Communication Quarterly* 15 (2001): 103-110.

McCaleb, Joseph L., and Kevin W. Dean. "Ethics and Communication Education: Empowering Teachers." *Communication Education* 36 (1987): 410-416.

McEuen, Viva S., Ronald D. Gordon, and William R. Todd-Mancillas. "A Survey of Doctoral Education in Communication Research Ethics." *Communication Quarterly* 38 (1990): 281-290.

McGuire, John, Cherise Stauble, David Abbott, and Rand Fisher. "Ethical Issues in the Treatment of Communication Apprehension: A Survey of Communication Professionals." *Communication Education* 44 (1995): 98-110.

Medhurst, Martin J. "Ghostwritten Speeches: Ethics Isn't the Only Lesson." *Communication Education* 36 (1987): 241-249.

Muir, Star A. "A Defense of the Ethics of Contemporary Debate." *Philosophy and Rhetoric* 26 (1993): 277-295.

Murray, Jeffrey W. "Bakhtinian Answerability and Levinasian Responsibility: Forging a Fuller Dialogical Communicative Ethics." *Southern Communication Journal* 65 (2000): 133-150.

———. "The Face in Dialogue: Emmanuel Levinas and Rhetorics of Disruption and Supplication." *Southern Communication Journal* 68 (2003): 250-266.

———. *Face to Face in Dialogue: Emmanuel Levinas and (the) Communication (of) Ethics*. Washington, DC: U of America P, 2003.

———. "An Other Ethic for Kenneth Burke." *Communication Studies* 49 (1998): 29-48.

———. "An Other-Burkean Frame: Rhetorical Criticism and the Call of the Other." *Communication Studies* 54 (2003): 169-187.

———. "The Paradox of Emmanuel Levinas: Knowledge of the Absolute Other." *Communication Quarterly* 49 (2001): 39-46.

Nichols, Marie H. "When you set out for Ithaka ..." *Central States Speech Journal* 28 (1977): 145-156.

Nkomo, Stella M. "Teaching Business Ethically in the 'New' South Africa." *Management Communication Quarterly* 17 (2003): 128-135.

Pinchevski, Amit. "Ethics on the Line." *Southern Communication Journal* 68 (2003): 152-166.

Pym, Anne. "Beyond Postmodernity: Grounding Ethics in Spirit." *Electronic Journal of Communication* 7.1 (1997). Retrieved March 14, 2005, from http://www.cios.org/getfile/Pym_V7N197.

Reich, Warren Thomas. "Experiential Ethics as a Foundation for Dialogue Between Health Communication and Health-Care Ethics." *Journal of Applied Communication Research* 16 (1988): 16-28.

Reinsch, Lamar N., Jr. "Management Communication Ethics Research: Finding the Bull's-eye." *Management Communication Quarterly* 9 (1996): 349-358.

Rimal, R. N., B. J. Fogg, and J. A. Flora. "Moving Toward a Framework for the Study of Risk Communication: Theoretical and Ethical Considerations." *Communication Yearbook 18*. Ed. B. R. Burleson. Thousand Oaks, CA: Sage, 1995. 320-342.

Rorty, Richard. *Philosophy and the Mirror of Nature*. Princeton, NJ: Princeton UP, 1979.

Schrag, Calvin O. *Communicative Praxis and the Space of Subjectivity*. Bloomington: Indiana UP, 1986.

Schwarze, Steve. "Corporate-state Irresponsibility, Critical Publicity, and Asbestos Exposure in Libby, Montana." *Management Communication Quarterly* 16 (2003): 625-633.

Seeger, Matthew W. *Ethics in Organizational Communication*. Cresskill, NJ: Hampton, 1997.

Seeger, Matthew W., and Robert R. Ulmer. "Explaining Enron: Communication and Responsible Leadership." *Management Communication Quarterly* 17 (2003): 58-84.

Sillars, Malcolm O. "Audiences, Social Values, and the Analysis of Argument." *Speech Teacher* 22 (1973): 291-303.

Sproule, J. Michael. "Whose Ethics in the Classroom? An Historical Overview." *Communication Education* 36 (1987): 317-326.

Stablein, Ralf. "Teaching Business Ethics or Teaching Business Ethically?" *Management Communication Quarterly* 17 (2003): 151-154.

Steiner, Linda. "Feminist Theorizing and Communication Ethics." *Communication* 12 (1991): 157-173.

Stewart, John, and Karen Zediker. "Dialogue as Tensional, Ethical Practice." *Southern Communication Journal* 65 (2000): 224-242.

Struever, Nancy S. "The Rhetoric of Familiarity: A Pedagogy of Ethics." *Philosophy and Rhetoric* 31 (1998): 91-106.

Tocqueville, Alexis de. *Democracy in America*. 1835. Trans. George Lawrence. Ed. J. P. Mayer. Garden City, NJ: Anchor Books, 1969.

Tompkins, Paula. "Exploring the Tension Between the First Amendment and Ethics in the Case of 'Outing'." *Electronic Journal of Communication* 7.1 (1997). Retrieved March 14, 2005, from http://www.cios.org/getfile/Tompkins_V7N197.

Tompkins Pribble, Paula. "Making an Ethical Commitment: A Rhetorical Case Study of Organizational Socialization." *Communication Quarterly* 38 (1990): 255-267.

Ulmer, Robert R., and Timothy L. Sellnow. "Strategic Ambiguity and the Ethic of Significant Choice in Tobacco Industry's Crisis Communication." *Communication Studies* 48 (1997): 215-233.

Vico, Giambattista. *On Human Education: Six Inaugural Orations, 1699-1707*. Trans. Giorgio A. Pinton and Arthur W. Shippee. Ithaca, NY: Cornell UP, 1987.

Wallace, Karl R. "An Ethical Basis of Communication." *Speech Teacher* 4 (1955): 1-9.

Whaley, Bryan B., Anne Maydan Nicotera, and Wendy Samter. "African American Women's Perception of Rebuttal Analogy: Judgments Concerning Politeness, Likeability, and Ethics." *Southern Communication Journal* 64 (1998): 48-58.

Winegarden, Alan D., and Marilyn Fuss-Reineck. "Using 'Star Trek: The Next Generation' to Teach Concepts in Persuasion, Family Communication, and Communication Ethics." *Communication Education* 42 (1993): 179-188.

Wood, Julia T. "Ethics, Justice, and the 'Private Sphere'." *Women's Studies in Communication* 21 (1998): 127-149.

Wood, Julia T. Foreword. *Dialogic Civility in a Cynical Age: Community, Hope, and Interpersonal Relationships*. By Ronald C. Arnett and Pat Arneson. Albany: State U of New York P, 1999. xi-xv.

Bibliography of Communication Ethics Scholarship in Communication Journals (1985-2004)

Democratic Communication Ethics

Arnett, Ronald C. "The Practical Philosophy of Communication Ethics and Free Speech as the Foundation for Speech Communication." *Communication Quarterly* 38 (1990): 208-217.

Batt, Shawn. "Keeping Company in Controversy: Education Reform, Spheres of Argument, and Ethical Criticism." *Argumentation and Advocacy* 40 (2003): 85-104.

Dowling, Ralf E., and Gabrielle Marraro. "Grenada and the Great Communicator: A Study in Democratic Ethics." *Western Journal of Speech Communication* 50 (1986): 350-367.

Garver, Eugene. "Essentially Contested Concepts: The Ethics and Tactics of Argument." *Philosophy and Rhetoric* 23 (1990): 251-270.

———. "The Ethical Criticism of Reasoning." *Philosophy and Rhetoric* 31 (1998): 107-130.

Haas, Tanni. "Toward an Ethic of Futurity." *Management Communication Quarterly* 16 (2003): 612-618.

Johnstone, Christopher L. "Reagan, Rhetoric, and the Public Philosophy: Ethics and Politics in the 1984 Campaign." *Southern Communication Journal* 60 (1995): 93-108.

Muir, Star A. "A Defense of the Ethics of Contemporary Debate." *Philosophy and Rhetoric* 26 (1993): 277-295.

Schwarze, Steve. "Corporate-state Irresponsibility, Critical Publicity, and Asbestos Exposure in Libby, Montana." *Management Communication Quarterly* 16 (2003): 625-633.

Tompkins, Paula. "Exploring the Tension Between the First Amendment and Ethics in the Case of 'Outing'." *Electronic Journal of Communication* 7.1 (1997). Retrieved March 14, 2005, from http://www.cios.org/getfile/Tompkins_V7N197.

Ulmer, Robert R., and Timothy L. Sellnow. "Strategic Ambiguity and the Ethic of Significant Choice in Tobacco Industry's Crisis Communication." *Communication Studies* 48 (1997): 215-233.

Universal-Humanitarian Communication Ethics

Arnett, Ronald C. "The Responsive 'I': Levinas's Derivative Argument." *Argumentation and Advocacy* 40 (2003): 39-50.

Condit, Celeste Michelle. "Crafting Virtue: The Rhetorical Construction of Public Morality." *Quarterly Journal of Speech* 73 (1987): 79-98.

DiTomaso, Nancy, Rochelle Parks-Yancy, and Corinne Post. "Structure, Relationships, and Community Responsibility." *Management Communication Quarterly* 17 (2003): 143-150.

Ferré, John P. "Communication Ethics and the Political Realism of Reinhold Niebuhr." *Communication Quarterly* 38 (1990): 218-225.

Fischer, Norman. "Frankfurt School Marxism and the Ethical Meaning of Art: Herbert Marcuse's *The Aesthetic Dimension*." *Communication Theory* 7 (1997): 362-381.

Ford, Wendy S. Zabava. "Ethics in Customer Service: Critical Review and Research Agenda." *Electronic Journal of Communication* 6.4 (1996). Retrieved March 14, 2005, from http://www.cios.org/getfile/Ford_V6N496.

Griswold, Charles L., Jr. "Rhetoric and Ethics: Adam Smith on Theorizing about the Moral Sentiments." *Philosophy and Rhetoric* 24 (1991): 213-237.

Gunson, Darryl, and Chik Collins. "From the 'I' to the 'We': Discourse, Ethics, Identity and the Pragmatics of Partnership in the West of Scotland." *Communication Theory* 7 (1997): 277-300.

Herrick, James A. "Rhetoric, Ethics, and Virtue." *Communication Studies* 43 (1992): 133-149.

McCaleb, Joseph L., and Kevin W. Dean. "Ethics and Communication Education: Empowering Teachers." *Communication Education* 36 (1987): 410-416.

Pym, Anne. "Beyond Postmodernity: Grounding Ethics in Spirit." *Electronic Journal of Communication* 7.1 (1997). Retrieved March 14, 2005, from http://www.cios.org/getfile/Pym_V7N197.

Seeger, Matthew W., and Robert R. Ulmer. "Explaining Enron: Communication and Responsible Leadership." *Management Communication Quarterly* 17 (2003): 58-84.

Codes, Procedures, and Standards in Communication Ethics

Anderson, James A. "Forum Response: Ethics in Business and Teaching." *Management Communication Quarterly* 17 (2003): 155-164.

Bloom, Melanie M. "Sex Differences in Ethical Systems: A Useful Framework for Interpreting Communication Research." *Communication Quarterly* 38 (1990): 244-254.

Boynton, Lois A. "Professionalism and Social Responsibility: Foundations of Public Relations Ethics." *Communication Yearbook 26*. Ed. William B. Gudykunst. Mahwah, NJ: Lawrence Erlbaum, 2002. 230-265.

Jaques, Elliot. "Ethics for Management." *Management Communication Quarterly* 17 (2003): 136-142.

Kirkwood, William G., and Steven M. Ralston. "Ethics and Teaching Employment Interviewing." *Communication Education* 45 (1996): 167-179.

Tompkins Pribble, Paula. "Making an Ethical Commitment: A Rhetorical Case Study of Organizational Socialization." *Communication Quarterly* 38 (1990): 255-267.

Contextual Communication Ethics

Arnett, Ronald C., and Pat Arneson. "Interpersonal Communication Ethics and the Limits of Individualism." *Electronic Journal of Communication* 6.4 (1996). Retrieved March 14, 2005, from http://www.cios.org/getfile/Arnett_V6N496.

Booth-Butterfield, Steve, and Rocco R. Cottone. "Ethical Issues in the Treatment of Communication Apprehension and Avoidance." *Communication Education* 40 (1991): 172-179.

Cameron, Kenzie A., Shelly Campo, and Dominique Brossard. "Advocating for Controversial Issues: The Effect of Activism on Compliance-Gaining Strategy Likelihood of Use." *Communication Studies* 54 (2003): 265-281.

Granville, King, III, and Amy Hermodson. "Peer Reporting of Coworker Wrongdoing: A Qualitative Analysis of Observer Attitudes in the Decision to Report versus Not Report Unethical Behavior." *Journal of Applied Communication Research* 28 (2000): 309-330.

Hallstein, D. Lynn O'Brien. "A Postmodern Caring: Feminist Standpoint Theories, Revisioned Caring, and Communication Ethics." *Western Journal of Communication* 63 (1999) 32-56.

Jaffe, Cella I. "Ethics in the Family: A Ninth Century Mother Trains Her Sons." *Electronic Journal of Communication* 7.1 (1997). Retrieved March 14, 2005, from http://www.cios.org/getfile/Jaffe_V7N197.

Johannesen, Richard L. "The Ethics of Plagiarism Reconsidered: The Oratory of Martin Luther King, Jr." *Southern Communication Journal* 60 (1995): 185-194.

Lepper, Tammy Swenson. "Ethical Sensitivity, Cognitive Mapping, and Organization Communication: A Different Approach to Studying Ethics in Organizations." *Electronic Journal of Communication* 6.4 (1996). Retrieved March 14, 2005, from http://www.cios.org/getfile/Lepper_V6N496.

Marin, Mary J., John C. Sherblom, and Therese B. Shipps. "Contextual Influences on Nurses' Conflict Management Strategies." *Western Journal of Communication* 58 (1994): 201-228.

McGuire, John., Cherise Stauble, David Abbott, and Rand Fisher. (1995). "Ethical Issues in the Treatment of Communication Apprehension: A Survey of Communication Professionals." *Communication Education* 44 (1995): 98-110.

Medhurst, Martin. J. "Ghostwritten Speeches: Ethics Isn't the Only Lesson." *Communication Education* 36 (1987): 241-249.

Nkomo, Stella M. "Teaching Business Ethically in the 'New' South Africa." *Management Communication Quarterly* 17 (2003): 128-135.

Reinsch, Lamar N., Jr. "Management Communication Ethics Research: Finding the Bull's-eye." *Management Communication Quarterly* 9 (1996): 349-358.

Stablein, Ralf. "Teaching Business Ethics or Teaching Business Ethically?" *Management Communication Quarterly* 17 (2003): 151-154.

Steiner, Linda. "Feminist Theorizing and Communication Ethics." *Communication* 12 (1991): 157-173.

Winegarden, Alan D., and Marilyn Fuss-Reineck. "Using 'Star Trek: The Next Generation' to Teach Concepts in Persuasion, Family Communication, and Communication Ethics." *Communication Education* 42 (1993): 179-188.

Wood, Julia T. "Ethics, Justice, and the 'Private Sphere'." *Women's Studies in Communication* 21 (1998): 127-149.

Narrative Communication Ethics

Hyde, Michael J., and Kevin D. Sargent. "The Performance of Play, the 'Great Poem,' and Ethics." *Text and Performance Quarterly* 13 (1993): 122-138.

Mattson, Marifran, and Patricia M. Buzzanell. "Traditional and Feminist Organizational Communication Ethical Analyses of Messages and Issues." *Journal of Applied Communication Research* 27 (1999): 49-72.

Struever, Nancy S. "The Rhetoric of Familiarity: A Pedagogy of Ethics." *Philosophy and Rhetoric* 31 (1998): 91-106.

Whaley, Bryan B., Anne Maydan Nicotera, and Wendy Samter "African American Women's Perception of Rebuttal Analogy: Judgments Concerning Politeness, Likeability, and Ethics." *Southern Communication Journal* 64 (1998): 48-58.

Dialogic Communication Ethics

Arnett, Ronald C. "Dialogic Civility as Pragmatic Ethical Praxis: An Interpersonal Metaphor for the Public Domain." *Communication Theory* 11 (2001): 315-338.

Deetz, Stanley. "Reclaiming the Subject Matter as a Guide to Mutual Understanding: Effectiveness and Ethics in Interpersonal Interaction." *Communication Quarterly* 38 (1990): 226-243.

Engnell, Richard A. "Toward an Ethic of Evocative Language: Contemporary Uses of Holocaust-related Terminology." *Southern Communication Journal* 66 (2001): 312-322.

Fenske, Mindyl. "The Aesthetic of the Unfinished: Ethics and Performance. *Text and Performance Quarterly* 24 (2004): 1-19.

Fulkerson, Gerald. "The Ethics of Interpersonal Influence: A Critique of the Rhetorical Sensitivity Construct." *Journal of Communication and Religion* 13 (1990): 1-14.

Garvey, Gregory T. "The Value of Opacity: A Bakhtinian Analysis of Habermas's Discourse Ethics." *Philosophy and Rhetoric* 33 (2000): 370-390.

Johannesen, Richard L. "Nel Noddings's Uses of Martin Buber's Philosophy of Dialogue." *Southern Communication Journal* 65 (2000): 151-160.

Jovanovic, Spoma. "Difficult Conversations as Moral Imperative: Negotiating Ethnic Identities During War." *Communication Quarterly* 51 (2003): 57-72.

Lipari, Lisabeth. "Listening for the Other: Ethical Implications of the Buber-Levinas Encounter." *Communication Theory* 14 (2004): 122-141.

Mattson, Marifran, and Christina W. Stage. "Toward an Understanding of Intercultural Ethical Dilemmas as Opportunities for Engagement in New Millennium Global Organizations." *Management Communication Quarterly* 15 (2001): 103-110.

Murray, Jeffrey W. "Bakhtinian Answerability and Levinasian Responsibility: Forging a Fuller Dialogical Communicative Ethics." *Southern Communication Journal* 65 (2000): 133-150.

———. "The Face in Dialogue: Emmanuel Levinas and Rhetorics of Disruption and Supplication." *Southern Communication Journal* 68 (2003): 250-266.

———. "An Other Ethic for Kenneth Burke." *Communication Studies* 49 (1998): 29-48.

———. "An Other-Burkean Frame: Rhetorical Criticism and the Call of the Other." *Communication Studies* 54 (2003): 169-187.

———. "The Paradox of Emmanuel Levinas: Knowledge of the Absolute Other." *Communication Quarterly* 49 (2001): 39-46.

Pinchevski, Amit. "Ethics on the Line." *Southern Communication Journal* 68 (2003): 152-166.

Reich, Warren Thomas. "Experiential Ethics as a Foundation for Dialogue Between Health Communication and Health-Care Ethics." *Journal of Applied Communication Research* 16 (1988): 16-28.

Stewart, John, and Karen Zediker. "Dialogue as Tensional, Ethical Practice." *Southern Communication Journal* 65 (2000): 224-242.

History of Communication Ethics

Arnett, Ronald C. "The Status of Communication Ethics Scholarship in Speech Communication Journals from 1915-1985." *Central States Speech Journal* 38 (1987): 44-61.

Chesebro, James. "A Construct for Assessing Ethics in Communication." *Central States Speech Journal* 20 (1969): 104-114.

Christians, Clifford G., and Edmund B. Lambeth. "The State-of-the-Art in Teaching Communication Ethics." *Communication Education* 45 (1996): 236-243.

Jensen, J. Vernon. "An Analysis of Recent Literature on Teaching Ethics in Public Address." *Speech Teacher* 8 (1959): 219-228.

———. "Teaching Ethics in Speech Communication." *Communication Education* 34 (1985): 324-331.

Johannesen, Richard L. "Communication Ethics: Centrality, Trends, and Controversies." *Communication Yearbook 25*. Ed. William B. Gudykunst. Mahwah, NJ: Lawrence Erlbaum, 2001. 201-235.

McEuen, Viva S., Ronald D. Gordon, and William R. Todd-Mancillas. "A Survey of Doctoral Education in Communication Research Ethics." *Communication Quarterly* 38 (1990): 281-290.

Sproule, J. Michael. "Whose Ethics in the Classroom? An Historical Overview." *Communication Education* 36 (1987): 317-326.

Contributors

Kenneth E. Andersen (Ph.D., University of Wisconsin, 1961) is Professor Emeritus in the Department of Speech Communication at the University of Illinois Urbana-Champaign. Dr. Andersen's teaching and research center on ethics of communication; persuasion theory; ethos and source credibility; and philosophy of communication. His service to the profession includes serving as President of the National Communication Association, the Central States Communication Association, and the Association of Communication Administrators. He is author of *Persuasion: Theory and Practice* (Allyn and Bacon, 1978), *Introduction to Communication Theory and Practice* (Cummings, 1972), *Speech Communication: Analysis and Readings* with Howard H. Martin (Allyn and Bacon, 1968). He served as editor to two journals, and has published articles in scholarly journals including *Speech Monographs*, *Journal of the American Forensics Association* and *Central States Speech Journal* among other publications.

Pat Arneson (Ph.D., Ohio University, 1987) is Associate Professor in the Department of Communication & Rhetorical Studies at Duquesne University. Dr. Arneson's work examines issues of human communication from philosophical perspectives. Her research interests include rhetoric, philosophy of communication, interpretive approaches to research, interpersonal communication ethics, and educational assessment. She has published over 25 book chapters, journal articles, or research reports and is co-author with Ronald C. Arnett of *Dialogic Civility in a Cynical Age: Communication, Hope, and Interpersonal Relationships* (State University of New York Press, 1999). She is editor of *Perspectives on Philosophy of Communication* (Purdue University Press, in press). Her work appears in *Integrative Explorations: Journal of Culture and Consciousness*, *Women's Studies in Communication*, *Communication Studies*, *The Review of Communication*, *The Electronic Journal of Communication/La Revue Electronique de Communication*, and *Journal of the Association for Communication Administration* among other publications.

Ronald C. Arnett (Ph.D., Ohio University, 1978) is Professor and Chair in the Department of Communication & Rhetorical Studies at Duquesne University. Additionally, he was the Chair at Marquette University and Vice-President at Manchester College. Dr. Arnett's research and teaching interests include managerial communication, communication ethics, philosophy of communication, interpretive research, religion and communication, and dialogic theory. His work examines the presuppositions and the implications of philosophy of communication authors such as Martin Buber, Emmanuel Levinas, Hans Gadamer and Paul Ricoeur in applied communication contexts. He is the author of four books: *Dialogic Confession: Bonhoeffer's Rhetoric of Responsibility for a World Come of Age* (Southern Illinois University Press, 2005), *Dialogic Education: Conversation About Ideas and Between Persons* (Southern Illinois University Press, 1992), *Communication and Community: Implications of Martin Buber's Dialogue* (Southern Illinois University Press, 1986) and *Dwell in Peace: Applying Nonviolence to Everyday Relationships* (Brethren Press, 1980). He is co-author with Pat Arneson of *Dialogic Civility in a Cynical Age: Community, Hope, and Interpersonal Relationships* (State University of New York Press, 1999). He is co-editor with Josina M. Makau of *Communication Ethics in an Age of Diversity* (University of Illinois Press, 1996) and co-editor with Rob Anderson and Kenneth N. Cissna of *The Reach of Dialogue: Confirmation, Voice, and Community* (Hampton Press, 1994). He is the author of more than 50 articles appearing in scholarly journals including *Western Journal of Speech Communication*, *Religious Communication Today*, *Journal of Communication and Religion*, *Central States Speech Journal*, *Communication Quarterly*, *The Review of Communication*, and *Communication Education* among other publications.

Leeanne M. Bell (M.A., University of West Virginia, 2003) is a Ph.D. student in the Department of Communication & Rhetorical Studies at Duquesne University. Ms. Bell's work examines communication ethics and communication education. She has presented scholarship at professional conferences and her work appears in *The Review of Communication* and *Journal of the Pennsylvania Communication Association*.

Sharon L. Bracci (Ph.D., Ohio State University, 1994) is Associate Professor in the Department of Communication at University of North Carolina-Greensboro. Dr. Bracci's teaching and research focus on interdisciplinary connections among communication ethics, public argument, and practical moral reasoning in contemporary social, media, and health care contexts. She is co-editor, with Clifford G. Christians, of *Moral Engagement in Public Life: Theorists for Contemporary Ethics* (Peter Lang, 2002). She has published numerous book chapters and articles in scholarly journals including *Qualitative Inquiry, Argumentation and Advocacy,* and *Journal of Applied Communication Research* among other publications.

Clifford G. Christians (Ph.D., University of Illinois, 1974) is Professor in the College of Communications at University of Illinois. Clifford Christians's work integrates the humanities into communications scholarship, linking communication issues with ethical theory. His aim is to construct a normative discourse for applied ethics generally. His work on dialogic communication is characterized by a symbolic approach to issues in terms of a theory of culture. He has co-authored *Responsibility in Mass Communications* with William L. Rivers and Wilbur Schramm; *Media Ethics: Cases and Moral Reasoning* with Mark Fackler, Kim Rotzoll, and Kathy McGee (2004/7th ed.), and *Good News: A Social Ethics of the Press* with John Ferré and Mark Fackler. He has co-edited *Jacques Ellul: Interpretive Essays* with Jay M. Van Hook; *Communication Ethics and Universal Values* with Michael Traber, and *Moral Engagement in Public Life: Theorists for Contemporary Ethics* with Sharon Bracci. He has published numerous book chapters and articles in scholarly journals including *Journalism Monographs, Journal of Broadcasting, Journalism History, Ethical Perspectives: Journal of the European Ethics Network, Ethical Space: The International Journal of Communication Ethics, Journal of Communication, Journal of Mass Media Ethics, Media Development, Communication, Qualitative Inquiry, European Journal of Communication* and the *International Journal of Mass Communication Research* among other publications.

Michael J. Hyde (Ph.D., Purdue University, 1977) is The University Distinguished Professor of Communication Ethics in the Department of Communication at Wake Forest University and a Fellow of the W. K. Kellogg Foundation. Dr. Hyde's research and teaching interests consider the study of public moral argument, the ethics of rhetoric, computer-mediated communication, and the ethics and rhetoric of medicine. He has published five books, including *The Call of Conscience: Heidegger and Levinas, Rhetoric and the Euthanasia Debate* (University of South Carolina Press, 2001), which received the 2001 National Communication Association Diamond Anniversary Book Award and the 2001 Marie Hochmuth Nichols Award for Outstanding Scholarship in Public Address. Hyde's most recent book is *The Life-Giving Gift of Acknowledgment (A Philosophical and Rhetorical Inquiry)* (Purdue University Press, 2006). He has received national, state, and university research grants for his work in the rhetoric of medicine. He has written more than 50 articles and critical reviews in scholarly texts and journals including *Quarterly Journal of Speech, Philosophy and Rhetoric, Journal of Applied Communication Research, Rhetoric and Public Affairs, Journal of Medical Humanities*, and *Text and Performance Quarterly*.

Richard L. Johannesen (Ph.D., University of Kansas, 1964) is Professor Emeritus in the Department of Communication at Northern Illinois University. Dr. Johannesen's research and teaching centers around Contemporary Rhetorical Theory & Criticism, Communication Ethics, Richard M. Weaver's philosophy of rhetoric, Martin Buber's philosophy of dialogue, and the jeremiad as a rhetorical genre. He has authored and edited several books including *Ethics in Human Communication* (Waveland Press, 2002/5th ed.), *Contemporary American Speeches* (Kendall/Hunt, 2000/9th ed.), *Language Is Sermonic: Richard M. Weaver on the Nature of Rhetoric* (Louisiana State University Press, 1970), and *Ethics and Persuasion: Selected Readings* (Random House, 1967). He has published numerous articles in scholarly journals including *Southern Communication Journal, Communication Yearbook, Journal of Mass Media Ethics, Central States Speech Journal, Communication Monographs, Western Speech, Quarterly Journal of Speech*, and *Journal of the American Forensic Association*.

Christopher Lyle Johnstone (Ph.D., University of Wisconsin-Madison, 1976) is Associate Professor of Communication Arts and Sciences at The Pennsylvania State University. Dr. Johnstone's teaching and research center around Communication Ethics, the History of Rhetorical Theory, Classical Rhetoric and Philosophy, Communication and Friendship, Rhetoric and Local Political Activism, and Speech Pedagogy. He edited and contributed to *Theory, Text, Context: Issues in Greek Rhetoric and Oratory* (State University of New York Press, 1996). Dr. Johnstone has published scholarly articles in *Philosophy and Rhetoric, Quarterly Journal of Speech, Advances in the History of Rhetoric, Southern Communication Journal, Central States Speech Journal*, and *Western Journal of Speech Communication* among other publications.

Josina M. Makau (Ph.D., UC Berkeley, 1980) is Professor of Philosophy and Communication and Co-Coordinator of the Program in Practical and

Professional Ethics at California State University, Monterey Bay. Dr. Makau's research and teaching interests center around communication ethics, moral development, higher education, and practical reasoning. She has authored or edited three books: *Cooperative Argumentation: A Model for Deliberative Community,* with Debian L. Marty (Waveland, 2002), *Communication Ethics in an Age of Diversity,* with Ronald C. Arnett (University of Illinois Press, 1997), and *Reasoning and Communication* (Wadsworth, 1992). She has published numerous book chapters and articles in scholarly journals including *Communication Studies, Argumentation and Advocacy, Women's Studies in Communication, Quarterly Journal of Speech,* and *Communication Education* among other publications.

Julia T. Wood (Ph.D., Pennsylvania State University, 1975) is the Lineberger Distinguished Professor of Humanities in the Department of Communication Studies at the University of North Carolina at Chapel Hill. Dr. Wood's teaching and research focus on gender, communication, and culture; personal relationships; intimate partner violence, and feminist theories. She has authored and edited numerous books including *Communication Theories in Action: An Introduction* (Wadsworth, 2004), *Interpersonal Communication: Everyday Encounters* (Thomson Wadsworth, 2004), *Gendered Lives: Communication, Gender, and Culture* (Wadsworth, 2004), *Composing Relationships: Communication in Everyday Life* with Steve Duck (Wadsworth, 2005), *Communication Mosaics: An Introduction to the Field of Communication* (Wadsworth, 2004), *Communication in Our Lives* (Wadsworth, 2003), *Relational Communication: Continuity and Change in Personal Relationships* (Wadsworth, 2000), *Communication Theories in Action: An Introduction* (Wadsworth, 2000), *Case Studies in Interpersonal Communication: Processes and Problems* with Dawn O. Braithwaite (Wadsworth, 2000), *But I Thought You Meant: Misunderstandings in Human Communication* (Mayfield, 1998), *Gendered Relationships* (Mayfield, 1996), *Under-studied Relationships: Off the Beaten Track* with Steve Duck (Sage, 1995), *Toward the Twenty-First Century: The Future of Speech Communication* with Richard B. Gregg (Hampton Press, 1995), *Relational Communication: Continuity and Change in Personal Relationships* (Wadsworth, 1995), *Confronting Relationship Challenges* (Sage, 1995), *Who Cares?: Women, Care, and Culture* (Southern Illinois University Press, 1994), *Spinning the Symbolic Web: Human Communication as Symbolic Interaction* (Ablex, 1992), *Speech Communication: Essays to Commemorate the 75th anniver-

sary of the Speech Communication Association with Gerald M. Phillips (Southern Illinois University Press, 1990), *Group Discussion: A Practical Guide to Participation and Leadership* with Gerald M. Phillips and Douglas J. Pedersen (Harper & Row, 1986), and *Emergent Issues in Human Decision Making* (Southern Illinois University Press, 1984). She has published numerous book chapters and articles in scholarly journals including *Journal of Social and Personal Relationships, Southern Journal of Communication, Feminist Teacher, Qualitative Research in Review, Journal of Applied Communication Research, Communication Studies, Quarterly Journal of Speech, Western Journal of Communication, Communication Quarterly*, and *Communication Education* among other publications.

Index

Abbott, David, 161, 176, 181
acknowledgment, 106–108, 115, 150
agency, 3, 18, 24, 55, 56, 58
agent, xx, 42–43, 58–59, 61–62, 64–66, 127, 132, 144, 147, 160, 164–165; embedded, xx, 59, 65, 144, 164; ethical, 43, 147
Alcoff, Linda, 124, 128
Allen, M. W., 145, 170
Anaximander, 2, 20
Andersen, Kenneth E., i, xxi–xxii, 130-142, 145, 159, 170
Anderson, James A., xv, xvii–xviii, xxii, 43, 50, 159, 170, 180
Anderson, Rob, xxii, 39, 50, 51, 186
Ardener, Edwin, 122, 128
Ardener, Shirley, 122, 128
Arendt, Hannah, 55, 57, 66, 67
argumentation, 21–22, 35, 67, 70–71, 75–77, 80, 87, 141, 154, 157, 161, 171, 179, 187, 189; competitive, 81; cooperative, xxiii, 75, 80–82, 86, 189; moral, 24-25, 35, 37
Aristotle, xix, 1–3, 5–6, 9, 14–15, 18–19, 21, 26–28, 32, 35–36, 43, 54–55, 66, 70, 79, 85, 89, 102–103, 109–110, 113, 131–133, 137–138, 141–142, 160, 164, 166, 170
Arneson, Pat, xi, xiv, xxi, 57, 67, 85, 89, 128, 142–143, 145, 151, 161, 171, 178, 180, 185–186
Arnett, Ronald C., xiv, xxi, xxiii, 39–41, 50–51, 53–67, 79, 81, 85–86, 118, 121, 128–129, 142–143, 145–147, 150–162, 165–167, 169–171, 176, 178–180, 182–183
Arnold, Caroll C., 140, 142, 145, 159, 170
Auer, J. Jeffrey, 37, 51

Bacon, Francis, 1, 18–19
Bakhtin, Mikhail, 40, 165, 173, 176, 182–183
Batt, Shawn, 156, 171, 179

Baudrillard, Jean, 99, 103
Baxter, Leslie, 50, 103
Bauman, Zygmunt, 15, 19, 25, 35
Belenky, Mary Field, 83, 85
Bell, Leeanne M., xiv, xxi, 57, 67, 143, 186
Bellah, Robert N., 59, 67, 143, 165, 169, 171
Benhabib, Seyla, 26–27, 31, 33–35, 43, 56, 67, 74, 82, 85, 172
Bentham, Jeremy, 1, 19
Berlin, Isaiah, 26, 36
bioethics, 21–22, 26
Bloom, Melanie M., 145, 159, 171, 180
Bok, Derek, 143
Bok, Sissela, 45–46, 50, 78, 83, 85, 142
Bonhoeffer, Dietrich, 55–57, 59–61, 66–67, 153, 170, 186
Booth, Wayne, 70, 85
Booth-Butterfield, Steve, 161, 171, 181
Boynton, Lois A., 145, 159–160, 171, 180
Bracci, Sharon L., xx, 21–35, 40, 50, 57, 67, 83, 86, 145, 152, 170–171, 176
Brossard, Dominique, 161, 171, 181
Brown, Dale, 54
Brown, Wendy, 126, 128
Brown, William J., 171
Buber, Martin, 39–40, 42, 50–51, 53–55, 58–59, 64–67, 81, 86, 165–167, 171, 175, 182, 186, 188
Burke, Kenneth, 13, 19, 43, 70, 86, 108, 115, 176, 183
Buzzanell, Patrice M., 163, 176, 182

Cameron, Glen T., 145, 171
Cameron, Kenzie A., 161, 171, 181
Campo, Shelly, 161, 171, 181
Camus, Albert, 55, 58, 67
Caputo, John, 4, 12, 14, 17, 19
Carter, Stephen, xvii
Casmir, Fred L., 149, 171
character, xii–xiv, xix, xxi, 1–2, 28, 41, 43, 48, 52, 68, 95, 97–98, 101–102, 144; ethical, 41, 48; moral, xvii, xxi,

41, 107, 111, 131, 152. *See also* ethos
Chesebro, James, 56, 67, 146–147, 155, 166, 172, 183
Christians, Clifford G., xxi, 40, 44–46, 50, 57, 62, 67, 83, 86, 88–103, 145, 149–150, 152, 154–155, 170–173, 176, 183
Cicero, xii, 26, 27, 36, 109, 110, 115
Cissna, Ken, 39, 50–51, 186
civic culture, xxi, 140, 142, 145, 151, 153, 159, 170
Clandinin, D. Jean, xix, xxiii
codes. *See* communication ethics
Collins, Chik, 158, 173, 180
communication ethics: codes, procedures, and standards, 159-160, 180; contextual, 160-162, 180-182; define, 1-4, 22, 37–38, 56-59, 72, 73, 91-95, 105-106, 132-133; democratic, 156-157, 178–179; dialogic turn, 166-169, 182-183; historical periods, 27–29; 183-184; in postmodernity, 14-18, 30-32, 61–63, 83-85, 114-115, 120-121, 127-128; universal, 10-14, 76, 111-113, 121-122, 137–138, 157-159, 179–180. *See also* communitarian ethics, dialogic ethics, ethics, narrative ethics, rhetorical ethics, social ethics
communicative action. *See* Habermas, Jürgen
communitarian ethics, xxi, 91, 94, 97
community of memory, 143, 145, 167, 169
Condit, Celeste M., 158, 172, 179
confession, 58, 94, 153; dialogic, 58, 66, 153, 170, 186
Connelly, F. Michael, xix, xxiii
conscience, xvi, 105, 107–108, 112; call of, 47, 51, 96, 107, 109–111, 115, 152, 174
Cooper, Lane, 141
Cooper, Martha, 43, 51

Cooper, Thomas W., 148, 173
Cornford, Francis Macdonald, 151, 153, 172
Cottone, Rocco R., 161, 171, 181
Cribbet, John, 136
critical theory, 105
Curtin, Patricia A., 145, 171
cyberspace, 33, 44, 51, 77, 92–94, 147

Dallmayr, Fred, 148, 172
Day, Dorothy, 56, 67
Dean, Kevin W., 158, 176, 180
deconstruction, 19, 105, 113
Deetz, Stanley, 55, 145, 165, 170, 172, 182
Deigh, John, xii, xxiii
deliberation, xv, xx, xxi, 3, 5–6, 23–24, 26–28, 33–34, 74–75, 78–79, 83, 85, 124, 146
Denton, Robert E., Jr., 41, 44, 51–52, 148, 151, 172
Derrida, Jacques, 15, 19, 105, 108, 111, 113, 115, 145, 168, 172
Descartes, René, 28, 36, 70, 86
Dewey, John, 1–3, 5–6, 14, 19, 20, 88, 103
dialectic, 56–58, 67, 73, 84, 98, 100–101, 113
dialogic ethics, 24–25, 64–65, 164-166
dialogic turn. *See* communication ethics.
dialogue, xviii, 6, 8, 20, 27, 30, 32–33, 40, 42, 50–51, 53, 55, 57, 64–67, 73–74, 79–85, 149, 151–152, 164–166, 170, 175–178, 182–183
Diggs, B. J., 141
DiTomaso, Nancy, 158, 172, 179
Dowling, Ralf E., 156, 172, 179
Dryzek, John, 26, 36
Duncan, Ronald, 169, 172
Dunne, Joseph, 30, 36

Ellul, Jacques, 95–101, 103, 187
Engelhardt, Elaine, xv, xvii–xviii, xxii, 43, 50, 151, 172

Engnell, Richard A., 165, 173, 182
Enlightenment, 3, 18, 111, 144, 150, 157–158
epistemology, xii, 22, 29–30, 69, 73, 80–81, 83–84, 98, 120, 152, 164
ethics: applied, xii, 38, 118, 150, 187; feminist, 26, 41–46, 51–52, 71, 102, 119, 128, 147, 174, 176, 178, 181–182; philosophical, 7-8, 22-23, 73-74.
ethos, xvii, xxi, 1–2, 106, 112, 115, 131, 141
Eubank, Henry, 37, 51
Eubanks, Ralph, 4, 19
existentialism, 55, 58, 59, 105, 111, 113, 173

Fackler, Mark, 40, 50, 103, 187
Farrell, Thomas, xviii, xix, xxiii
Faulk, W. D., 4
Fenske, Mindyl, 165
Ferré, John P., 40, 50, 103, 145, 158, 173, 179
Fischer, Norman, 158, 173, 179
Fisher, Rand, 161, 176, 181
Fisher, Walter, R., xix, xxiii, 163, 173
Fletcher, Joseph, 160, 173
Flora, J. A., 145, 177
Fogg, B. J., 145, 177
Follette, Charles, 141
Ford, Wendy S. Zabava, 145, 158, 173, 180
Foucault, Michel, 15, 19, 43–44, 126–128
free speech, xiii, xvi, xvii, 39, 52–54, 142, 153, 156–157, 171, 178
Freire, Paulo, 67, 89, 101, 103, 167, 169, 170
Friedman, Maurice, 50, 169, 173
Fulkerson, Gerald, 165, 173, 182
Fuss-Reineck, Marilyn, 161, 178, 182

Gadamer, Hans-Georg, 55, 64, 68, 105, 113, 115, 186

Gandhi, Mahatma, 53–55, 63–64, 68, 169, 172
Garver, Eugene, 156, 173, 179
Garvey, Gregory T., 165, 173, 182
Gerbner, George, 77, 86, 148, 173
Gilligan, Carol, 41, 51
Glover, Jonathan, 32, 36
Gorgias, 8, 15, 20
Gordon, Ronald D., 145, 155, 176, 184
Gotcher, J. M., 145, 170
Granville, King, III, 161, 173, 181
Greenberg, Karen Joy, xxii–xxiii, 148, 174
Griswold, Charles L., Jr., 158, 173, 180
Gross, Daniel, 109, 115–116
Gross, Larry, 49, 51, 86
Guinier, Lani, 82, 86
Gunkel, David, 44, 51
Gunson, Darryl, 158, 173, 180
Gutmann, Amy, 26, 36

Haas, Tanni, 156, 174, 179
Haberman, Fred, 131
Habermas, Jürgen, 26–27, 36, 44, 57, 62–63, 68, 105, 112, 115, 153, 173–174, 182
Haiman, Franklyn, 39, 51, 142
Halley, Janet, 126, 128
Hallstein, D. Lynn O'Brien, 43, 51, 161, 174, 181
Haraway, Donna, 121, 128
Harding, Sandra G., 58, 68, 162, 174
Hauerwas, Stanley, 59, 68
Havelock, Eric, 2, 19
Hawhee, Debra, 44, 51
Hegel, Georg, 91, 103
Heidegger, Martin, 51, 105, 107–113, 115–116, 152, 174
Heraclitus, 15, 18, 20
hermeneutics, 61, 105, 108, 110, 113, 128, 147
Hermodson, Amy, 161, 173, 181
Herrick, James A., 158, 174, 180
Hesiod, 2, 19

Hobbes, Thomas, 1, 19
Homer, 2, 8, 19
hooks, bell, 82, 86
human rights, xvi, xxiii, 16–17, 32, 76, 126, 137
Hume, David, 111–112, 115
Hyde, Michael J., xxi, 47, 51, 105-115, 152–153, 163, 174, 182

information age. *See* technology
Innis, Harold, 95, 103

Jaffe, Clella I., 145, 161, 174, 181
Jaksa, James A., i, xii–xiv, xxiii, 142, 145, 148–149, 174
Jaques, Elliot, 159, 174, 180
Jaspers, Karl, 113, 116
Jensen, J. Vernon, xiii, xvi–xvii, xxii–xxiii, 146–148, 150, 155, 168, 174, 183
Johannesen, Richard L., xiii–xviii, xx, xxiii, 37-51, 86, 142, 145–147, 152, 155, 161, 165–166, 168, 174, 181–183
Johnstone, Christopher Lyle, xx, 1-19, 156–158, 175, 179
Jonsen, Albert, 26, 36, 113, 116
Jovanovic, Spoma, 165, 175, 182
justice, 28–29, 34, 36, 46, 74–76, 80, 84–85, 87, 89, 91–94, 101–102, 104, 126, 129, 140, 142, 150, 156, 178, 182

Kane, Robert, 45, 52
Kant, Immanuel, xxi, xxiii, 28, 31, 36, 63, 102, 103, 143, 147, 153, 160, 168–169, 175
Keller, Paul, 55, 67
Kemmann, Ansgar, 109, 115–116
Kernisky, Debra A., 145, 175
Kernisky, Ivan F., 145, 175
Kierkegaard, Søren, 61, 68, 98, 103, 113, 116, 168, 175
Kirkwood, William G., 159, 175, 180

Lambeth, Edmund B., 155, 172, 183
Langsdorf, Lenore, xix, xxiii
Lasch, Christopher, 55, 68
Lepper, Tammy Swenson, 145, 161, 175, 181
Levinas, Emmanuel, 51, 55–58, 62, 66–68, 102–103, 105, 107–108, 110–113, 115–116, 152–153, 167, 171–172, 174–177, 179, 183
Lipari, Lisabeth, 165, 175, 183
Locke, John, xvii, 91, 103
Lugones, María, 127–128
Lyotard, Jean-François, 43, 58, 68, 163, 175

MacIntyre, Alasdair, xii, 15, 20, 56, 58–59, 68, 144, 161, 168, 175
Madsen, Richard, 67, 143, 167, 169, 171
Makau, Josina M., xv, xxi, xxiii, 21, 41, 51, 69-86, 118, 121, 129, 145, 150, 152–153, 176
Manning, Rita, 41, 52
Marin, Mary J., 161, 176, 181
Marraro, Gabrielle, 156, 172, 179
Marty, Debian, xv, xxiii, 75, 86
Marx, Karl, 91, 95, 103, 173, 179
Mattson, Marifran, 163, 165, 176, 182, 183
McCaleb, Joseph L., 158, 176, 180
McDaniel, James, 44, 51
McEuen, Viva S., 145, 155, 176, 184
McGuire, John, 161, 176, 181
McLuhan, Marshall, 95, 103
Medhurst, Martin J., 161, 176, 181
metaphysical, xii, xxiii, 1, 18, 22, 30, 36, 98, 99, 107, 111, 114–115, 175
Mill, John Stuart, 1, 20, 81, 86, 102–103
Minnick, Wayne, 37, 52
Morris, David, 21, 36
Muehlhoff, Tim, 119, 125, 129
Muir, Star A., 156–157, 176, 179
Murray, Jeffrey W., 152–153, 165, 176, 183

narrative, i, xiv, xix–xxiii, 26, 29, 31, 33, 35, 42, 54–59, 61, 64–67, 72–74, 77–78, 82–84, 92, 116, 120–121, 124–125, 144, 146, 150–151, 155, 160, 162–164, 166, 168–170, 182; ethics, 59-61, 162-164, 182
negotiating social goods. *See* communication ethics, dialogic turn; deliberation
Nichols, Marie Hochmuth, 143, 177
Nicotera, Anne Maydan, 163, 178, 182
Niebuhr, Reinhold, 102, 104, 173, 179
Nietzsche, Friedrich, 113, 116
Nilsen, Tom, 39, 52, 142
Nkomo, Stella, 161, 177, 181
Noddings, Nel, 41–42, 51–52, 126, 129, 165, 168, 175, 182
nonviolence, 50, 53, 55, 67, 68, 101
Nordenstreng, Kaarle, 40, 50, 94, 103
Nussbaum, Martha, 32, 36, 79, 82, 86

Okin, Susan Moller, 29, 36, 126, 129
Oliver, Robert, 37, 52
Ong, Walter, xviii, xxiii
ontology, 1, 46, 68, 91, 98, 105, 107–111, 113, 152, 160, 163
ought. *See* Kant, Immanuel

Parks-Yancy, Rochelle, 158, 172, 179
Pateman, Carole, 91, 104
Perelman, Chaïm, 69, 70
phenomenology, xxiii, 59, 105, 110, 113
philosophical ethics. *See* ethics
philosophical anthropology, 94, 97
phronesis, 5, 21, 26, 28, 30, 36, 70, 160
Pinchevski, Amit, 165, 177, 183
Pinker, Steven, 114, 116
Plato, xix, 8, 20, 27–28, 36, 38, 88, 104, 157
Porter, James, 43, 52
Post, Corinne, 158, 179
postmodern. *See* communication ethics
practical wisdom. *See* phronesis

praxis, xix, 118, 142, 150, 170, 177, 182; communicative, xxiii, 66, 68, 154, 160, 163, 165, 177
Pritchard, Michael S., xii–xiv, xxiii, 142, 148–149, 174
protonorm, 46, 98
Pym, Anne, 145, 158, 177, 180
Pythagoras, 15, 19

Ralston, Steven M., 159, 175, 180
Rawls, John, 141–142
Reich, Warren Thomas, 165, 177, 183
Reinsch, Lamar N., Jr., 161, 177, 181
relativism, 16, 46, 65, 127
rhetorical ethics, 8-10, 23, 106-107, 133-134. *See also* communication ethics
Riessman, Catherine Kohler, xix, xxiii
Ricoeur, Paul, 105, 116
Rimal, R. N., 145, 177
Rogers, Carl, 40, 50–51, 64–65, 68
Rorty, Richard, 151, 177
Rosaldo, Renato, 82, 87
Ross, Veronica, xxii
Ross, W. David, 102, 104

Sallot, Lynne M., 145, 171
Samter, Wendy, 163, 178, 182
Sandel, Michael, 91, 104
Sargent, Kevin D., 163, 174, 182
Sartre, Jean-Paul, 61, 68
Schrag, Calvin O., xxi–xxiii, 57, 66, 68, 105, 154, 157–158, 160, 162–163, 165, 170, 177
Schwarze, Steve, 156, 177, 179
Schweitzer, Albert, 53, 68
Seeger, Matthew W., 150–151, 158, 177, 180
Seibert, J. H., 145, 170
Sellnow, Timothy L., 156, 178–179
shame, 23, 47, 147, 166. *See also* conscience
Sherblom, John C., 161, 176, 181
Shipps, Therese B., 161, 176, 181
Sillars, Malcolm O., 161, 177

Singhal, Arvind, 145, 171
Sloop, John, 44, 51
social ethics, 40, 50, 68, 89–91, 102–103
social justice. *See* justice
Socrates, xv, xix, 11, 153, 172
Sontag, Susan, 25, 36
Sproule, J. Michael, 155, 177, 184
Stablein, Ralf, 161, 177, 181
Stage, Christina W., 165, 176, 183
standpoint, xxii, 25, 39, 43, 51, 56, 58–59, 66, 81, 105, 120, 122–123, 144, 161–164, 174, 181
Stauble, Cherise, 161, 176, 181
Steiner, Linda, 161, 178, 181
Stewart, John, 164–167, 178, 183
Stuever, Nancy S., 109, 116, 163–164, 178, 182
Sullivan, William M., 67, 143, 167, 169, 171
Swidler, Ann, 67, 143, 167, 169, 171

Taylor, Charles, 27, 36, 56, 68, 91, 104
technology, xix, xvi, xxiii, 14, 30, 34, 73, 75–78, 84–86, 92–101, 103, 105, 107–108, 115, 125, 149
Thales, 2, 19
Thompson, Dennis, 26, 36
Tipton, Steven M., 67, 143, 167, 169, 171
Tocqueville, Alexis, 143–144, 178
Todd-Mancillas, William R., 145, 155, 176, 184
Tompkins Pribble, Paula, 145, 156, 159, 177–180
Torres, Gerald, 82, 86
Toulmin, Stephen, 26, 36, 70, 87, 92, 104, 113, 116
Traber, Michael M., 40, 45–46, 50, 62, 67, 83, 86, 103, 149–150, 172
Tronto, Joan, 41, 52

Ulmer, Robert R., 156, 158, 177–180
Universal Declaration of Human Rights. *See* human rights

Vico, Giambattista, 169, 178
visual communication, 25, 48–49, 93, 95

Wallace, Karl R., 39, 52, 156, 178
Weber, Max, 95, 101, 104
Whaley, Bryan B., 163, 178, 182
Wheeler, Tom, 49, 52
Winegarden, Alan D., 161, 178, 182
Wood, Julia T., xxi–xxiii, 42, 52, 58, 67, 117-129, 151, 155, 161, 168, 178, 182
Wyschogrod, Edith, 102, 104

Yoder, John Howard, 54, 68

Zediker, Karen, 164–167, 178, 183
Zinn, Howard, 121, 129